BESTSELLING
BOOK SERIES

A+® Certification Work[book] For Dummies®

W9-AYN-035

Cheat Sheet

CPU Packaging

	Manufacturer	Packaging (Including # of Pins)	Bits (32 or 64)
Pentium III	Intel	370, or SEC2 cartridge	32
Pentium 4	Intel	423 or 478	32
Xeon	Intel	603, or SEC cartridge	32
Itanium	Intel	418	64
Athlon XP	AMD	462	32
Duron	AMD	462	32
Opteron	AMD	940	64

Socket Types

Socket	Compatible CPUs	Number of Pins
Socket A	Later Athlon, Duron, and Athlon XP	462
Slot A	Athlon	242
Socket 370	Celeron, Pentium III	370
PAC 418 / Socket 418	Itanium	418
Socket 423	Pentium 4	423
Socket 478	Celeron, Pentium 4	478
Socket 603	Xeon	603
PAC 611	Itanium	611
Socket 940	Opteron	940
Slot 1	Pentium II, Pentium III	
Slot 2	Xeon	

Default Resource Assignments

Port	Standard IRQ Assignment	Standard I/O Address Range
COM2	3	2F8-2FF
COM4	3	2E8-2EF
COM1	4	3F8-3FF
COM3	4	3E8-3EF
Floppy drive	6	03F0 to 03F7
LPT2	5	278-27F
LPT1	7	378-37F
Primary IDE	14	01F0 to 01F7
Secondary IDE	15	0170 to 0177

PC Card Types

Slot Type	Thickness	Device Type
Type 1	3.3 mm	Memory cards
Type 2	5.0 mm	Modems, network cards, and so on
Type 3	10.5 mm	Removable drives

Printer Technologies

	Laser	Inkjet	Thermal (Solid Ink)	Dot Matrix
Impact or nonimpact?	Nonimpact	Nonimpact	Nonimpact	Impact
Ink type	Toner	Liquid	Wax	Ribbon
Sheet-fed or tractor-fed?	Sheet	Sheet	Sheet	Tractor
Page printer or line printer?	Page	Line	Page	Line

For Dummies: Bestselling Book Series for Beginners

A+® Certification Workbook For Dummies®

Cheat Sheet

Laser Printer Process Steps

1. Charging (Conditioning)
2. Writing
3. Developing
4. Transferring
5. Fusing
6. Cleaning*

* Note that some reference guides place cleaning at the beginning rather than the end.

Windows Startup Modes

Startup Mode	Description	Windows Versions
Safe Mode	Starts with a minimal set of drivers	95, 98, Me, 2000, XP
Safe Mode with Network Support	Same as Safe Mode but includes networking	95, 2000, XP
Safe Mode Command Prompt Only	Boots to a command prompt and bypasses all startup files	95, 98
Safe Mode with Command Prompt	Same as Safe Mode except a command prompt window opens within Safe Mode	2000, XP
VGA Mode / Enable VGA Mode	Starts normally but uses the plain VGA video driver	NT, 2000, XP

Windows Requirements

Version	CPU	Memory	Hard Drive
Windows NT Workstation 4	Pentium	16MB (32MB recommended)	110MB
Windows 95	386DX (486 recommended)	4MB (8MB recommended)	50 to 55MB
Windows 98	486DX 66 (Pentium recommended)	16MB (24MB recommended)	165 to 355MB
Windows Me	150 MHz Pentium	32MB	480 to 645MB
Windows 2000 Professional	133 MHz Pentium	64MB	2GB with at least 650MB free
Windows XP	233 MHz	64MB (128MB recommended)	1.5GB
Windows Vista Home Basic	1 GHz	512MB	20GB with at least 15GB free
Windows Vista Premium, Business, or Ultimate	1 GHz	1GB	40GB with at least 15GB free

UTP Cable Categories

Category	Speed
CAT3	10 Mbps
CAT5	100 Mbps
CAT5e	1,000 Mbps
CAT6/6a	10 Gbps

For Dummies: Bestselling Book Series for Beginners

CompTIA A+® Certification Workbook

FOR DUMMIES®

by Faithe Wempen

BICENTENNIAL
1807
WILEY
2007
BICENTENNIAL

Wiley Publishing, Inc.

Comp TIA A+® Certification Workbook For Dummies®

Published by
Wiley Publishing, Inc.
111 River Street
Hoboken, NJ 07030-5774
www.wiley.com

WILEY

About the Author

Faithe Wempen, M.A., has passed every version of the A+ exams that have ever been offered. She is the author of over 90 books, including *PC Maintenance: Preparing for A+ Certification, A+ Jumpstart,* and *A+ Fast Pass.* She teaches Computer Hardware and Software Architecture at Indiana University/Purdue University in Indianapolis, and she writes and facilitates online courses on PC hardware and software for corporate clients including Hewlett Packard, Sony, and CNET. She also owns and operates Sycamore Knoll Bed and Breakfast (`www.sycamoreknoll.com`).

Dedication

To Margaret

Author's Acknowledgments

A big thanks to my great team of editors at Wiley, including Katie Feltman, Paul Levesque, Virginia Sanders, and Dan DiNicolo. They're all true professionals, and they make my job a lot easier.

Publisher's Acknowledgments

We're proud of this book; please send us your comments through our online registration form located at www.dummies.com/register/.

Some of the people who helped bring this book to market include the following:

Acquisitions, Editorial, and Media Development

Senior Project Editor: Paul Levesque

Senior Acquisitions Editor: Katie Feltman

Copy Editor: Virginia Sanders

Technical Editor: Dan DiNicolo

Editorial Manager: Leah Cameron

Media Development and Quality Assurance: Steven Kudirka

Media Development Coordinator: Jenny Swisher

Media Project Supervisor: Laura Moss-Hollister

Editorial Assistant: Amanda Foxworth

Sr. Editorial Assistant: Cherie Case

Cartoons: Rich Tennant (www.the5thwave.com)

Composition Services

Project Coordinator: Jennifer Theriot

Layout and Graphics: Stacie Brooks, Brooke Graczyk, Denny Hager, Stephanie D. Jumper, Jennifer Mayberry, Julie Trippetti, Christine Williams, Erin Zeltner

Proofreaders: Henry Lazarek, Dwight Ramsey

Indexer: Broccoli Information Management

Anniversary Logo Design: Richard Pacifico

Publishing and Editorial for Technology Dummies

Richard Swadley, Vice President and Executive Group Publisher

Andy Cummings, Vice President and Publisher

Mary Bednarek, Executive Acquisitions Director

Mary C. Corder, Editorial Director

Publishing for Consumer Dummies

Diane Graves Steele, Vice President and Publisher

Joyce Pepple, Acquisitions Director

Composition Services

Gerry Fahey, Vice President of Production Services

Debbie Stailey, Director of Composition Services

Contents at a Glance

Table of Contents

Table of Exercises

Introduction

*T*he *A+ Certification Workbook For Dummies* is a very different kind of study guide. It assumes that you want to not only pass the A+ exams, but be *good at the job* you get with that certification. This book tries to make you a good PC technician by giving you the theory and practice you need to succeed in the field.

Pretty radical, eh?

Most exam prep study guides spoon-feed you test questions in exactly the same format that you'll find on the exam. For the A+ exams, that would involve endless streams of multiple choice questions. And that study approach does have its benefits: It helps you become familiar with the exam format, and it gives you a sense of the scope of the questions the exam asks. And in fact, if you want that type of practice, I've provided such questions on the CD that accompanies this book. But that kind of studying can't really make you a better technician.

This book can, though.

I've been teaching PC hardware and A+ technician courses at Indiana University/Purdue University in Indianapolis for many years, and my students often cite the course as one of the most helpful they took in preparing for Computer Technology careers. Why? Primarily because of all the hands-on lab work we do. We dive right in there and supplement all the theory with some real practice. So in developing this book, I've put together dozens of hands-on exercises you can complete. Go into these exercises with a willingness to learn something, and you'll come out with some of the real experience that the A+ exam is supposed to measure.

Hands-on effort alone won't get you through the test, though, so other sections in each chapter review the concepts and principles that you need to know. These aren't questions that you can guess at, though, or get by with luck. The review questions in this book expect you to really *know* what you're talking about. They don't just ask what; they ask *why.* Do you need to know the "why" to pass the A+ exam? No, not really. But if you know why something works the way it does, you can reason out the answer to any question about it, no matter how it's asked. If you really know the answers to the questions asked in this book, you'll find the A+ exams a piece of cake.

How to Study

First of all, this shouldn't be your only A+ study guide book, because this book doesn't actually *teach* you anything. (Okay, I'm saying that facetiously, but it's partly true.) This workbook is a tool for reviewing what you already know — or should know — and cementing that knowledge with hands-on experience.

In this workbook, I'm assuming that you are also studying other reference guides. A good place to start is the *CompTIA A+ Certification All-in-One Desk Reference For Dummies,* by Glen E. Clarke and Ed Tetz (Wiley Publishing). Most of the answers to the questions asked in this book — and on the A+ exam — can be found there.

So what's the best way to prepare? To pick up the basic theory, read an A+ study guide and, if possible, get out into the industry and get a little hands-on experience. Nobody will hire you? Offer to fix your friends' PCs for free or for barter.

Then, when you get to the point where you think you have this stuff down cold, start in on this workbook. Go through each chapter, answering the questions and doing the exercises. Check your answers to the questions in the answer sections at the back of each chapter, to see how you did. Between the review questions and the hands-on practice, you'll top off your knowledge and be able to take the exams with confidence.

How This Book Is Organized

This book breaks down PC hardware and software into the following parts:

Part I: Basic Components

This part reviews the essential innards of a PC, including components like CPUs, motherboards, memory, BIOS, disk storage, and power supplies, and makes sure you know how to protect a PC (and yourself) from damage.

Part II: Peripherals

In this part, you check your knowledge of the "outards," the components that exist separately from the big gray box, such as cables, printers, input/output devices, monitors, and video adapters. (Okay, so technically a video adapter is an innard, but it interfaces with a monitor, so I'm lumping it in here.)

Part III: Operating System Basics

This part reviews the basic skills for managing Windows. It includes installing and upgrading Windows, working with files and folders in a GUI environment and at a command prompt, running and configuring applications, and allocating system resources and device drivers to the hardware.

Part IV: Maintaining and Troubleshooting the Operating System

In this part, you look at the various utilities and commands you can use when a system isn't performing up to its potential or when some action is required to make sure it continues to do so. This section covers task and application management, boot sequences, system files, as well as troubleshooting hardware and boot problems.

Part V: Networking

This part reviews what you need to know in terms of setting up and maintaining networks. These days, a basic understanding of networking procedures is necessary for any techie, because nearly all computers are networked in some way. This part reviews peer-to-peer and client server, networking architectures, topologies and devices, and setting up networking in Windows. It also covers basic file sharing, network troubleshooting, and Internet e-mail and security settings.

Part VI: The Part of Tens

As is traditional in *For Dummies* books, this book ends with several handy Top Ten lists. The selection here includes ten things end users do to mess up their PCs (and how to fix them), ten (more or less) Windows system files you need to know, and ten command prompt commands that can save the day.

Appendixes

The book contains two appendixes. The first one, "About the A+ Certification Exams," explains the A+ certification exams and what they cover. The second one, "About the CD-ROM," explains how to use the CD-ROM that accompanies this book to load a testing engine and practice questions that will further help you prepare for exam success.

Icons Used in This Book

Throughout this book, icons in the margins alert you to important types of information:

This icon indicates a question-and-answer pairing that helps tie the concepts covered under a topic with how you might use the concepts in the software.

This icon gives you a dash of extra information, such as background explanations or alternatives you might see with specific nonstandard hardware or software.

Tips offer helpful hints and shortcuts for accomplishing something more easily.

Warnings point out potential pitfalls and dangers — things that could hurt the computer, hurt you, or make life more difficult for you or the users you support.

Where to Go from Here

From here, you're ready to go! Dive into the first chapter and see how much you already know. Then check your answers by using the answer key at the end of each chapter.

If you find yourself lost and unable to answer any of the questions posed, try working through the hands-on exercises provided. Consult a reference manual such as *CompTIA A+ Certification All-in-One Desk Reference For Dummies,* by Glen E. Clarke and Ed Tetz, to see whether you can come up with the missing answers. (You can also look at the answers in the answer key as a shortcut, but you'll remember it better if you expend some effort to find the answer on your own.)

Part I
Basic Components

"You know, this was a situation question on my A+ Certification exam, but I always thought it was just hypothetical."

In this part . . .

You start here with the basics, the most critical components that all PCs share. You test your knowledge of essential hardware components, including CPUs, memory, disk storage, and the electrical system. You review the parts of a portable PC and check your knowledge of ergonomic practices, safety issues, and proper cleaning procedures.

Chapter 1

Protecting Yourself and Your PC

● ●

● ●

*1*n this chapter, you practice procedures for ensuring that your PC doesn't hurt you — or your environment — and vice versa.

Preventing ESD Damage

Electrostatic discharge (ESD), also known as *static electricity,* is an insidious destroyer of computer and electronic components. Even the smallest, most harmless-seeming jolt of ESD can ruin a circuit board or chip. The damage can be immediately apparent, or it can weaken the component in such a way that it fails days, weeks, or even months later.

ESD is caused by electrical potential equalizing itself between a higher and a lower source. Think about what would happen, for example, if two sides of a gate had different water levels. When the gate is opened, the water from the higher-level side rushes into the lower-level side to equalize the level. Well, when electrical potential rushes from the higher-potential side to the lower-potential one, it zaps the component on the lower side, and that's what causes the damage.

Humans don't even notice ESD unless it's thousands of volts in strength (because the amperage is so low), but much lower levels can damage equipment. Therefore you can't use "Can I feel it?" as a reliable indicator of whether ESD damage is taking place. Instead, you must take precautions to ensure that ESD doesn't happen in the first place.

As a PC technician, you need to know how to set up a work environment so that the risk of ESD damage is minimized as much as possible. This includes wearing certain clothing/fabrics, using antistatic equipment and mats, and controlling environmental conditions, such as humidity in the room.

1. What is the optimal humidity level in a work area, as a percentage?

   _____

2. Describe the characteristics of the optimal clothing you should wear while working on a PC in order to avoid ESD.

   A. What material should your clothing be made of?

   _____

   B. What material should you especially avoid?

   _____

   C. What type of shoes should you wear?

   _____

   D. Should you work in socks (no shoes)? Why or why not?

   _____

3. Describe the characteristics of the optimal flooring for avoiding ESD.

   A. What types of floor covering generate the least ESD risk?

   _____

   B. What type of floor covering should you especially avoid?

   _____

4. What is the purpose of an antistatic wrist strap?

   _____

   _____

5. Where does an antistatic wrist strap attach at each end?

   _____

   _____

6. What is the purpose of an antistatic grounding mat?

   _____

   _____

7. If a cable is leading from the grounding mat, what should it plug into, and why?

    _____

    _____

8. When working inside a PC without an antistatic wrist strap, experts recommend that you frequently touch the metal frame of the PC case or the power supply box. What does that do?

    _____

    _____

    _____

Cleaning a PC

Keeping a PC clean takes only a little time and pays off by extending the life of the equipment and making it more pleasant to use on a daily basis. If you've ever tried to use a PC with a sticky mouse, a grimy keyboard, or a dusty screen, you know firsthand about that! Even though in most organizations, end-users are responsible for cleaning their own PCs, in practice a technician may find that PC cleaning is sometimes a part of his or her job.

To clean a PC, you need the following equipment and supplies:

- Compressed air
- Lint-free cleaning cloths (paper towels are acceptable for cleaning keyboards)
- Ammonia-free monitor cleaner
- Mild general-purpose cleaner for external plastic parts, or mild soapy water
- Cotton swabs and alcohol (if you have a ball-style mouse)

9. How do dust and dirt inside a PC make the PC more prone to failure?

    _____

    _____

10. Why is it important to use ammonia-free products on a monitor screen?

    _____

    _____

11. Why should you avoid using alcohol to clean the rubber ball of a ball-style mouse?

    _____

    _____

12. Why is it preferable that cleaning cloths be made of natural materials (such as cotton) rather than synthetic materials?

_____

_____

13. Describe the qualities of an appropriate general-purpose cleaner for use on the external parts of a PC.

_____

_____

14. Most PC technicians would not take the time to disassemble a keyboard for cleaning (that is, to pull off the keys and clean underneath them). Why is that?

_____

_____

_____

_____

Exercise 1-1: Cleaning a Desktop PC

Follow these steps to practice cleaning a desktop PC:

1. Shut down the computer and unplug it.

2. If you have a ball-style mouse, disassemble it and clean out the inside of the mouse casing with alcohol and a cotton swab. Clean the mouse ball itself with mild soapy water.

3. Using general-purpose cleaner or mild soapy water and either a paper towel or a lint-free cloth, clean the keyboard as thoroughly as possible without disassembling it.

   It isn't worth disassembling most keyboards because putting them back together again is extremely difficult.

4. Using monitor cleaner and a lint-free cloth, clean the monitor glass.

5. Using general-purpose cleaner and a lint-free cloth, clean the plastic surfaces of the monitor.

6. Using general-purpose cleaner and a lint-free cloth, clean the plastic surfaces of the outside of the PC.

7. Open the PC case and, using your fingers, fish out any clumps of dust or hair that you can reach.

8. Using compressed air, blow out any remaining clumps of dust or hair from inside the PC case.

9. Using compressed air, blow out any dust from the fans inside the PC, including the fan on the power supply.

10. Close the PC case.

Disposing of Hazardous Components

The United States Environmental Protection Agency (EPA) publishes standards dealing with the proper disposal of electronics components (such as computer hardware) and of cleaning supplies and consumables (such as toner cartridges). It's important to follow these standards, not only because it's the right thing to do for the environment, but also because in many cases, it's the law. These guidelines are published at www.epa.gov/epaoswer/osw/hazwaste.htm.

Many cleaning supplies also have their own specific disposal guidelines contained in a Material Safety Data Sheet (MSDS). You can obtain the MSDS for a chemical from the manufacturer, usually from its Web site. In some cases, the proper disposal procedure for a chemical is also printed on its container.

To effectively deal with equipment and consumables that are potential environmental hazards, you should not only be able to enumerate what items require special disposal, but you should also understand *why* they do. When you know why things are hazardous, you can make judgment calls when you encounter new equipment in the future that isn't on the specific list to which you normally refer.

15. For each of the following items, specify how they should be handled and explain what the hazard is for each one.

Component/Material	Proper Disposal	Reason
Notebook PC battery		
Standard alkaline battery, such as in a flashlight		
Coin-style battery, such as on a motherboard		
CRT-style monitor		
Toner cartridge		

Exercise 1-2: Determining Disposal and Recycling Options

When the time comes to get rid of cleaning products and electronics, take these steps:

1. Look on the packaging of the cleaning products you used to clean your PC earlier in this chapter and find the Web sites for the manufacturers.

2. Visit those Web sites and attempt to locate Material Safety Data Sheets for each of the cleaning products. (Not all products have them.)

3. Visit www.epa.gov/epr/products/ele-resources.htm and review the information about electronics disposal and recycling.

Identifying Good Ergonomic Practices

Ergonomics is the science of designing equipment and setting up work areas in a way that reduces or prevents discomfort and injury in workers. The most common type of injury caused by poor ergonomics is *repetitive strain injury* (RSI), which is an injury to the muscles and tendons caused by repeatedly performing the same movement in a way that stresses them.

Here are the three components to good ergonomic practices:

✔ Purchase ergonomically sound equipment that's appropriate for the user.

✔ Set up workstations so that the user is positioned in a way that avoids stress.

✔ Use equipment in a way that avoids stress.

PRACTICE

16. Describe the features that differentiate an ergonomic keyboard from a standard one.

_____

_____

_____

_____

17. Where should a monitor be positioned in relation to the user's eyes?

_____

_____

_____

18. Describe the appropriate body posture a computer user should maintain when using a PC in order to avoid body stress and strain, including the angles at which arms and legs should be positioned in relation to the floor.

_____

_____

_____

19. Describe how a user can avoid eyestrain when working at a computer for a long stretch of time.

_____

_____

_____

Exercise 1-3: Making a Workstation Ergonomically Correct

Follow these steps to help prevent RSI:

1. Go to www.osha.gov/SLTC/etools/computerworkstations and read the information about creating an ergonomically sound computer work area.

2. Evaluate and correct your current workstation for ergonomic problems:

- Reposition the monitor if needed.

- Check the keyboard and mouse positioning. Adjust them if needed so that your arms are positioned correctly when using them.

- Check the chair height. Adjust the chair if needed so that your feet and legs are positioned correctly.

- Evaluate the design of the keyboard to determine whether it could potentially cause RSI. If it could cause RSI, consider replacing it, or reassign it to a workstation that is used less frequently than others.

Answers to Questions in This Chapter

The following are the answers to the practice questions presented earlier in this chapter:

1. **What is the optimal humidity level in a work area, as a percentage?**

The optimal humidity level is between 50 and 80 percent. If the humidity is less than that, static electricity is more prevalent; more than that, and moisture tends to collect on parts, possibly causing short-circuiting.

2. **Describe the characteristics of the optimal clothing you should wear while working on a PC in order to avoid ESD.**

A. What material should your clothing be made of?

Clothing should be made of natural fibers.

B. What material should you especially avoid?

Avoid polyester and other synthetic fibers because they generate ESD.

C. What type of shoes should you wear?

Wear rubber- or leather-soled shoes.

D. Should you work in socks (no shoes)? Why or why not?

No, you should not go shoeless, because socks, especially those made with synthetic fibers, can rub against a carpet, rug, or other surface to create static electricity.

3. **Describe the characteristics of the optimal flooring for avoiding ESD.**

A. What types of floor covering generate the least ESD risk?

A rubber floor mat is best; a tile floor is also acceptable.

B. What type of floor covering should you especially avoid?

Avoid synthetic-fiber carpeting.

Remember back when you were a kid and you used to scuff your stocking feet on the carpet and then zap your little brother with static electricity? That's what you want to avoid doing to your PC. Avoid working in your socks, especially on carpet.

4. **What is the purpose of an antistatic wrist strap?**

An antistatic wrist strap equalizes the electrical potential between you and the PC. It doesn't "ground" you per se, unless you use it in conjunction with a grounding mat; it simply keeps the potential the same between you and the parts that you don't want to accidentally zap.

5. **Where does an antistatic wrist strap attach at each end?**

The wrist strap attaches to your wrist, of course. The alligator clip at the other end attaches to the PC's frame or to its power supply — anything that's metal and not a circuit board.

6. **What is the purpose of an antistatic grounding mat?**

A grounding mat dissipates any excess electrical potential that builds up in your body, channeling it out to a ground source.

7. **If a cable is leading from the grounding mat, what should it plug into, and why?**

   A grounding mat typically plugs into a three-prong electrical outlet; the third prong (the grounding prong) channels ESD away from your body — and from anything else placed on the mat.

8. **When working inside a PC without an antistatic wrist strap, experts recommend that you frequently touch the metal frame of the PC case or the power supply box. What does that do?**

   Touching the metal frame equalizes the charge between you and the PC's frame, keeping excess charge from building up. If you touch the metal frame, the electrical potential in your body flows harmlessly into that nonelectronic source. If you touched a sensitive circuit board instead with excess charge built up in your body, it would get zapped.

9. **How do dust and dirt inside a PC make the PC more prone to failure?**

   Dust is an insulator, so heat builds up to a greater degree on a dusty chip than on a clean one. This causes the chips to run hotter and to fail more quickly. Dusty fan blades circulate air less efficiently than clean ones, and clumps of dirt or hair inside a component can impede the free flow of air within it.

10. **Why is it important to use ammonia-free products on a monitor screen?**

    Ammonia can destroy the antiglare coating on monitor glass and can damage LCD screens.

11. **Why should you avoid using alcohol to clean the rubber ball of a ball-style mouse?**

    Alcohol can dry out the rubber in the ball.

12. **Why is it preferable that cleaning cloths be made of natural materials (such as cotton) rather than synthetic materials?**

    There are two reasons. One is that some synthetic materials react with chemicals to cause color bleeds or to break down the fibers in the fabric. Another is that synthetic fibers are more prone to generating ESD.

13. **Describe the qualities of an appropriate general-purpose cleaner for use on the external parts of a PC.**

    A cleaner should be nonabrasive and should not contain harsh chemicals such as benzene or ammonia. Mild soapy water (made with dishwashing detergent) is inexpensive and works well for external parts; for internal areas, where water is a no-no, consider an alcohol-based product.

14. **Most PC technicians would not take the time to disassemble a keyboard for cleaning (that is, to pull off the keys and clean underneath them). Why is that?**

    Keyboards are inexpensive, so it doesn't make financial sense for a skilled technician to spend a lot of time cleaning one meticulously. In addition, the keycaps can be difficult to remove and replace, and some keyboards have a spring under the spacebar that's hard to reinstall.

15. **For each of the following items, specify how they should be handled and explain what the hazard is for each one.**

Component/Material	Proper Disposal	Reason
Notebook PC battery	Take to recycling center or hazardous waste center	Batteries can contain heavy metals such as nickel and cadmium.
Standard alkaline battery, such as in a flashlight	Okay to throw in regular trash	This type of battery doesn't require special handling.
Coin-style battery, such as on a motherboard	Okay to throw in regular trash	This type of battery doesn't require special handling.
CRT-style monitor	Donate to charity or take to recycling center or hazardous waste center	Phosphors and lead are used in the monitor; in addition, the large, boxy nature of such a monitor means it takes up lots of space in a landfill.
Toner cartridge	Return to manufacturer for recycling or disposal, or take to recycling center or hazardous waste center	The fine powder in toner can present a breathing hazard if it's dispersed in the air, and the plastic cartridge can take up space in a landfill.

16. **Describe the features that differentiate an ergonomic keyboard from a standard one.**

An ergonomic keyboard typically has a built-in wrist rest and might also have a split design that enables your wrists to point at more natural angles than with a standard keyboard.

17. **Where should a monitor be positioned in relation to the user's eyes?**

The monitor should be at eye level so that the user doesn't have to bend or stretch his or her neck to look at it. Also, the monitor should be about two feet away from the eyes.

18. **Describe the appropriate body posture a computer user should maintain when using a PC in order to avoid body stress and strain, including the angles at which arms and legs should be positioned in relation to the floor.**

Forearms and thighs should be parallel to the ground. Calves and upper arms should be perpendicular to it. The shoulders should be relaxed, and the lower back should be supported.

19. **Describe how a user can avoid eyestrain when working at a computer for a long stretch of time.**

Users should blink their eyes frequently as they work. They should focus on a distant object for a few seconds every 15 to 20 minutes. Users should keep eyedrops handy if dryness is a problem because they forget to blink.

Chapter 2

Motherboards and CPUs

● ●

In This Chapter

▶ Identifying the parts of a motherboard

▶ Identifying motherboard form factors

▶ Understanding bus architectures and slots

▶ Differentiating between CPUs

▶ Identifying CPU socket types

▶ Installing a CPU

▶ Cooling a CPU

● ●

A sk a techie what the most important part of a computer is, and he'll probably say it's the central processing unit (CPU). The CPU and the motherboard on which it is mounted largely distinguish a good PC (that is, a revved up powerful one) from a bad PC (an old lame one).

For the A+ exam, you should know how to distinguish between motherboards and CPUs and how to install, configure, and troubleshoot them. In this chapter, you test your knowledge of motherboards and CPUs.

Identifying Parts of a Motherboard

A motherboard is a large circuit board containing a complex assortment of slots, sockets, chips, and traces (that is, connecting pathways between them). The exact shapes, sizes, and quantities of components vary from board to board, but a technician should be able to recognize the common components no matter what form they take.

1. Label the photos using these terms. Not every term is used on every photo.

AGP

Floppy

PCIe 1X

AMR slot

PATA (IDE)

Power

Battery

PCI

RAM slots

CPU socket

PCIe 16X

SATA

Exercise 2-1: Checking Out the Motherboard

1. Shut down your computer and unplug it.

2. Open the case so that the motherboard is visible.

3. Identify as many of the components as possible from the previous section.

4. Close the case and restart the PC.

Identifying Motherboard Form Factors

When selecting a motherboard for a system, it's important to choose one that has the features and components you want (for example, the right slots and sockets), but it's equally important that the motherboard you select fits into the case you plan to use. Different case sizes and shapes call for different *form factors*. A form factor is a size and shape of motherboard, but it's also more than that because different form factors position components in different places. For example, some form factors position expansion slots parallel to the wide edge of the board, whereas others position them perpendicular.

Match up the following descriptions with the motherboard form factor:

A. ATX

B. BTX

C. Baby AT

D. NLX

E. Mini-ITX

F. MicroATX

G. WTX

H. Full AT

2. _____ 12" x 13.8" board containing only a keyboard connector built in and no other I/O ports

3. _____ 8.5" x 13" board with a DIN keyboard connector in the top-right corner and no other I/O ports

4. _____ 9" x 13.6" board with a riser card for the expansion slots, suitable for slim-line cases

5. _____ 9.6" x 12" board with most of the I/O ports integrated directly into the side of the board

6. _____ 9.6" x 9.6" board with most of the I/O ports integrated directly into the side of the board

7. _____ 16.75" x 14" board designed for use in servers, similar to an ATX except for size and power

8. _____ 12.8" x 10.5" board, similar to ATX but with improved design so that components don't block airflow

9. _____ 6.7" x 6.7" board, a very small board used in home theater PCs and other nontraditional units

Exercise 2-2: Taking a Look at the Form Factor

1. Shut down your computer and unplug it.

2. Open the case so that the motherboard is visible.

3. Identify the motherboard's form factor. Use a ruler or tape measure to identify its dimensions if needed to make a determination.

4. Close the case.

Understanding Bus Architectures and Slots

Within a motherboard are several *buses* (electrical pathways) of various types, speeds, and widths. Some of these buses, like the system bus, exist to carry data between the built-in parts of the motherboard like the CPU socket and the memory slots. Other buses connect various types of expansion slots to the CPU.

A PC technician should be able to identify various bus types both by description and by sight. A technician should also know what type of device would be serviced by each.

Match up the following bus types to the descriptions and pictures provided. Some letters are used more than once; others are not used at all.

A. Accelerated (or Advanced) Graphics Port (AGP)

B. Audio/Modem Riser

C. Peripheral Component Interconnect (PCI)

D. VESA Local Bus (VLB)

E. PCI Express

F. Industry Standard Architecture (ISA)

10. _____ 32-bit bus used only for video cards. Different varieties are available, ranging from 1X (66 MHz) to 8X (533 MHz).

11. _____ 32-bit or 64-bit bus used for general-purpose expansion boards, including modems, sound cards, and network cards. Supports Plug and Play resource assignments for IRQs and I/O addresses. Runs at 33 MHz for 32-bit or 66 MHz for 64-bit.

12. _____ A high-speed serial bus that transfers 250 Mbps per channel. Multiple channels can be combined for high-data-rate usage such as with a video card. Slots are available for x1, x2, x4, x8, x16, and x32; the slots get larger with each multiplier.

13. _____ The oldest expansion bus type, operating at only 8 MHz. Slots can be 8-bit or 16-bit, although 8-bit is seldom seen anymore. This expansion bus type is largely obsolete.

14. _____ A small slot used to connect a special-purpose expansion board that combines multiple functions.

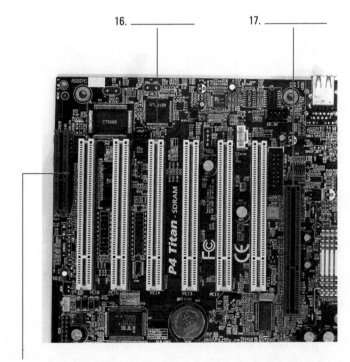

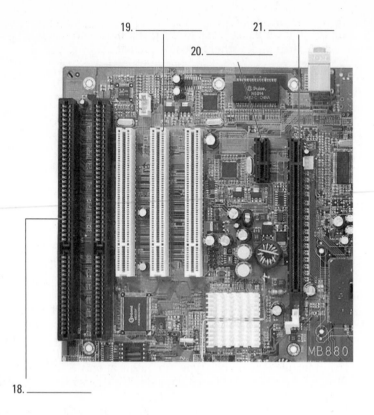

Exercise 2-3: Scoping Out the Slots

1. Shut down your computer and unplug it.

2. Open the case so that the motherboard is visible.

3. Identify the motherboard's slots, noting which slots are occupied (and by what) and which slots are available.

4. Suppose you were going to add a second video card to your system. Of the slots available, think about which one you would use and why.

5. Close the case.

Differentiating between CPUs

A *central processing unit* (CPU) is the main brain of the PC and — along with the RAM — is the primary factor that determines the system's capability.

The following factors are involved in selecting a CPU:

✔ **Manufacturer:** Intel and AMD are the two top competitors. The motherboard must be designed to work with one or the other, as their architectures are not compatible.

✔ **Chip class:** Each manufacturer has families of CPUs that share common basic characteristics. For example, Intel has the Pentium 4, and AMD has the Athlon.

- **Single core or dual core:** A dual-core processor combines two independent processors on a single chip, for executing multiple threads at the same time.

- **Hyperthreading:** This technology enables a single processor to execute two simultaneous threads, as if it were dual core (although it isn't actually so).

- **Throttling:** This technology enables the CPU to gauge its own temperature and reduce its speed if it gets too hot.

- **Packaging:** Different CPUs come in different chip sizes and shapes, designed to fit into the slot or socket on a compatible motherboard. The Pin Grid Array (PGA) is the most popular style; different CPUs have different numbers and arrangements of pins. Other styles include Single Edge Contact (SEC), SEC2 (a newer variant of SEC), Pin Array Cartridge (PAC), and Organic Land Grid Array (OLGA).

- **Cache:** Because data that has just been used may soon be needed again, a CPU maintains a holding area on its chip for recently used data so that the data need not be fetched from RAM each time. A Level 1 (L1) cache is built into the CPU itself. The L2 cache is built into the chip but is separate from the CPU portion of the circuitry. Higher-end CPUs tend to have larger L1 and L2 caches.

- **Speed:** Each CPU has an internal speed measured in megahertz or gigahertz; this is the rate at which it operates internally. It's usually a multiple of the motherboard's system bus speed (also called the *external speed*).

- **Bits:** A processor can be 32-bit (standard on most entry-level PCs) or 64-bit (becoming more common recently, especially on servers and high-end systems). Special 64-bit versions of Windows XP and Windows Vista that are available can take advantage of the extra capability.

22. Fill out the following chart to describe the characteristics of some popular CPUs.

CPU	Manufacturer	Packaging (including # of pins)	Bits (32 or 64)
Pentium III			
Pentium 4			
Xeon			
Itanium			
Athlon XP			
Duron			
Opteron			

Exercise 2-4: Researching Your CPU

1. Use System Information in Windows to determine what CPU your system has.

2. Visit www.intel.com or www.amd.com and get the specs for your CPU.

3. Imagine that your motherboard needed replacing. Visit www.motherboards.org and find a replacement motherboard with the same CPU.

Identifying CPU Sockets

A technician should be able to identify CPU socket types to determine the overall class of the motherboard and the family of CPUs that might work with it. Different CPUs have different numbers and arrangements of pins. Not all motherboards that are pin-compatible with a certain CPU will actually work with it; you need to check the documentation for the motherboard to answer that question for sure.

23. Fill out the following chart to describe the sockets.

Socket	Compatible CPUs
Socket 370	
PAC 418	
Socket 423	
Socket 478	
Socket 603	
PAC 611	
Socket 940	
Slot A	
Slot 1	
Slot 2	

Installing a CPU

Almost all CPUs today use *zero insertion force* (ZIF) sockets and *Pin Grid Array* (PGA) *packaging*. Therefore, they all install approximately the same way: Lift the lever, insert the chip, and lower the lever.

The CPU must be oriented in such a way that pin 1 on the CPU aligns with pin 1 on the socket. Pin 1 is usually marked on the CPU by a dot or triangle in one corner or by a rounded-off edge on the ceramic block to which the chip is mounted. On the socket, the pin 1 corner has a different pin arrangement than the other three corners.

On each of the following pictures, draw an arrow pointing to Pin 1.

24.

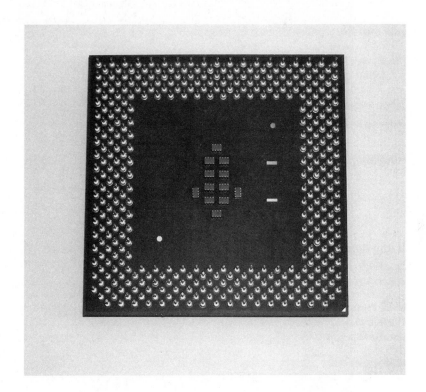

25.

26.

Cooling a CPU

CPUs generate a lot of heat as they operate, and aggressive cooling methods are needed to prevent them from overheating. A technician should be able to list and compare/contrast the various cooling methods that are available and should be able to install a heat sink and fan.

27. What are the pros and cons of liquid cooling systems?

_____

_____

_____

_____

28. What is the purpose of using a thermal compound when attaching a heat sink to a chip?

_____

_____

_____

_____

29. What is the difference between an active and a passive heat sink?

_____

_____

_____

_____

30. What is the relationship between CPU temperature and overclocking?

_____

_____

_____

_____

Exercise 2-5: Keeping Your Cool

1. Turn off your PC and open the case.

2. Locate the CPU and identify the type of cooling system in use on it. If you find an unknown type of cooling system, use Web resources as needed to identify it.

3. Close the case.

4. If your current cooling system failed (for example, if the fan stopped working), what would you replace it with? Shop online for an appropriate replacement.

Answers to Questions in This Chapter

The following are the answers to the practice questions presented earlier in this chapter:

1.

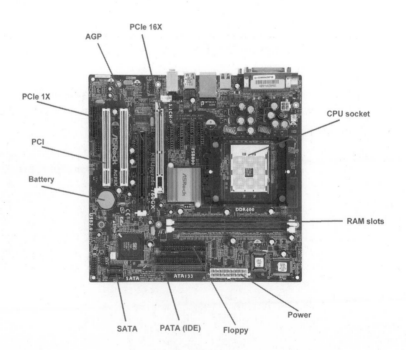

2. H

3. C

4. D

5. A

6. F

7. G

8. B

9. E

10. A

11. C

12. E

13. F

14. B

15-17.

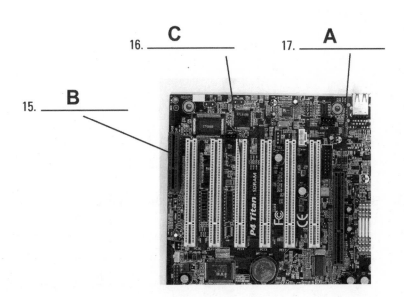

18-21.

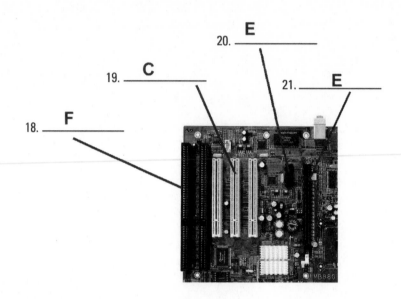

20. _____ E _____

19. _____ C _____

21. _____ E _____

18. _____ F _____

22. **Fill out the following chart to describe the characteristics of some popular CPUs.**

CPU	Manufacturer	Packaging (including # of pins)	Bits (32 or 64)
Pentium III	Intel	370, or SEC2 cartridge	32
Pentium 4	Intel	423 or 478	32
Xeon	Intel	603, or SEC cartridge	32
Itanium	Intel	418	64
Athlon XP	AMD	462	32
Duron	AMD	462	32
Opteron	AMD	940	64

23. **Fill out the following chart to describe the sockets.**

Socket	Compatible CPUs
Socket 370	Celeron, Pentium III
PAC 418	Itanium

Socket	Compatible CPUs
Socket 423	Pentium 4
Socket 478	Celeron, Pentium 4
Socket 603	Xeon
PAC 611	Itanium
Socket 940	Opteron
Slot A	Athlon
Slot 1	Pentium II, Pentium III
Slot 2	Xeon

24.

25.

26.

27. **What are the pros and cons of liquid cooling systems?**

The benefit of a liquid cooling system is the reduced noise and often superior cooling capacity. The drawbacks are the amount of space needed and the risk of leaking if it isn't installed properly.

28. **What is the purpose of using a thermal compound when attaching a heat sink to a chip?**

Thermal compound is a paste that creates a closer connection between the processor and the heat sink by filling in the gap with a heat-conductive material.

29. **What is the difference between an active and a passive heat sink?**

An active heat sink has a fan on it; a passive heat sink doesn't.

30. **What is the relationship between CPU temperature and overclocking?**

Overclocking increases the CPU's temperature, so more aggressive cooling measures might be required.

Chapter 3
Memory, BIOS, and CMOS

∙∙∙

In This Chapter

▶ Understanding memory types

▶ Identifying and selecting RAM

▶ Installing RAM

▶ Examining memory usage

▶ Understanding basic BIOS settings

▶ Troubleshooting and updating a BIOS

∙∙∙

In this chapter, you review information about identifying, selecting, installing, and troubleshooting memory in a PC.

Understanding Memory Types

Even though the term *memory* has come to refer mostly to RAM, it's actually a much broader term than that. It includes both RAM and ROM, both static and dynamic memory, and various types and speeds.

Use the following review questions to test your knowledge of memory types and your ability to differentiate one type from another:

1. What is the difference between RAM and ROM?

_____

_____

_____

_____

2.   What is the difference between static RAM and dynamic RAM?

_____

_____

_____

_____

3.   What is EEPROM and what is it used for?

_____

_____

_____

_____

4.   Name two ways to measure DRAM speed.

_____

_____

_____

_____

5.   Is CMOS a type of RAM or a type of ROM? Explain why.

_____

_____

_____

_____

6.   What is synchronous DRAM synchronized with?

_____

_____

_____

_____

7. How is DDR SDRAM different from regular SDRAM?

_____

_____

_____

_____

8. What is the purpose of a parity bit?

_____

_____

_____

_____

9. What is ECC memory?

_____

_____

_____

_____

_____

Identifying and Selecting RAM

When searching for RAM that will work in upgrading a certain PC, you should be able to identify various types of RAM visually. That way, even if you can't find any identifying markings, you still have at least an idea of what you're holding in your hands.

From the outside, you can differentiate one type of RAM from another by its packaging — that is, the size and style of circuit board to which the RAM chips are mounted. These little circuit boards, as they appear in modern PCs, are known as *dual inline memory modules* (DIMMs), and there are various types of them. Earlier systems (Pentium and below) used *single inline memory modules* (SIMMs).

For each of the following RAM sticks, write the following letters next to it:

- Write A next to all the SIMMs
- Write B next to all the DIMMs
- Write C next to parity SIMMs
- Write D next to 72-pin SIMMs
- Write E next to 30-pin SIMMs
- Write F next to SDRAM (all types)
- Write G next to SO-DIMMs
- Write H next to DDR or DDR2 SDRAM

10. _____

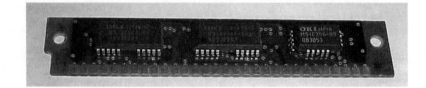

11. _____

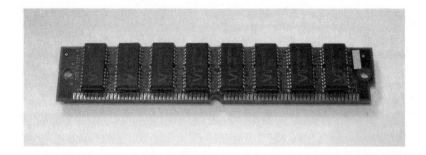

12. _____

13. ____

14. ____

15. ____

16. ____

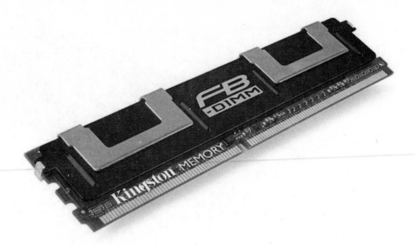

Exercise 3-1: Looking at RAM Types

Follow these steps to explore the types of RAM available:

1. Visit the Kingston Memory Web site at www.kingston.com.

2. View the memory products available there and examine the pictures of each type to familiarize yourself with their appearance.

3. Leaving that window open, use System Information on your PC to identify the type of RAM you currently have installed. (In Windows XP, choose Start⇨All Programs⇨Accessories⇨System Tools⇨System Information.)

4. Use the Memory Tools section of the Kingston Web site to find memory that you can use in your current system.

Installing RAM

Ninety percent of the tricky stuff involved in working with memory is choosing the appropriate type. After that's done, the process of actually installing the stuff is a piece of cake.

On an older system using SIMMs, you typically install RAM at a 45-degree angle to the motherboard and then push it up to a 90-degree angle. Make sure you get the RAM in the slot facing the right direction; use the existing RAM's positioning as a guide.

Newer systems that use DIMMs have RAM slots in which the RAM goes down into the slots at a straight 90-degree angle. Press the RAM firmly into the slot, seesawing it if needed, until the retaining clips pop into place at both ends. DIMMs fit into the slots only one way because of the notches in the DIMMs and in the slots.

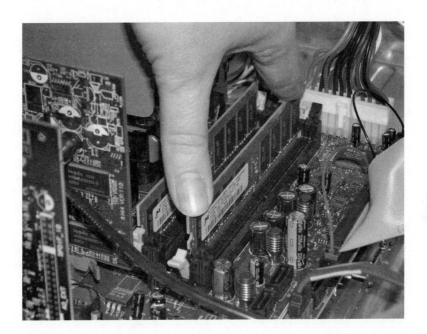

Exercise 3-2: Practicing RAM Installation

Follow these steps to practice installing RAM:

1. Turn off your PC and open the case.

2. Remove one stick of RAM.

3. Examine its markings and make a mental note of its type.

4. Reinstall the RAM.

5. Close the case and restart your PC.

Examining Memory Usage

Many times when evaluating the memory in a system, you don't have to open the case and physically inspect the SIMMs or DIMMs. Instead, you can rely on memory utilities either present within the operating system itself or provided by third parties.

The Windows OS provides basic memory information via its System Information utility, including the total amount of physical and virtual memory and the available amounts of each. It also reports specific memory addresses that various devices are using, and it displays what programs and processes are running and how much RAM they're occupying. Other information utilities include the command-line MEM command and the Performance tab of the Task Manager.

Test your knowledge of the types of memory usage that system information and memory utilities typically report on:

17. What is the first 640K of RAM called?

_____

_____

18. What is the RAM between 640K and 1MB called?

_____

19. What is the RAM above 1MB called?

_____

20. What type of memory does HIMEM.SYS work with, and what does it do to the memory?

_____

_____

_____

21. What type of memory does the EMM386.EXE driver enable?

_____

Exercise 3-3: Collecting Memory Information

Follow these steps to practice collecting memory information from a Windows XP or Vista system:

1. In Windows XP or Windows Vista, choose Start➪All Programs➪Accessories➪ System Tools➪System Information to open the System Information dialog box.

2. Click System Summary and then scroll down in the right pane to find the following information:

- Total Physical Memory: _____

- Available Physical Memory: _____

- Total Virtual Memory: _____

- Available Virtual Memory: _____

- Page File Space: _____

- Page File: _____

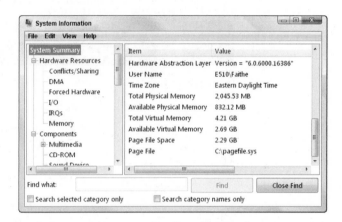

3. Expand the Software Environment group and click Running Tasks. Examine the running tasks.

4. Expand the Hardware Resources group and click Memory. Examine the memory addresses in use for the hardware.

5. Close the System Information dialog box.

6. Right-click the taskbar and click Task Manager.

7. On the Performance tab, gather the following information:

- Physical Memory (Total): _____

- Physical Memory (Cached): _____

- Kernel Memory (Total): _____

- Kernel Memory (Paged): _____

8. Close the Task Manager window.

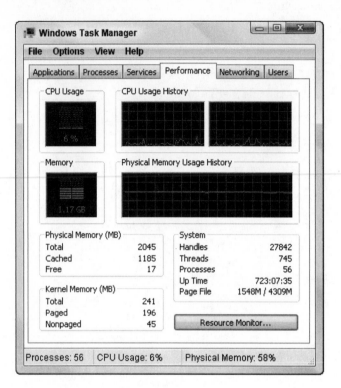

Working with Virtual Memory

Virtual memory isn't really memory at all; it's storage space that is used to help extend the memory capacity on a system. On Windows systems, a file called `pagefile.sys` is used to set aside the space for use by virtual memory. Whenever the system runs out of real RAM, it moves the least-recently used contents of RAM out to the hard drive, into a paging file, freeing up some blocks of real RAM for new content. When the content in `pagefile.sys` is needed again in RAM, Windows performs another swap to bring the data back to its original location, from which it can be accessed. For that reason, another name for the paging file is *swap* file.

Most of the time, Windows manages virtual memory nicely all by itself. You don't have to do anything special to it. However, sometimes it can be advantageous in certain situations to specify which hard drive will be used for virtual memory and/or to limit the size of the paging file.

Exercise 3-4: Changing Virtual Memory Settings

Follow these steps to practice configuring virtual memory:

1. In Windows XP or Windows Vista, choose Start⇨Control Panel⇨Click Classic View.

2. Double-click the System icon.

3. In Windows Vista, double-click Advanced system settings. (This step is not necessary in Windows XP.)

4. Click the Advanced tab.

5. Under Performance, click the Settings button.

6. Click the Advanced tab.

7. Under Virtual Memory, click the Change button.

8. Clear the Automatically Manage Paging File Size for All Drives check box.

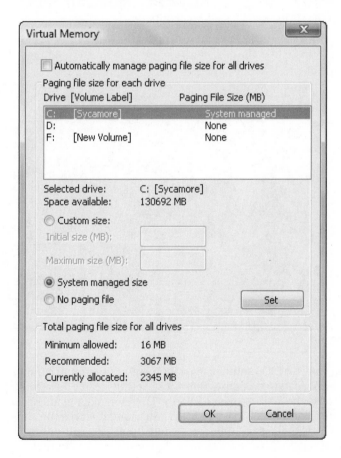

9. Choose the desired hard drive for the paging file from the drives listed.

10. Click Custom size.

11. Look at the recommended size and then type that amount into the Maximum Size text box.

12. Click OK and restart the PC when prompted.

13. Return the system to the original configuration by selecting the Automatically Manage Paging File Size for All Drives check box.

Understanding the BIOS and CMOS

The *Basic Input/Output System* (BIOS) is the instruction set that tells the PC how to start, including recognizing its basic hardware and transferring control to the operating system. The BIOS chip is typically a *dual inline pin package* (DIPP), which is a rectangular chip with "legs" on two sides, like a centipede.

BIOS chip

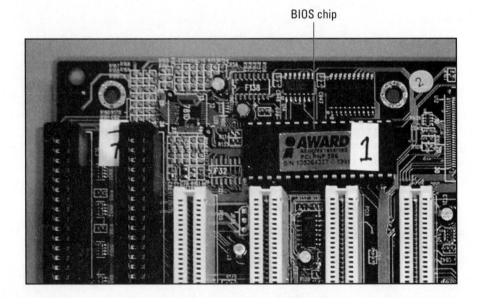

You can edit BIOS settings via a BIOS setup utility that's built into the motherboard. The only catch, though, is that those settings can't be saved on the BIOS chip itself because the BIOS chip is read-only. Therefore a companion *Complementary Metal-Oxide Semiconductor* (CMOS) chip is available, and it stores the changes you make to the BIOS's defaults. Each time the system boots, the settings in BIOS load, and then any variations to those settings load from CMOS on top of that.

Technically yes, the BIOS chip *can* be changed via a special BIOS updater utility. However, that utility is used only to provide a new read-only version of the BIOS, not to make configuration changes to the system.

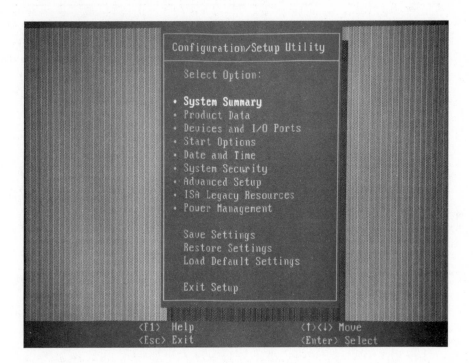

Test your knowledge of all things BIOS and CMOS:

22. Describe how to enter a CMOS Setup program, starting with the computer powered off.

_____

_____

_____

_____

23. What are hard drive type numbers, and why aren't they used today when setting up modern drives?

_____

_____

_____

24. Suppose you want to boot from a DVD, but the PC keeps booting from the hard drive instead. What CMOS setting can you change to ensure that the PC boots from the DVD?

_____

_____

25. In CMOS Setup, you might be able to set both an administrator password and a power-on password.

A. If you don't know the administrator password, what can't you do?

_____

_____

B. If you don't know the power-on password, what can't you do?

_____

_____

26. How can you reset the CMOS password on a system where it has been forgotten?

_____

_____

_____

_____

27. What three conditions are necessary for Plug and Play to work correctly?

_____

_____

_____

_____

28. List three components that might be built into a motherboard and enabled/disabled via the CMOS Setup program.

_____

_____

_____

Exercise 3-5: Mastering the CMOS Setup Program

Follow these steps to practice working with a CMOS Setup program:

1. Start your PC and press whatever key is specified to run CMOS Setup.

2. Locate the Date/Time setting, and change the time two minutes ahead of its current time; then change it back again.

3. Locate the floppy disk controller in CMOS Setup. If you have a floppy drive, it's probably enabled; disable it and then re-enable it. If you don't have a floppy drive, it's probably disabled; enable it and then disable it again.

4. If your system has a parallel port, check to see what mode it's in (SPP, EPP, or ECP). Change its mode to any of the other modes, disable the port entirely, and then change it back to its original mode.

5. If your system has a serial port, check to see what address and IRQ are assigned to it.

6. Locate the USB controller settings in CMOS Setup. Disable the USB controller and then re-enable it.

7. Exit from CMOS Setup and don't save your changes.

Troubleshooting and Updating a BIOS

Sometimes the root cause of a system problem turns out to be the BIOS. This can happen for any of several reasons:

✔ Someone might have made inappropriate changes to CMOS settings.

✔ The BIOS might have an error or bug in it.

✔ The BIOS might be incompatible with a new piece of hardware you just installed.

In such cases, you might first try resetting the BIOS to factory settings by clearing the CMOS. (You can do that via the BIOS Setup program itself or via a reset jumper on the motherboard.)

If that doesn't solve the problem, you might consider updating the BIOS by using a BIOS update utility. You can download such a utility — and the needed update — from the PC manufacturer's Web site. In most cases, you should go directly to the PC manufacturer and look up the PC by model number and serial number to confirm that you're getting the correct update. If the PC manufacturer doesn't have a Web site (for example, if it's out of business), you might try a third-party site such as a BIOS archive or the site of the BIOS chip's manufacturer.

See how much you know about BIOS updates and troubleshooting:

29. List at least two ways of finding out what BIOS version you have currently.

_____

_____

_____

_____

30. Suppose you need to install a BIOS update on a system, and the update you've downloaded needs to extract itself to a floppy disk, from which you're then supposed to boot. The PC doesn't have a floppy disk, however. What can you do?

_____

_____

_____

_____

31. If you can't locate an update for your specific BIOS, is it okay to install a BIOS update for a different model as long as it's from the same BIOS manufacturer? Why or why not?

_____

_____

_____

_____

Exercise 3-6: Updating the BIOS

Follow these steps to update your BIOS:

1. Determine your BIOS model and version number. Write them here:

_____

2. Go to the PC manufacturer's Web site and determine whether an update to your BIOS is available.

3. Download the update.

4. Install the update according to the instructions provided with it.

5. Determine your BIOS version number to confirm that the update took place. Write the current version number here: _____

Answers to Questions in This Chapter

The following are the answers to the practice questions presented earlier in this chapter:

1. What is the difference between RAM and ROM?

Random Access Memory (RAM) can be written to, whereas Read-Only Memory (ROM) permanently retains its original content, except when changed using some special update method, such as running a BIOS update utility.

2. What is the difference between static RAM and dynamic RAM?

Static RAM retains whatever information it holds indefinitely, whereas dynamic RAM requires constant electrical refreshing to retain its information, so it loses information if the power goes off.

3. What is EEPROM and what is it used for?

Electrically Eraseable Programmable Read-Only Memory (EEPROM) is the type of ROM used on most systems to store the BIOS. This type of ROM is erasable and rewriteable using a utility program that increases the voltage delivered to the chip temporarily, wiping out its contents, and then writes new information to it.

4. Name two ways to measure DRAM speed.

Older DRAM is measured in nanoseconds of delay, such as 60 ns, with lower numbers being faster. Modern RAM is synchronized with the speed of the system bus and is measured in megahertz, with higher numbers being faster.

5. Is CMOS a type of RAM or a type of ROM? Explain why.

CMOS is a type of dynamic RAM. It requires electrical refreshing, like other DRAM, but it requires less electrical power than most RAM, so it gets what it needs from the motherboard's battery.

6. What is synchronous DRAM synchronized with?

The motherboard's system bus speed. The DRAM can be either the same speed as the motherboard bus or a multiple of it.

7. How is DDR SDRAM different from regular SDRAM?

DDR stands for Double Data Rate. This type of RAM can process two operations per clock cycle (that is, the motherboard's system bus clock tick), so DDR SDRAM's speed is twice as fast as that of the motherboard system bus.

8. What is the purpose of a parity bit?

A parity bit is for error checking. Parity RAM ensures that no storage mistakes occur in the RAM banks. If a parity bit detects an error, the system shuts down.

9. What is ECC memory?

ECC stands for Error Correcting Code. ECC memory is like parity memory except that when it identifies an error, it attempts to correct the error, rather than shut down the system.

10. A, E

11. A, D

12. B, F

13. B, F, G

14. B, F, H

15. B, F, H

16. B, F, H

17. **What is the first 640K of RAM called?**

Conventional memory

18. **What is the RAM between 640K and 1MB called?**

Upper memory

19. **What is the RAM above 1MB called?**

Extended memory

20. **What type of memory does `HIMEM.SYS` work with, and what does it do to the memory?**

`HIMEM.SYS` works with extended memory; it converts the memory to XMS so the operating system (such as Windows) can use it.

21. **What type of memory does the `EMM386.EXE` driver enable?**

Expanded memory

22. **Describe how to enter a CMOS Setup program, starting with the computer powered off.**

As the PC is booting, a message appears on-screen telling you what key to press to enter the Setup utility. Press that key. Depending on the BIOS manufacturer, it might be Del, F10, F1, or F2. If the operating system begins to load, you didn't press the key at the right time; reboot and try again.

23. **What are hard drive type numbers, and why aren't they used today when setting up modern drives?**

Hard drive type numbers were used in the very early days of computing to designate a particular size of hard drive and all its settings. They're no longer used because the old type definitions are out of date and because modern systems use Plug and Play to automatically detect the drive's capacity and settings, so manually configuring the drive's type is no longer an issue.

24. **Suppose you want to boot from a DVD, but the PC keeps booting from the hard drive instead. What CMOS setting can you change to ensure that the PC in fact boots from the DVD?**

    In CMOS Setup, change the boot order so that the system prefers the DVD drive over the hard drive (that is, boots from it first).

25. **In CMOS Setup, you might be able to set both an administrator password and a power-on password.**

    A. If you don't know the administrator password, what can't you do?

    You can't enter CMOS Setup to make changes there.

    B. If you don't know the power-on password, what can't you do?

    You can't boot the PC.

26. **How can you reset the CMOS password on a system where it has been forgotten?**

    You can move the Reset jumper to Reset position, power the system on for several seconds, and then power it off again and put the jumper back to Normal position. This causes all data stored in CMOS to be flushed, not just the passwords.

27. **What three conditions are necessary for Plug and Play to work correctly?**

    Plug-and-play–compatible BIOS

    Plug-and-play–compatible hardware

    Plug-and-play–compatible operating system

28. **List three components that might be built into a motherboard and enabled/disabled via the CMOS Setup program.**

    Built-in components might include the display adapter, sound card, network card, and modem.

29. **List at least two ways of finding out what BIOS version you have currently.**

    You can find the BIOS information in the CMOS Setup program or on-screen when the PC starts. You can also get it from the System Information utility in Windows XP and Windows Vista.

30. **Suppose you need to install a BIOS update on a system, and the update you've downloaded needs to extract itself to a floppy disk, from which you're then supposed to boot. The PC doesn't have a floppy disk, however. What can you do?**

    Some BIOS updates come in two forms, one for a floppy and one without; check to see whether an alternative version is available. If not, use a USB-based floppy disk drive.

31. **If you can't locate an update for your specific BIOS, is it okay to install a BIOS update for a different model as long as it's from the same BIOS manufacturer? Why or why not?**

    No, it is not okay to install an update that isn't specifically created for the exact BIOS you have, because incompatibilities can result, causing your system to be unusable.

Chapter 4

Disk Storage

- -

In This Chapter

▶ Understanding hard drive terminology

▶ Reviewing IDE standards

▶ Understanding IDE capacity limitations

▶ Configuring PATA disk drives

▶ Understanding SCSI drives

▶ Configuring SCSI drives

- -

In this chapter, you practice procedures for working with disks and drives of various types.

Understanding Hard Drive Terminology

All hard drives store data in basically the same way — they divide the available surfaces into individually addressable areas, and then they maintain a record of what data is stored where. The way the drive is divided into addressable units is called its *geometry*.

When selecting and configuring hard drives, it's helpful to understand how they're categorized, benchmarked, and sold. A drive's specs can tell you how large it is, its geometry, what type of interface it uses, how fast it can perform, and more.

1. On a hard drive, what is a track? What is a cylinder? What is the relationship between them?

_____

_____

_____

_____

2. How many bytes are in a sector on a hard drive?

_____

3. What is the formula for calculating a hard drive's capacity based on its cylinders, heads, and sectors?

   _____

4. Suppose you have a drive that reports 4,960 cylinders, 15 heads, and 63 sectors per track. What is that drive's capacity?

   _____

5. In Question 4, is the answer the drive's actual physical geometry, or translated? How can you tell?

   _____

   _____

   _____

   _____

6. What is the relationship between a sector and a cluster?

   _____

   _____

   _____

7. What is seek time and how is it measured?

   _____

   _____

   _____

8. What is latency and how is it measured?

   _____

   _____

   _____

Exercise 4-1: Evaluating Hard Drives, Part I

Follow these steps to practice working with hard drive geometry and performance measurement:

1. Enter CMOS Setup for your PC and look at the drive settings for your primary hard drive. Identify the drive's geometry (cylinders, heads, and sectors) and the sector translation method being used.

2. Use the Web to find a hard drive–benchmarking utility. Use it to determine your drive's seek time, latency, and access time.

3. Compare the measurements from Step 2 with the advertised specifications for your drive as reported on its manufacturer's Web site. Based on those comparisons, are the manufacturer's claims about drive performance accurate?

Understanding IDE Standards

IDE stands for *Integrated Drive Electronics*. In a nutshell, that means that the controller for the drive is built into the package with the drive platters. The operating system talks to the drive controller, which in turn talks to the drive. The modern version of IDE is known as *Advanced Technology Attachment* (ATA). (All other versions of IDE are long obsolete, so ATA and IDE can be considered roughly the same thing for most purposes.)

IDE is the most common type of drive interface, by far. (The other type is SCSI, which is covered in the next section.) Almost any hard drive you buy for a system will therefore be an IDE of some type.

The two types of connections for ATA drives are *Parallel ATA* (PATA), which is the traditional type with a ribbon cable, and *Serial ATA* (SATA), the newer type, using a smaller, thinner cable.

PATA has been around for a long time, and many iterations of the standard have been released, starting with ATA-1 and running to the current version, ATA-6. Each of these standards has its own top speed and specifications.

Match up the following descriptions with the IDE standard:

    A. IDE/ATA

    B. EIDE/ATA-2

    C. ATA-3 (ATAPI)

    D. UltraDMA/33

    E. UltraDMA/66

    F. UltraDMA/133

    G. SATA

9. ____ An UltraDMA version that operates at 66 Mbps

10. ____ The first version to allow for a dual-channel controller that has two drives on the same cable

11. ____ The first version to allow other drives, such as CD-ROM drives, to be used on an ATA/IDE controller

12. ____ The fastest available parallel ATA version

13. _____ Also known as ATA-1, the original ATA standard

14. _____ The only UltraDMA version that can work at its top speed with a regular 40-wire ribbon cable

15. _____ A serial type of ATA, expected to soon replace UltraDMA as the dominant standard

---

Exercise 4-2: Evaluating Hard Drives, Part II

Suppose you have a motherboard with an ATA-4–compliant PATA controller built into it, supporting UltraDMA/66, and you need to purchase a hard drive for it. Go online and locate an appropriate hard drive. Keep the following in mind:

- ATA-4 compliant hard drives are no longer being made, so you need to get one that supports a higher standard. It will be backward-compatible, however.

- ATA-6 is required for the BIOS to support a hard drive larger than 137GB, so a drive larger than that is a waste.

- On a system where the data transfer rate will be limited to ATA-4 speeds (66 Mbps), it would be especially useful for the drive to have a low access time. A higher RPM (revolutions per minute) would mean less latency, which is one factor in access time. The less latency, the better.

Understanding Hard Drive Capacity Limitations

The original IDE specification limited drive size to 540MB. It wasn't that the drive individually or the system BIOS individually couldn't handle more, but the combination of the two couldn't. Physically, the drive could have a lot more cylinders than the BIOS could keep track of, but fewer heads than the BIOS could manage. To overcome this limitation — and other limitations that came after — various translation and enhancement schemes have been developed over the years to enable systems to recognize drives with larger and larger capacities.

These capacity limitations (and limitation-breakers) fall into two main categories:

- **BIOS support:** Newer BIOSes support larger hard drives because of their support of modern sector translation methods.

- **OS support:** New operating systems support larger hard drives because of their file systems (FAT32, NTFS) and because of their tie-in with the BIOS support.

Test your knowledge of hard drive capacity limitations:

16. What do the acronyms CHS, ECHS, and LBA stand for, and what do they have in common?

_____

_____

_____

_____

17. What is the size limit for a drive that uses 28-bit LBA addressing?

_____

18. What does 48-bit LBA addressing achieve, and what operating systems support its use?

_____

_____

_____

_____

19. What is *Enhanced BIOS Services for Disk Drives,* and what does it do?

_____

_____

_____

20. What is the size limit per logical drive under FAT16?

_____

21. Suppose you just bought a used 20GB hard drive for an old PC. You install it, but the BIOS autodetects it as a 528MB drive. What is happening, and what can you do, if anything, to make the BIOS see it as a larger size?

_____

_____

_____

_____

22. Suppose you have that same 20GB hard drive, and you install it in a different PC (still an older one, but not as old as the one in Question 21). The BIOS autodetects it as an 8GB drive. What is happening, and what can you do, if anything, to make the BIOS see it as a larger size?

_____

_____

_____

_____

23. You have managed to make the BIOS recognize the drive as its full 20GB, and you're ready to partition and format it. You boot from a Windows 95 startup floppy and use FDISK to partition the drive, but it won't let you create partitions larger than 2GB. What is causing this problem, and what can you do to solve it?

_____

_____

_____

_____

Exercise 4-3: Identifying Hard Drive Limitations

Follow these steps to practice identifying BIOS-based and OS-based drive capacity limitations:

1. Enter CMOS Setup and locate the settings for the primary hard drive.

2. Find the settings that enable/disable LBA or other sector translation.

3. Disable LBA and check the drive's reported capacity in CMOS Setup. Then re-enable LBA.

4. Exit CMOS Setup without saving your changes and then boot into Windows.

5. Using System Information, collect the following information about the primary hard drive:

    - Size _____
    - Free space _____
    - File system _____
    - Bytes per sector _____
    - Sectors per track _____
    - Total cylinders _____
    - Total sectors _____
    - Tracks per cylinder _____

Configuring PATA Disk Drives

Each parallel ATA controller can support up to two drives using a single ribbon cable. The first drive is the master, and the second one is the slave. The faster drive of the two should be set as the master because the master receives and processes all commands; the slave drive receives only the commands that the master passes on to it.

You have two ways of specifying which drive will be the master and which the slave. You can set jumpers on the drives for master or slave status, or you can set the jumper to Cable Select, in which case the drives rely on their relative positions on the ribbon cable to determine which is which. (The drive farthest away from the end connected to the controller is the master.)

Some hard drives have a separate jumper setting for Single (that is, for when it is the only drive on the cable); others use the Master setting both for single-drive usage and for cases where the drive is a master that has a slave.

An older motherboard typically has two PATA controllers: IDE0 and IDE1. The drives attached to IDE0 are primary, and the drives attached to IDE1 are secondary. For example, the master on IDE0 is the Primary Master and is typically the boot drive (usually the main hard drive).

24. How is pin 1 marked on a motherboard's PATA connector?

_____

_____

25. How is pin 1 marked on a PATA ribbon cable?

_____

_____

26. How many pins are in a PATA connector on a motherboard?

_____

_____

Suppose that the following chart appears on a hard drive's label:

J5

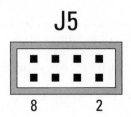

	J5 (7–8)	J5 (5–6)	J5 (3–4)	J5 (1–2)
ATA Master Only	▪ ▪	▪ ▪	▪ ▪	▪ ▪
ATA Slave	[▪ ▪]	▪ ▪	▪ ▪	▪ ▪
ATA Master with Slave	▪ ▪	[▪ ▪]	▪ ▪	▪ ▪
Cable Select	[▪ ▪]	[▪ ▪]	▪ ▪	▪ ▪

On the following diagrams, if a jumper cap is necessary, indicate where it should be positioned.

27.   Master with no slave

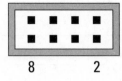

28.   Master with slave

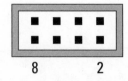

29. Slave

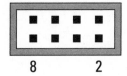

8   2

30. Cable Select

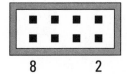

8   2

Now suppose there is no label on the drive, but some letters are above the jumper pins, as shown here:

On the following diagrams, draw the jumper positions needed.

31. Master with no slave

32.   Master with slave

33.   Slave

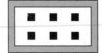

34.   Cable Select

Exercise 4-4: Working with Jumper Settings

1. Open your computer's case and locate all the PATA drives.

2. Remove each PATA drive and examine its jumper settings. Write them down if needed.

3. If any ribbon cable contains two drives, switch which one is the master and which one is the slave. Reboot and examine the drive settings in CMOS Setup and then shut down again and put the drives back to their original master/slave settings.

4. If possible, rearrange the cabling on the PATA drives so that the fastest PATA hard drive is on its own cable, separate from the other PATA drives, if possible. (This isn't possible if you have four PATA drives.)

Understanding SCSI Drives

SCSI stands for *Small Computer System Interface.* It's a venerable technology for connecting disk drives, but it's been updated many times, so it holds its own favorably with IDE.

One of the benefits of SCSI is that a single host adapter can support many drives without appreciable slowdown in performance. IDE, on the other hand, suffers from performance issues when even two drives share a cable. The fastest SCSI drives today can also outperform the fastest IDE devices.

SCSI hasn't caught on in the mainstream primarily because of its higher cost, coupled with the fact that most motherboards don't have a SCSI controller, necessitating the use of an add-on board. SCSI is popular in RAIDs, however, and in high-end storage systems.

Test your knowledge of SCSI terminology:

35. How many devices can a standard (narrow) SCSI host adapter support?

_____

36. How many devices can a wide SCSI host adapter support?

_____

37. Which of these types of connectors are used for SCSI devices? Choose as many as apply.

    _____A. 50-pin IDC (internal ribbon cable)

    _____B. 40-pin IDC (internal ribbon cable)

    _____C. 68-pin high density

    _____D. 80-pin SCSI SCA

    _____E. DB-25

    _____F. 50-pin Centronics

    _____G. 50-pin high density

    _____H. 68-pin high density

    _____I. 68-pin very high density

38. What is the difference between passive and active termination?

_____

_____

_____

_____

39. Of the following types of devices, which can coexist on the same chain?

Standard SCSI

Low-Voltage Differential (LVD)

High-Voltage Differential (HVD)

_____

_____

_____

_____

40. If your SCSI host adapter has a combination of internal and external devices attached to it, should the host adapter itself be terminated? Why or why not?

_____

_____

_____

_____

41. What is the bus width on Ultra Wide SCSI, and what is its maximum data transfer rate in Mbps?

_____

_____

Exercise 4-5: Working with SCSI Drives

Suppose you want to add SCSI capability to your system, and you need both internal and external SCSI support. Follow these steps:

1. Go to www.adaptec.com and select a moderately priced SCSI host adapter that will work for this purpose.

2. Locate a moderately priced SCSI hard drive at www.maxtor.com and determine what type of SCSI connector it uses.

3. Shop online for a cable that you can use to connect the drive from Step 2 with the host adapter from Step 1.

Configuring SCSI Drives

Selecting the appropriate SCSI devices is half the battle; the other half is installing them correctly. SCSI has a reputation for being tricky to configure, but that reputation was earned back in the old days before automatic configuration was the norm.

Even though most SCSI devices are automatically configured these days, you still need to know how to set termination and IDs manually for the A+ exam and for those cases where you have to deal with older equipment in the field.

Exercise 4-6: Installing SCSI Devices

The general process for installing SCSI devices is as follows:

1. If needed, install the host adapter card and install drivers for it.

2. Set unique ID numbers on each device if needed. Give the host adapter its own ID, too.

3. Connect the SCSI devices to the host adapter by using appropriate cables.

4. Terminate both ends of the chain.

Some devices have internal termination that you can enable with jumpers or through the device's properties; others require a terminator block to be attached. Some devices set their ID via a wheel or jumper; others are software-configured.

For devices that are jumper-configured, a chart explaining the jumper settings might be printed on the device. If you don't find a chart, you can generally assume that the jumper pins represent binary numbering, from right to left, as shown in this image:

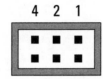

With no jumper caps (as shown here), the SCSI ID is 0 (zero). With a cap over any of the other pin sets, the SCSI ID number is the sum of all the pins with caps. For example, the ID if all three sets of pins are capped would be 7 (4+2+1).

Test your knowledge of SCSI configuration:

What SCSI ID are the following jumpers set to?

42. ____

43. ____

44. ____

For the following questions, suppose you have a drive with the following label on it:

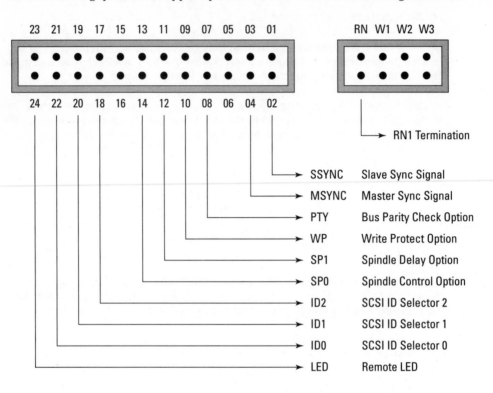

SCSI ID	ID2	ID1	ID0
0	N	N	N
1	N	N	Y
2	N	Y	N
3	N	Y	Y
4	Y	N	N
5	Y	N	Y
6	Y	Y	N
7	Y	Y	Y

45. Draw the jumpers for setting the drive to SCSI ID 6.

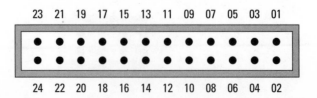

46. Draw the jumpers for setting the drive to SCSI ID 1.

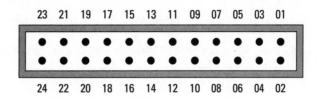

47. Draw the jumpers for setting the drive to SCSI ID 5.

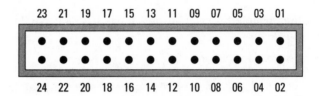

Exercise 4-7: Configuring a SCSI Drive

1. Install a SCSI host adapter in your PC. Boot into Windows and install a driver for it.

2. Review the documentation for the host adapter, or explore its Properties in Windows from Device Manager, and then determine how to set the adapter's SCSI ID number. Set it to 7.

3. Turn off the PC and attach two SCSI devices to the adapter. Terminate them as needed. Assign IDs to them as needed. (Don't use 7, because that's already in use.)

4. Restart Windows and check that each SCSI device works correctly.

5. Turn off the PC and change the ID number for each of the devices. (Do not duplicate.)

6. Restart Windows and check that each SCSI device works correctly.

Answers to Questions in This Chapter

The following are the answers to the practice questions presented earlier in this chapter:

1. **On a hard drive, what is a track? What is a cylinder? What is the relationship between them?**

   A track is a concentric ring on a disk platter. A stack of tracks that are all at the same in/out position of the read/write heads in a hard drive is known collectively a cylinder.

2. **How many bytes are in a sector on a hard drive?**

   512

3. **What is the formula for calculating a hard drive's capacity based on its cylinders, heads, and sectors?**

   Cylinders × Heads × Sectors × 512

4. **Suppose you have a hard drive that reports 4,960 cylinders, 15 heads, and 63 sectors per track. What is that drive's capacity?**

   $4,960 \times 15 \times 63 \times 512 = 2,399,846,400$, or approximately 2.4GB

5. **In Question 4, is the answer the drive's actual physical geometry, or translated? How can you tell?**

   No, the answer to Question 4 isn't the physical geometry. One way to tell is that it has an odd number of heads, but on an actual drive each platter is double-sided so the number of heads would be even.

6. **What is the relationship between a sector and a cluster?**

   A cluster, also called an allocation unit, is a group of sectors that the operating system addresses as a single unit.

7. **What is seek time and how is it measured?**

   Seek time is the amount of time it takes for the read/write heads to find a particular sector, on the average.

8. **What is latency and how is it measured?**

   Latency is the time it takes for the appropriate sector to move under the read/write head. It is measured in milliseconds.

9. **An UltraDMA version that operates at 66 Mbps.**

   E

10. **The first version to allow for a dual-channel controller that has two drives on the same cable.**

    B

11. **The first version to allow other drives, such as CD-ROM drives, to be used on an ATA/IDE controller.**

    C

12. **The fastest available parallel ATA version.**

    F

13. **Also known as ATA-1, the original ATA standard.**

    A

14. **The only UltraDMA version that can work at its top speed with a regular 40-wire ribbon cable.**

    D

15. **A serial type of ATA, expected to soon replace UltraDMA as the dominant standard.**

    G

16. **What do the acronyms CHS, ECHS, and LBA stand for, and what do they have in common?**

    CHS stands for Cylinder/Head/Sector. ECHS stands for Extended Cylinder/Head/Sector. LBA stands for Logical Block Addressing. These are all methods used by the BIOS when interpreting the available storage locations on a hard drive.

17. **What is the size limit for a drive that uses 28-bit LBA addressing?**

    8.4GB

18. **What does 48-bit LBA addressing achieve, and what operating systems support its use?**

    48-bit LBA addressing breaks the 137GB barrier for hard drive size. It's supported in Windows 2000 Service Pack 4 and higher and Windows XP Service Pack 1 and higher.

19. **What is *Enhanced BIOS Services for Disk Drives,* and what does it do?**

    It's a BIOS feature that enables hard drives to break the 8.4GB barrier.

20. **What is the size limit per logical drive under FAT16?**

    2GB

21. **Suppose you just bought a used 20GB hard drive for an old PC. You install it, but the BIOS autodetects it as a 528MB drive. What is happening, and what can you do, if anything, to make the BIOS see it as a larger size?**

    The drive is set to use CHS values in CMOS Setup. You need to set it to LBA.

22. **Suppose you have that same 20GB hard drive, and you install it in a different PC (still an older one, but not as old as the one in Question 21). The BIOS autodetects it as an 8GB drive. What is happening, and what can you do, if anything, to make the BIOS see it as a larger size?**

    You need Enhanced BIOS Services for Disk Drives, which can generally be obtained via a BIOS update.

23. **You have managed to make the BIOS recognize the drive as its full 20GB, and you're ready to partition and format it. You boot from a Windows 95 startup floppy and use FDISK to partition the drive, but it won't let you create partitions larger than 2GB. What is causing this problem, and what can you do to solve it?**

A Windows 95 boot disk doesn't support FAT32. Booting from a Windows 98 boot disk will solve the problem.

24. **How is pin 1 marked on a motherboard's PATA connector?**

It is marked with an arrow or triangle printed on the motherboard next to one end of the connector.

25. **How is pin 1 marked on a PATA ribbon cable?**

With a red stripe.

26. **How many pins are in a PATA connector on a motherboard?**

40

27. **Master with no slave**

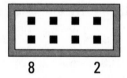

28. **Master with slave**

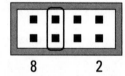

29. **Slave**

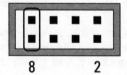

30. **Cable select**

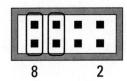

31. **Master with no slave**

32. **Master with slave**

33. **Slave**

34. **Cable select**

35. 3

36. 5

37. 0

38. **What is the difference between passive and active termination?**

Passive termination uses a resistor; active termination uses voltage regulation. Passive termination is cheap and not as effective; use it only on chains with two or fewer devices.

39. **Of the following types of devices, which can coexist on the same chain?**

Standard SCSI

Low-Voltage Differential (LVD)

High-Voltage Differential (HVD)

Standard and LVD can be used on the same chain.

40. **If your SCSI host adapter has a combination of internal and external devices attached to it, should the host adapter itself be terminated? Why or why not?**

No, it should not, because the host adapter is not the end of the chain.

41. **What is the bus width on Ultra Wide SCSI, and what is its maximum data transfer rate in Mbps?**

16-bit width, and 20 MB/sec

42. 3

43. 5

44. 0

45.

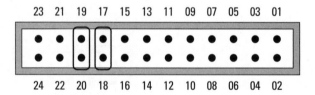

46.

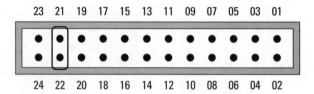

47.

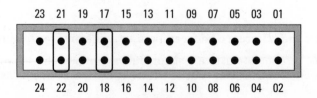

Chapter 5

Power Supplies and Portable PCs

• •

• •

*I*n this chapter, you practice procedures for working with power supplies and portable PCs.

Understanding Electricity

Electrical systems in computers fail fairly often in comparison to other components, and yet they're one of the last things many people suspect when troubleshooting, simply because people forget about it. Folks get so used to relying on consistent, clean electrical power coming from a wall outlet to whatever devices need it that it's easy to forget that a lot happens to that power between its entry into the PC case and its delivery to the motherboard and other components.

To perform electrical testing, you must first understand the core concepts and vocabulary of electricity, such as volts, amps, ohms, and watts.

Match up the following descriptions with the electricity-related term.

A. Volt

B. Amp

C. Ohm

D. Watts

E. Resistance

F. Continuity

G. AC

H. DC

1. _____ The unit of measure for power delivered, equal to one joule per second

2. _____ The unit of measure for electrical impedance

3. _____ The unit of measure for electrical potential difference

4. _____ The type of current that alternates between positive and negative

5. _____ The unit of measure for the rate of electrical flow

6. _____ The type of current that does not alternate

7. _____ The condition of a pathway existing through which electricity can flow

8. _____ The general term for electrical impedance

9. Using the terms *amp, volt,* and *watt,* write the formula for calculating the wattage used by a specific component:

_____

10. Suppose a hard drive uses 0.4 amp of 5V DC and 0.27 amp of 12V DC. What is its total wattage consumed?

_____

Selecting Appropriate Power Supplies

To select a power supply for a computer system, you need to understand the criteria by which power supplies are evaluated. Some things to consider include:

✔ **Overall wattage:** How much power overall can the power supply deliver?

✔ **Wattage of each voltage:** How much power of each voltage can the power supply deliver? The +12V voltage is especially important because most high-wattage devices draw mostly from that voltage.

✔ **Form factor:** What's the size and shape of the power supply in comparison to the area of the case in which it needs to mount?

✔ **Connector types:** Does the power supply have the right connectors to the motherboard? Does it have enough connectors for all the drives you want to hook up?

When calculating overall wattage that a power supply can deliver, keep in mind that it can't actually deliver 100 percent of the wattage for which it's rated in most environments. Wattage ratings are often based upon a certain operating temperature, and it's usually lower than the actual temperature at which most PCs operate, so the wattage promises made by the specs are overly optimistic. For example, a certain wattage might be deliverable at 25 degrees Celsius (approximately 50 degrees Fahrenheit), but how many offices keep their thermostat set at 50? In addition, you must factor in the fact that most devices draw more power as they're starting up than they do while they're running — up to three times as much. Therefore you should buy a power supply that supports significantly greater wattage than you actually need.

Table 5-1 provides power consumption estimates, in watts, for many common devices. You need this information to complete some of the review questions that follow.

Table 5-1	Power Consumption by Product
Device	*Power Usage*
AGP video card	30–75W
PCI video card	30–35W
SLI video cards (pair)	200W
AMD Athlon XP 1.5 MHz–2.5 GHz	66–77W
AMD Athlon 64 3.0 GHz–3.4 GHz	89W
Intel Pentium 4 2.2 GHz–2.4 GHz	80–90W
Intel Pentium 4 2.4 GHz–3.0 GHz	90–105W
Intel Celeron Socket 478	45–65W
ATX motherboard	40–65W
PC133 RAM	12W
PC2100+ DDR RAM	10W
PC3200+ DDR2 RAM	7.5W
CD-ROM drive	20W
CD-RW drive	30W
DVD-ROM drive	25W
5,400 RPM IDE hard drive	15W

(continued)

Table 5-1 *(continued)*

Device	Power Usage
7,200 RPM IDE hard drive	25W
Floppy drive	5W
Network card or modem	5W
Sound card	7–18W
SCSI controller card	25W
FireWire or USB 2.0 controller card	40W
USB device	5W
FireWire device	8W
CPU or case fan	2W

11. Suppose you have 250W, 350W, and 500W power supplies available. For each of the following systems, state the minimum power supply that would work reliably with that system.

A. Pentium 4 3.0 GHz CPU, AGP video card, two sticks of PC3200+ DDR2 RAM, a CD-RW drive, a DVD-ROM drive, two 7,200 RPM IDE hard drives, a floppy drive, a USB 2.0 controller card, an ATX motherboard, a SCSI controller card, and seven USB devices.

B. ATX motherboard, Celeron Socket 478 CPU, two sticks of PC2100+ DDR RAM, one 5,400 RPM IDE hard drive, AGP video card, a sound card, a network card, a floppy drive, and a CD-ROM drive.

C. ATX motherboard, one stick of PC133 RAM, AMD Athlon XP 1.5 MHz, AGP video card, DVD-ROM drive, floppy drive, network card, two CPU/case fans.

12. Suppose a PCI card takes 5 amps of +5V, 0.5 amp of +12V, and 7.6 amps of +3.3V. What is the total wattage it draws?

13. On the label shown, what is the maximum amperage that can be drawn for each voltage?

```
Model : HP-235ATXAK
AC INPUT (60/50Hz): 115V~/6A , 230V~/3.5A
DC OUTPUT:    +5V ⎓/25A ,   +12V ⎓/8A
              −5V⎓/0.5A ,  −12V⎓/0.5A
MAX. OUTPUT POWER: 235W   +3.3V⎓/14A
FUSE RATING: T6.3AH/250V   +5VSB⎓/1A
```

A. +5V DC Output: _____

B. +12V DC Output: _____

C. +3.3V DC Output: _____

D. Total output (all voltages): _____

Exercise 5-1: Evaluating Power Supplies

Follow these steps to practice evaluating a power supply:

1. Shut down your PC and open the case.

2. Find the power supply label and note its wattage and the amounts of each voltage it can provide.

3. Take a quick inventory of the devices installed and use Table 5-1 to estimate the power draw.

4. Based on this estimate, determine whether the power supply is adequate for this PC. If it's adequate, determine how much more wattage can be drawn from it within a safe range. If the supply isn't adequate, figure out the amount of the shortfall.

Testing Power Supply Voltages

Computer technicians use a multimeter when taking electrical measurements. The "multi" refers to the fact that it's actually several meters in one: a voltmeter to measure volts, an ammeter to measure amps, and an ohmmeter to measure ohms. The meter has a dial or switch that you can change among the different measurements. The multimeter has two long, skinny probes, one red and one black. The red probe goes on the live wire; the black one on a ground wire. The gauge reports the measurement.

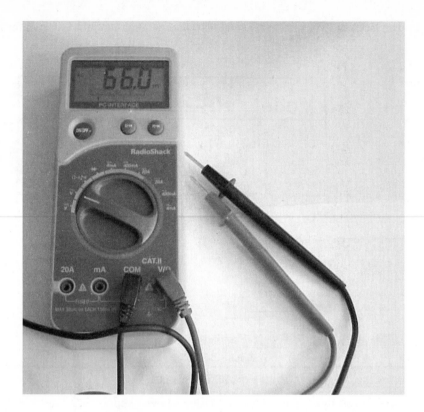

Voltage measures the strength of the electricity being delivered. Standard 110-volt power passes to the computer's power supply, which steps it down considerably and delivers it to components requiring various voltages. For example, a typical floppy disk requires some +5V and some +12V. Voltage can be either positive or negative. Computer power supplies are capable of supplying both to their components, but most components use only positive.

The most common use of voltage testing for a PC is to measure the voltage from a wire coming out of the computer's power supply to ensure that the correct voltages are being provided. Voltage must be tested with the computer on. Because the connector must not be unplugged while the PC is running, you have to stick the probe down into the back of the connector, where the wires come into it. This is called *back-probing*. For example, a red wire should deliver +5V. To test that, set your multimeter to volts. Then place the red probe as far down as possible inside the connector where the red wire enters the plug to the motherboard. Place the black probe down inside where a black wire (a ground wire) enters the same plug.

Different wire colors represent different voltages. These wire colors are somewhat different on AT versus ATX power supplies, so you should know the wire colors separately for each. The main difference is that AT power supplies predated the use of +3.3V power, so orange was assigned a different meaning in them than in the ATX.

The Power_Good wire, located on the connector to the motherboard, sends +5V (plus or minus a variance) to the motherboard whenever the power supply is operating correctly. When the correct voltage isn't coming through on the Power_Good wire, the motherboard shuts down for its own protection, so overvoltage doesn't damage its circuitry. One of the most basic tests, therefore, is to probe the Power_Good wire, looking for a measurement of somewhere between +3.5V and +6V.

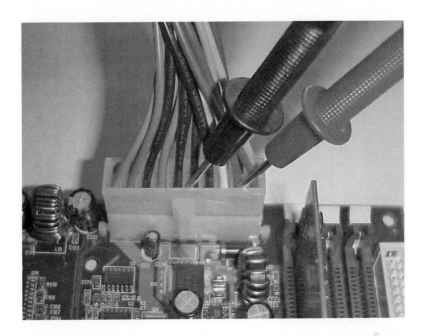

14. Fill in the following chart, matching up wire colors on an ATX power supply to the voltages at which their wires should test.

Wire Color	Voltage
Orange	
Black	
Red	
Yellow	
Blue	
White	

15. What is the wire color for the Power_Good wire:

A. AT system: _____

B. ATX system: _____

16. On an AT power supply, what are the P8 and P9 connectors for?

_____

17. On an ATX power supply, what is the purpose of the green wire?

_____

18. Suppose you have a multimeter that is not autoranging, so you have to set the testing range on it. For measuring the wires in Question 14, which would be the most appropriate setting: 2V, 20V, or 200V?

_____

19. On a Molex connector (a power connector to a disk drive), what wire colors are used and what voltages do they represent?

_____

Exercise 5-2: Testing Voltages

Follow these steps to practice testing power supply voltages:

1. Open your PC's case with the PC running.

2. Using a multimeter, back-probe each wire on the power supply connector to the motherboard and record the voltages you measure there. If you have only 20 pins, rather than 24, skip the bottom two rows.

Pin 1: _____   Pin 13: _____

Pin 2: _____   Pin 14: _____

Pin 3: _____   Pin 15: _____

Pin 4: _____   Pin 16: _____

Pin 5: _____   Pin 17: _____

Pin 6: _____   Pin 18: _____

Pin 7: _____   Pin 19: _____

Pin 8: _____   Pin 20: _____

Pin 9: _____   Pin 21: _____

Pin 10: _____   Pin 22: _____

Pin 11: _____   Pin 23: _____

Pin 12: _____   Pin 24: _____

Replacing a Power Supply

Power supplies are fairly easy to replace. Just detach the connector from the motherboard and remove the old power supply by removing the three or four screws that hold it in the case. Then pop the new one into place.

The only tricky part is that if it's an AT power supply, the power switch is attached to it via a thick black cable. You can detach the switch from the inside front of the case. (It's held there with a couple of screws.) On an ATX system, the power switch is wired to the motherboard, not to the power supply, so this isn't an issue.

On newer motherboards, in addition to connecting the main 20- or 24-pin ATX power block to the motherboard, you must connect an extra +12V four-wire connector, usually to a slot near the CPU. This connector feeds power directly to the CPU socket.

Exercise 5-3: Replacing Power Supplies

Follow these steps to practice replacing a power supply:

1. Shut down your PC.

2. Disconnect the power supply from the motherboard and from all drives and devices.

   If needed, make notes about what is connected where so that you can put things back together later.

3. Remove the screws holding the power supply in the case and remove the power supply.

4. Examine the label on the power supply. Evaluate its suitability for this PC.

5. Reinstall the power supply in the PC, or if you found it to be unsuitable, install a different, more suitable power supply instead.

Working with UPSes and Surge Suppressors

The AC power coming from a household wall outlet is sometimes unreliable. It surges and sags in voltage and sometimes cuts out completely, especially during bad weather conditions. To avoid such problems, many systems employ one or more power conditioning devices, such as UPSes, surge suppressors, and line conditioners.

PRACTICE

20. What is the difference between a standby power supply and an inline UPS?

_____

_____

_____

_____

21. What is the difference between a standard surge suppressor and a line conditioner?

_____

_____

_____

_____

22. UPSes are rated using VA. What does that stand for, and what is it?

_____

_____

23. What is a varistor and what does it do?

_____

_____

_____

24. How are UPSes rated?

_____

_____

_____

Match the following terms to their definitions:

A. Spike

B. Surge

C. Noise

D. Blackout

E. Brownout

25. _____ A total interruption in the line power

26. _____ A sharp, quick increase in voltage caused by a problem with power utility equipment or lightning strikes

27. _____ A temporary increase in voltage, typically lasting a few seconds

28. _____ Electrical interference caused by items not directly connected to the power system, such as florescent lights

29. _____ A temporary decrease in the line power, ranging from seconds to minutes

Exercise 5-4: Choosing the Correct UPS

Go to `www.apc.com/tools/ups_selector` and use the selector tool to select an appropriate UPS for your PC or workstation.

Configuring Power Management

Power management refers to saving electricity, either to cut down on your electric bill or to make your laptop battery last longer. Power management features vary among operating systems; the controls in the various versions of Windows differ in their details. They have many of the same features and functionality in common, though. In this section, you review them.

PRACTICE

Test your knowledge of power management:

30. What two computer components are most typically set to shut themselves off automatically after a specified period of inactivity?

_____

_____

31. When a PC goes into Sleep (or Standby) mode, what component(s) remain powered up?

_____

_____

32. What is the difference between Sleep and Hibernate?

_____

_____

_____

_____

33. What component does SpeedStep Technology slow down to increase battery life on a notebook PC?

_____

_____

34. What are APM and ACPI and which one is the most modern and desirable for a system to support?

_____

_____

_____

_____

35. What are three different things you can set the Start button to do when pressed?

_____

_____

_____

36. Other than waiting for idle time to elapse, how can you put a PC in Sleep (or Standby) mode from within Windows?

_____

_____

_____

_____

37. Suppose you have a PC on which Windows has just been installed, and you haven't gotten all the drivers installed for the various hardware components. You try to set up power management, but Windows won't let you specify that the PC should enter Standby mode when you press its power button. Which hardware device probably needs to have its driver installed before this feature will work?

_____

_____

Exercise 5-5: Configuring Power Management Options

Do the following to practice setting up power management. If you have access to both Windows XP and Windows Vista, perform both sets of steps.

In Windows Vista:

1. From the Control Panel, open Power Options.

2. Customize the High Performance power plan with the following settings:
   • Turn Off the Display: 1 hour
   • Put the PC to Sleep: Never

3. Change the Advanced Settings for this power plan with the following settings:
   • Require a Password on Wakeup: No
   • Allow Hybrid Sleep: On
   • Power Buttons and Lid/Lower Button Action: Setting: Standby

4. Put the computer into Standby mode and then wake it up again.

In Windows XP:

1. From the Control Panel, open Power Options.

2. Customize the Home/Office Desk power scheme as follows:
   • Turn Off Monitor: After 1 hour
   • Turn Off Hard Disks: After 1 hour

3. On the Advanced tab, set the When I Press the Power Button on My Computer option to Standby.

4. Put the computer into Standby mode and then wake it up again.

Selecting and Handling Batteries

In a desktop PC, the power supply performs two functions: It converts the power from AC to DC, and it steps down the voltage. In a notebook PC, those two functions are handled by an AC adapter built into the power cord.

When the AC adapter isn't plugged in, the power is provided by a battery. When running on battery power, the PC doesn't need either of the functions of the AC adapter because the battery is already DC and because the PC draws the voltage it needs from the battery directly. The AC adapter recharges the battery whenever it's plugged into an electrical outlet.

Test your knowledge of battery selection and handling:

Match up the following descriptions with the battery-related term.

    A. Alkaline

    B. Nickel-Cadmium (NiCad)

    C. Lithium-Ion (LI-Ion)

    D. Nickel-Metal Hydride (NiMH)

    E. CMOS Battery

    F. Smart battery

38. _____ Lightweight, expensive battery

39. _____ A battery with its own power circuitry for monitoring battery performance, output voltage, and temperature

40. _____ Heavy, inexpensive battery, needing to be recharged after 3–4 hours of use

41. _____ Battery installed directly on the motherboard

42. _____ Usually found in handheld/palmtop computers and calculators

43. _____ Environmentally friendly battery that does not contain toxic materials

---

Exercise 5-6: Working with Batteries

Do the following steps to practice working with batteries:

1. If you have a notebook PC available to work with, locate its battery and identify the battery's type and model number.

2. If you have a desktop PC to work with, locate the battery on the motherboard and identify the battery's type and voltage.

3. Use the Internet to locate at least two sources of replacement batteries for the batteries you worked with in Steps 1 and 2. If you didn't have both a desktop and a notebook PC to work with, pick a desktop or notebook PC available for sale online at a major PC manufacturer's Web site (such as Dell.com) and determine what battery you would buy for that unit.

4. Remove and reinstall the batteries from Steps 1 and 2 if possible.

Expanding a Notebook PC with PC Card Devices

Expanding a notebook can involve adding internal components — when you add memory or replace a hard drive with a larger-capacity model, for example — or it can involve plugging external devices into it like monitors, PC Card devices, USB devices, and so on.

Selecting memory or a hard drive for a laptop is much the same as selecting it for a desktop PC except that it's more likely that you need to remove some existing item(s) before installing the new one(s). For example, most notebook PCs have room for only one hard drive, so you need to swap the old hard drive for a new one rather than simply tack on an additional drive. Similarly, you can usually find only one or two RAM slots in a notebook PC, and they're usually filled, so you might need to remove some RAM and replace it with a higher-capacity stick.

The main unique component in a notebook PC is the PC Card (PCMCIA) slot. PC Card devices are credit-card size cartridges that add various capabilities, such as a network adapter or modem. PCMCIA was the original standard for these slots; the standard has been updated to PC Card, and then later to CardBus; all three of those terms are considered roughly equivalent because later slots are backward compatible with earlier devices.

PC Card devices were more popular in earlier days, before USB became popular, because they provided a size-conscious way of adding capabilities to a notebook PC. Nowadays, most devices that used to be practical to add to a PC only via a PCMCIA slot, such as a hard drive or network adapter, can be just as easily (and more inexpensively) added via USB interface.

PC Card devices are hot-swappable, just like USB devices, so you can disconnect and connect them without turning off the PC. You should, however, be sure that the device isn't in use before disconnecting it. One way to do this is to stop the device. From the notification area (system tray), click the Safely Remove Hardware icon and then use the dialog box that appears to stop the device.

Test your knowledge of PC Card devices:

44. List the three types of PC Card devices and the thickness of each in millimeters:

_____

_____

_____

_____

45. Of the three types of devices you listed for Question 44, which type is most likely to contain . . .

A. A network interface card?

_____

B. A hard drive?

_____

C. Memory?

_____

46. What are Socket services?

_____

_____

_____

47. What are Card services?

_____

_____

_____

48. What does PCMCIA stand for?

_____

_____

_____

Exercise 5-7: Mastering PC Cards

Do the following steps to practice working with PC Card devices:

1. If you have a notebook PC available to work with, insert a PC Card device into it.

2. If prompted, install a driver for the device.

3. Use the Safely Remove Hardware icon in the notification area to open the Safely Remove Hardware dialog box.

4. Stop the device.

5. Physically remove the device.

Answers to Questions in This Chapter

The following are the answers to the practice questions presented earlier in this chapter:

1. D

2. C

3. A

4. G

5. B

6. H

7. F

8. E

9. **Using the terms *amp, volt,* and *watt,* write the formula for calculating the wattage used by a specific component:**

   Amps × Volts = Watts

10. **Suppose a hard drive uses 0.4 amp of 5V DC and 0.27 amp of 12V DC. What is its total wattage consumed?**

    $(0.4 \times 5) + (0.27 \times 12) = 5.24$ watts

11. **Suppose you have 250W, 350W, and 500W power supplies available. For each of the following systems, state the minimum power supply that would work reliably with that system.**

    A. **Pentium 4 3.0GHz CPU, AGP video card, two sticks of PC3200+ DDR2 RAM, a CD-RW drive, a DVD-ROM drive, two 7,200 RPM IDE hard drives, a floppy drive, a USB 2.0 controller card, an ATX motherboard, a SCSI controller card, and seven USB devices.**

       405 is the raw total; 500W supply is most appropriate.

    B. **ATX motherboard, Celeron Socket 478 CPU, two sticks of PC2100+ DDR RAM, one 5,400 RPM IDE hard drive, AGP video card, a sound card, a network card, a floppy drive, and a CD-ROM drive.**

       288 is the raw total; 350W is most appropriate.

    C. **ATX motherboard, one stick of PC133 RAM, AMD Athlon XP 1.5MHz, AGP video card, DVD-ROM drive, floppy drive, network card, two CPU/case fans.**

       268 is the raw total; 350W is most appropriate.

12. **Suppose a PCI card takes 5 amp of +5V, 0.5 amp of +12V, and 7.6 amps of +3.3V. What is the total wattage it draws?**

    $(5 \times 5) + (0.5 \times 12) + (7.6 \times 3.3) = 56.08$ watts

13. **On the label shown, what is the maximum amperage that can be drawn for each voltage?**

A. +5V DC Output: 25 amps

B. +12V DC Output: 8 amps

C. +3.3V DC Output: 14 amps

D. Total output (all voltages) in watts: 235

14. **Fill in the following chart matching up wire colors on an ATX power supply to the voltages at which their wires should test.**

Wire Color	Voltage
Orange	+3.3V
Black	Ground
Red	+5V
Yellow	+12V
Blue	−12V
White	−5V

15. **What is the wire color for the Power_Good wire:**

A. **AT system:** Purple

B. **ATX system:** Gray

16. **On an AT power supply, what are the P8 and P9 connectors for?**

The P8 and P9 connectors attach to the motherboard, black wires together.

17. **On an ATX power supply, what is the purpose of the green wire?**

The green wire signals the motherboard to start the boot process; it connects to the power button.

18. **Suppose you have a multimeter that is not autoranging, so you have to set the testing range on it. For measuring the wires in Question 14, which would be the most appropriate setting: 2V, 20V, or 200V?**

20V is most appropriate because it's above the highest voltage you will be testing (12V) but not so far above it that the readings would be difficult to interpret.

19. **On a Molex connector (a power connector to a disk drive), what wire colors are used and what voltages do they represent?**

A Molex connector has one red (+5V), one yellow (+12V), and two black (ground) wires.

20. **What is the difference between a standby power supply and an inline UPS?**

A standby power supply starts providing power only when regular power is interrupted; an inline UPS powers the outlets at all times, so no switchover is needed.

21. What is the difference between a standard surge suppressor and a line conditioner?

A surge suppressor protects against overvoltage, but not undervoltage. A line conditioner evens out power in both directions, both over- and undervoltage.

22. UPSes are rated using VA. What does that stand for, and what is it?

VA stands for Volts/Amps. It's the raw calculation of volts times amps, which is approximately equal to watts.

23. What is a varistor and what does it do?

A varistor is a variable resistor. It is the resistor inside a surge suppressor that takes the hit, absorbing the excess voltage to protect the outlets. Over time, it weakens and is able to take less, so surge suppressors must be periodically replaced.

24. How are UPSes rated?

UPSes are generally rated by VA. They may also report a clamping voltage in joules, which is the amount of surge they can absorb and protect from.

25. D

26. A

27. B

28. C

29. E

30. What two components are most typically set to shut themselves off automatically after a specified period of inactivity?

Hard drive and monitor

31. When a PC goes into Sleep (or Standby) mode, what component(s) remain powered up?

Memory

32. What is the difference between Sleep and Hibernate?

With Sleep, memory remains powered on. With Hibernate, the content of RAM is copied to the hard drive and then everything is completely shut down.

33. What component does SpeedStep Technology slow down to increase battery life on a notebook PC?

The CPU

34. What are APM and ACPI and which one is the most modern and desirable for a system to support?

APM is Advanced Power Management. ACPI is Advanced Configuration and Power Interface, and it is the more modern and desirable because it has better power management capability and also plug-and-play features.

35. **What are three different things you can set the Start button to do when pressed?**

    Shut down the PC, place the PC in Standby, or place the PC in Hibernate

36. **Other than waiting for idle time to elapse, how can you put a PC in Sleep (or Standby) mode from within Windows?**

    From the Start menu, choose Shut Down, and then select Sleep or Standby from the menu that appears.

37. **Suppose you have a PC on which Windows has just been installed, and you haven't gotten all the drivers installed for the various hardware components. You try to set up power management, but Windows won't let you specify that the PC should enter Standby mode when you press its power button. Which hardware device probably needs to have its driver installed before this feature will work?**

    The display adapter (video card driver) is probably at fault. The generic VGA driver for the display does not support standby or hibernation. Install its driver, and those options will become available.

38. C

39. F

40. B

41. E

42. A

43. D

44. **List the three types of PC Card devices and the thickness of each in millimeters:**

    Type I: 3.3mm

    Type II: 5.5mm

    Type III: 10.5mm

45. **Of the three types of devices you listed for Question 44, which type is most likely to contain . . .**

    A. A network interface card?

    Type II

    B. A hard drive?

    Type III

    C. Memory?

    Type I

46. What are Socket services?

Socket services are BIOS-level routines that detect when a PCMCIA card is inserted into or removed from the system.

47. What are Card services?

Card services provide the interface between the card and the device driver, and manage the assignment of system resources such as IRQs.

48. What does PCMCIA stand for?

Personal Computer Memory Card Industry Association

Part II
Peripherals

The 5th Wave   By Rich Tennant

A+ Exam

"I'm not sure you really understand this test. When asked to give a description of a 'Repeater', you wrote, 'A large bean burrito and a cup of coffee'."

In this part . . .

You review your knowledge of the "outties" of a computer system — the parts that are either outside the main case or not essential to its operation. You test your knowledge of cabling and connectors, review monitors and display adapters, and identify types of printers and their internal processes, connectivity methods, and software queues. You also review scanners, sound cards, and other devices that specialize in I/O operations.

Chapter 6

Ports, Cables, and Connectors

• •

In This Chapter

▶ Identifying common computer ports

▶ Comparing cable connector types

▶ Selecting and installing adapters

▶ Using a pinout diagram and doing pin testing

▶ Understanding USB and FireWire standards

• •

*W*henever points A and B aren't on the same circuit board, they need some sort of connector to act as a pathway between them. In this chapter, you brush up your knowledge of the various ports, cables, and connectors used in PCs to connect disparate items.

Identifying Common Computer Ports

Depending on the age and type of computer, you'll run into a different set of available ports. Whether it's a notebook or desktop and whether it's a 10-year-old clunker or the latest and greatest model, you'll need to be able to identify the ports available so that you can match them to devices.

1. Match up the following uses to the connectors shown. Several letters are used more than once.

A. AT (DIN) keyboard

B. FireWire (IEEE 1394)

C. Docking station

D. Analog (VGA) monitor

E. AC power

F. Phone cable (modem)

G. Ethernet network

H. COM port

I. External speakers

J. PS/2 mouse or keyboard

K. PC card

L. Joystick/MIDI

M. USB

N. Parallel printer

O. Digital (DVI) monitor

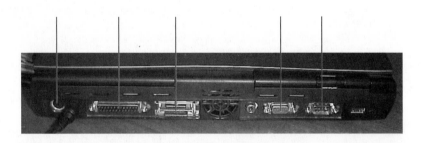

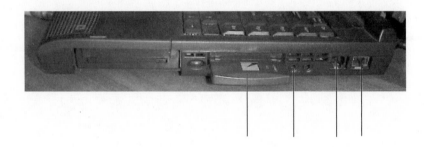

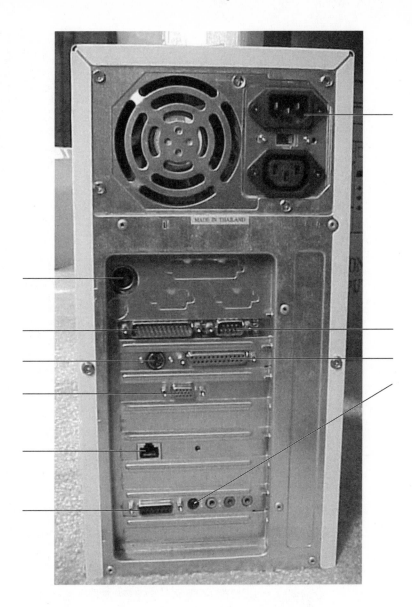

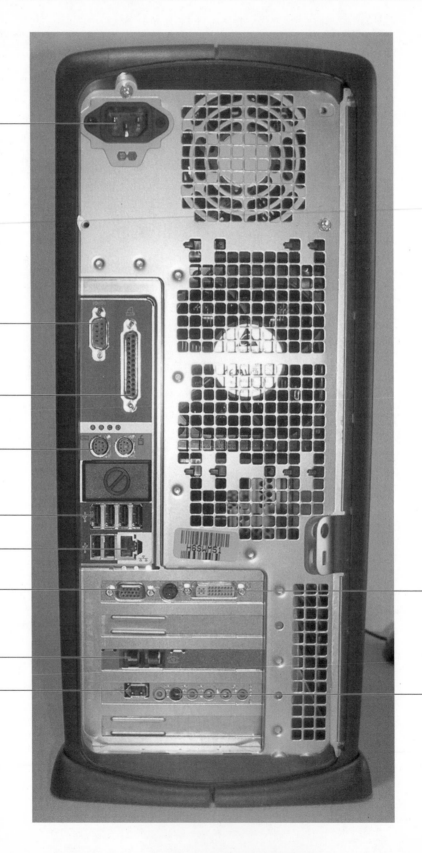

Comparing Cable Connector Types

Whenever you need to connect two pieces of hardware, a cable is required. A PC technician needs to be able to recognize and select from dozens of cable types, including ribbon cables, printer cables, and USB cables.

The A+ exam uses "official" names for connectors that you might not be familiar with, so brush up on this list:

- **BNC:** Bayonet Neill-Concelman or British Naval Connector; essentially, a metal threaded ring on a coaxial cable, used for Thinnet networking.

- **D-sub or DB:** A block of pins or holes with a D-shaped ring around them, usually containing either two or three offset rows.

- **Centronics:** A parallel connector consisting of a plastic bar on which rows of flat metal pieces are mounted.

- **RJ:** Registered Jack, a plastic block on a twisted pair cable, as on a phone cable or Ethernet network cable.

- **DIN:** An AT-style keyboard connector, consisting of a round plug with five fat metal pins.

- **PS/2 or mini-DIN 6:** An ATX-style keyboard connector, consisting of a round plug with six small metal pins.

- **Molex:** A power connector to CD-ROM drives, parallel ATA hard drives, and many other drive types.

- **Mini:** A power connector to a floppy drive.

Answer the questions that follow each cable photo.

2.   How many wires are in this cable?

_____

3.   Is this a parallel or serial cable?

_____

4.   This cable plugs into the _____ on one end and a _____ on the other.

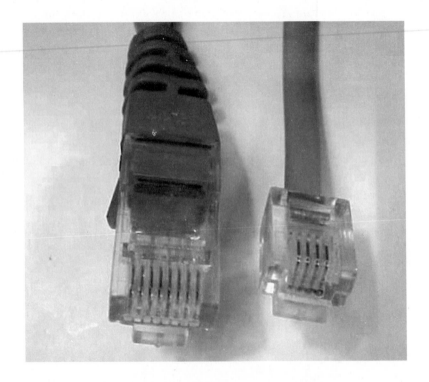

5.   Which connector, the right or the left one, would plug into a modem?

_____

6.   Which connector, the right or the left one, would plug into a 100BaseT Ethernet card?

_____

7.   How many wires does the connector on the left have?

_____

8.   What is the common name for the connector on the left?

_____

9. Is this a parallel or a serial cable?

_____

10. Which end connects to the PC: male or female?

_____

11. Give an example of a device that would use this cable.

_____

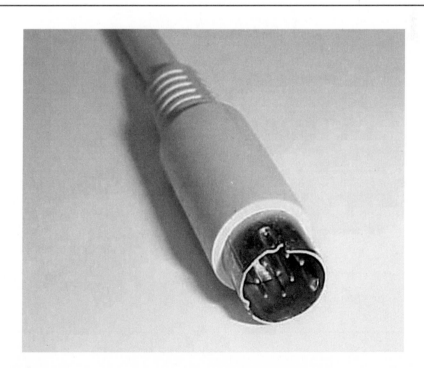

12. What is the common name for this type of connector?

_____

13. On an ATX system, name two devices that use this connector.

_____

14. On an AT system, name one device that uses this connector.

_____

15. What is the common name for this type of connector?

_____

16. What is the most common type of device that uses it?

_____

17. How many pins are in the D-sub connector at the other end of this cable?

_____

18. Does this connector plug into the PC or to the other device?

_____

19. These are opposite ends of the same cable. What type of cable is it?

_____

20. Which end, left or right, connects to the PC?

_____

21. Give an example of a device that would use this cable.

_____

Selecting and Installing Adapters

Sometimes the only thing standing in the way of a connection is the wrong type of connector. For example, a serial mouse can work in a PS/2 port if you have a converter plug that makes the connectors fit physically, and a 9-pin legacy serial device can work with a 25-pin legacy serial port. You can also adapt an AT keyboard for an ATX motherboard, and vice versa, and even convert a PS/2 or serial device to USB.

The tricky part when selecting a cable adapter is determining whether the connector at each side should be male or female. *Male* means it has pins; *Female* means it has holes. For example, if you have a PS/2 device, the PS/2 connector on the device is male, and the PS/2 connector on the PC is female. If you want to use an adapter to enable that device to plug into some other port on the PC, the PS/2 connector on the adapter must be female because it's simulating a PC's connector.

It makes sense in theory, but it's easy to get confused when you're standing there in the store staring at the endless racks of available converters and trying to remember what the connector looked like on the PC. In the following review exercise, try to work from memory rather than refer to a real PC, because that's what you'll probably need to rely on when shopping.

In the following sentences, fill in the blanks with the correct connector type. Choose from the following list of terms. (Some terms might be used more than once; some might not be used at all.)

DB-9 female

DB-9 male

DB-15 male

DB-15 female

DB-25 female

DB-25 male

PS/2 female

PS/2 male

DIN female

DIN male

RJ-45 male

36-pin Centronics

50-pin Centronics

USB male

USB female

22. To connect an external modem with a 25-pin serial connector to a 9-pin serial port on the PC, use a connector with _____ on one side and _____ on the other.

23. To patch together two 25-pin serial cables, use a connector with _____ on one side and _____ on the other.

24. To adapt a keyboard from an ATX system for use on an AT system, use a connector with _____ on one side and _____ on the other.

25. To adapt a serial mouse for use in a PS/2 mouse port, use a connector with _____ on one side and _____ on the other.

26. To adapt a PS/2 mouse for use in a 9-pin serial port, use a connector with _____ on one side and _____ on the other.

27. To connect a USB mouse to a 9-pin serial port, use a connector with _____ on one side and _____ on the other.

28. To connect two PCs together via their parallel ports, start with a parallel cable with straight pass-through wiring. If both ends are already _____, it is ready to use. If not, put an adapter on the _____ end of the cable that converts that end to _____.

29. To extend a monitor cable, use a cable with _____ on one end and _____ on the other.

30. To extend a USB printer cable, use a cable with _____ on one end and _____ on the other.

31. To use a PS/2 keyboard in a USB port, use a cable with _____ on one end and _____ on the other.

Using a Pinout Diagram and Doing Pin Testing

When you find a one-to-one relationship between two connectors at the two ends of a cable, the relationship between the pins is usually straightforward. On the female end, the pins are numbered from left to right, with the wider part at the top, like this:

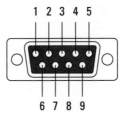

On the male end, the pins are numbered from right to left, like this:

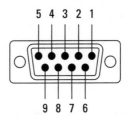

A pinout diagram for the preceding connectors would list only one column of data because the numbers represent the same thing on both ends:

1	Carrier Detect
2	Receive Data
3	Transmit Data
4	Data Terminal Ready

5	Signal Ground
6	Data Set Ready
7	Request to Send
8	Clear to Send
9	Ring Indicator

A pinout diagram is even more useful, however, when there isn't a one-to-one relationship between the different connectors at each end of a cable. For example, a legacy serial cable might be 25-pin at one end and 9-pin at the other. Which pins at the 25 end correspond to pins at the 9 end, and which ones are dead? You can determine this by testing each pin for continuity with a multimeter, but a diagram that maps the ends of the connectors to one another makes the task a lot easier.

32. Using a multimeter and any legacy serial 9-to-25 cable or adapter, determine which pin in the 9-pin connector corresponds to the pin in the 25-pin connector. The following pictures show a male 9-pin and female 25-pin; if yours are reversed, the numbering will be reversed as well.

9-pin male   25-pin female

1	
2	
3	
4	
5	
6	
7	
8	
9	

Understanding USB and FireWire Standards

USB and FireWire (IEEE 1394) are fast replacing the older and slower connector types on modern PCs. There have been several standards and connector types for both USB and FireWire, and you should be able to identify them, their top speeds, and their maximum numbers of devices for the A+ exam.

33. Fill in the following table of information about USB and FireWire standards.

	USB 1.0	USB 2.0	IEEE 1394a (FireWire)	IEEE 1394b (FireWire 800)
Top speed				
Number of devices in a chain				

Answers to Questions in This Chapter

The following are the answers to the practice questions presented earlier in this chapter:

1.

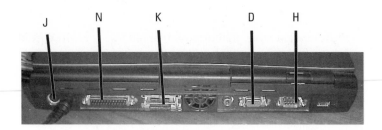

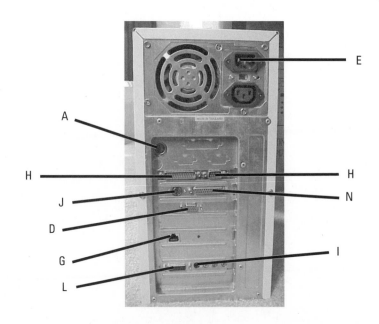

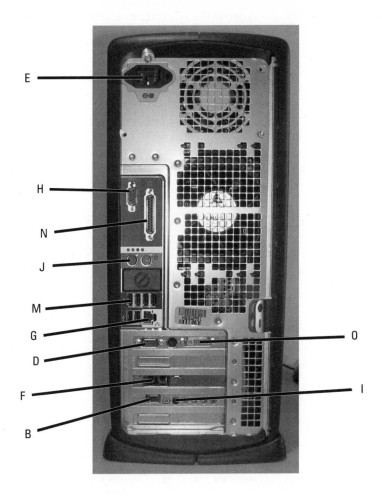

2. **How many wires are in this cable?**

    34

3. **Is this a parallel or serial cable?**

    Parallel

4. **This cable plugs into the <u>motherboard</u> on one end and a <u>floppy disk drive</u> on the other.**

5. **Which connector, the right or the left one, would plug into a modem?**

    Right

6. **Which connector, the right or the left one, would plug into a 100BaseT Ethernet card?**

Left

7. **How many wires does the connector on the left have?**

8

8. **What is the common name for the connector on the left?**

RJ-45

9. **Is this a parallel or a serial cable?**

Serial

10. **Which end connects to the PC: male or female?**

Female

11. **Give an example of a device that would use this cable.**

External modem, serial mouse, UPS, any other legacy serial device

12. **What is the common name for this type of connector?**

PS/2 or mini-DIN

13. **On an ATX system, name two devices that use this connector.**

Keyboard and mouse

14. **On an AT system, name one device that uses this connector**

Mouse (keyboard on an AT is a DIN, not a mini-DIN)

15. **What is the common name for this type of connector?**

Centronics

16. **What is the most common type of device that uses it?**

Parallel printer, or SCSI device

17. **How many pins are in the D-sub connector at the other end of this cable?**

25

18. **Does this connector plug into the PC or to the other device?**

The other device

19. **These are opposite ends of the same cable. What type of cable is it?**

    USB

20. **Which end, left or right, connects to the PC?**

    Right

21. **Give an example of a device that would use this cable.**

    Printer, keyboard, mouse, any other external serial device

22. **To connect an external modem with a 25-pin serial connector to a 9-pin serial port on the PC, use a connector with <u>DB-25 male</u> on one side and <u>DB-9 female</u> on the other.**

23. **To patch together two 25-pin serial cables, use a connector with <u>DB-25 male</u> on one side and <u>DB-25 female</u> on the other.**

24. **To adapt a keyboard from an ATX system for use on an AT system, use a connector with <u>PS/2 female</u> on one side and <u>DIN male</u> on the other.**

25. **To adapt a serial mouse for use in a PS/2 mouse port, use a connector with <u>DB-9 male</u> on one side and <u>PS/2 male</u> on the other.**

26. **To adapt a PS/2 mouse for use in a 9-pin serial port, use a connector with <u>PS/2 female</u> on one side and <u>DB-9 female</u> on the other.**

27. **To connect a USB mouse to a 9-pin serial port, use a connector with <u>USB female</u> on one side and <u>DB-9 female</u> on the other.**

28. **To connect two PCs together via their parallel ports, start with a parallel cable with straight pass-through wiring. If both ends are already <u>DB-25 female</u>, it is ready to use. If not, put an adapter on the <u>DB-25 male</u> end of the cable that converts that end to <u>DB-25 female</u>.**

29. **To extend a monitor cable, use a cable with <u>DB-15 female</u> on one end and <u>DB-15 male</u> on the other.**

30. **To extend a USB printer cable, use a cable with <u>USB male</u> on one end and <u>USB female</u> on the other.**

31. **To use a PS/2 keyboard in a USB port, use a cable with <u>PS/2 female</u> on one end and <u>USB female</u> on the other.**

32. Using a multimeter and any legacy serial 9-to-25 cable or adapter, determine which pin in the 9-pin connector corresponds to the pin in the 25-pin connector.

9-pin male   25-pin female

9-pin	25-pin
1	8
2	3
3	2
4	20
5	7
6	6
7	4
8	5
9	22

33. Fill in the following table of information about USB and FireWire standards.

	USB 1.0	USB 2.0	IEEE 1394a (FireWire)	IEEE 1394b (FireWire 800)
Top speed	12 Mbps	480 Mbps	400 Mbps	800 Mbps
Number of devices in a chain	127	127	63	63

Chapter 7

Monitors and Display Adapters

● ●

In This Chapter

▶ Identifying display adapter features

▶ Selecting an LCD monitor

▶ Selecting a CRT monitor

▶ Adjusting display settings in Windows

▶ Cleaning and adjusting a monitor

● ●

*T*he video subsystem includes the display adapter and whatever you plug into it. Most technicians don't have to repair monitors, but you will likely be called upon to troubleshoot display problems and to select display adapters and monitors for new installations and replacements.

Identifying Display Adapter Features

The display adapter takes commands from the operating system and turns them into instructions for lighting up various spots on the monitor with specified colors. It's kind of like a Lite-Brite.

When selecting a display adapter, here's what to keep in mind:

✔ **Chipset:** The chipset might or might not be made by the same company as the display adapter itself. It determines the basic set of features and commands that the board supports, such as 3D acceleration.

✔ **Memory:** A display adapter has its own memory (ideally; some built-in adapters share the motherboard's RAM). The more memory it has, the higher display resolutions it can support. For 32-bit color, figure on 4 bytes of RAM for each pixel at a particular display resolution. Then multiply that by 2 for double-buffered 3D acceleration or multiply that by 3 for triple-buffered.

✔ **Connectors:** Various types of connectors are available for plugging in monitors. The DB-15 VGA plug is the older standard, and DVI is the newer digital one, but you can also find some specialty types out there, such as S-video (seen primarily in home theater equipment), component/RGB, and HDMi.

✔ **Slot type:** Display adapter boards are designed to fit in a particular type of slot in the motherboard, such as PCI, PCI Express, or AGP.

Test your knowledge of display adapter selection criteria:

1. How much video RAM would a display adapter need to have in order to support a 32-bit color depth at 1,600 x 1,200 resolution, with no 3D acceleration? How do you calculate this?

2. How much video RAM would you need for the color depth and resolution from Question 1 with triple-buffered 3D acceleration? How do you calculate this?

3. List at least two ways of determining how much video RAM a display adapter has.

Identify the type of display connector shown in each picture:

4.

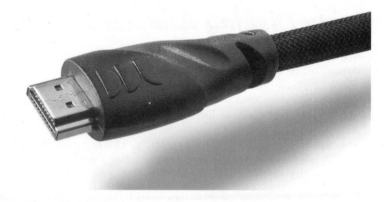

5.

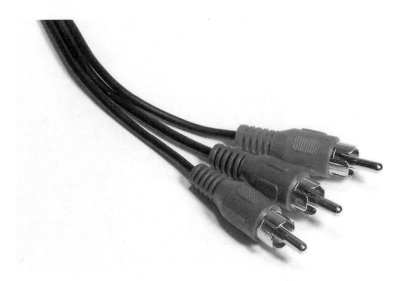

_____

6.

_____

7.

_____

8.

_____

9. Rank the following in order of preference for a display adapter interface, based on maximum speed, from most to least preferable: Vesa Local Bus (VLB), 8x AGP, ISA, 16x PCIe, and PCI.

_____

_____

_____

_____

_____

Exercise 7-1: Evaluating Display Adapters

1. Identify the following information about your computer's display adapter:

- Brand: _____
- Model: _____
- Amount of dedicated display memory: _____

2. Identify the slot type used by your display adapter (unless it's built into the motherboard).

3. Identify the connectors available on your display adapter.

4. Given the amount of video RAM you have, can your monitor support 32-bit color at 1,600 x 1,200 resolution in triple-buffered 3D display mode? To calculate this, refer to your answers to Questions 1 and 2 in the preceding Practice questions.

Selecting an LCD Monitor

Liquid crystal display (LCD) monitors are fast becoming the norm because they're thinner, lighter, and flatter than conventional cathode ray tube (CRT) models. Besides the obvious overall size difference, you can evaluate LCD monitors by looking at factors such as response time, contrast, and brightness.

Test how much you know about evaluating and selecting an LCD monitor:

10. If an LCD monitor is reported to be 19 inches, exactly what dimension is that a measurement of?

_____

11. What type of connector(s) would a high-end LCD monitor most likely have: VGA, DVI, or both?

_____

12. What is native resolution?

_____

_____

_____

_____

13. Is a higher native resolution always better? Why or why not?

_____

_____

_____

_____

14. What is response time a measurement of?

_____

_____

_____

15. What unit of measurement describes response time?

_____

16. When evaluating response time, is a higher or a lower number better?

_____

17. How is contrast measured on an LCD monitor?

_____

_____

18. When evaluating contrast, is a higher or a lower number better?

_____

19. How is brightness measured on an LCD monitor?

_____

_____

20. When evaluating brightness, is a higher or a lower number better?

_____

Exercise 7-2: Comparing LCD Monitors

Visit www.viewsonic.com or the Web site of some other monitor manufacturer and examine the specifications for at least three models of desktop LCD displays. Compare them using the following criteria:

Model
_____

Display area
_____

Brightness
_____

Contrast ratio
_____

Native (optimum) resolution
_____

Response time
_____

Viewing angle
_____

Selecting a CRT Monitor

Cathode ray tubes (CRTs) are the "boxy" kind of monitor, the traditional heavy behemoths that have been a staple of nearly every office for the last decade or so. This type of monitor is falling by the wayside lately because of the popularity and benefits of LCDs, but plenty of CRTs are still out there in the field.

The criteria for selecting a CRT monitor are quite different from those for an LCD monitor because of the technology behind them. For a CRT, the key factors are *dot pitch* (the spacing of the pixels), viewable image area, refresh rate, and the ability to make fine-tuning adjustments to the picture.

Test how much you know about evaluating and selecting a CRT monitor:

21. Are CRTs usually analog or digital?

_____

22. What is the most common connector type on a CRT monitor?

_____

23. Suppose a CRT's size is reported in its specs as 21/19.8 inches.

A. What is 21 inches a measurement of?

_____

_____

B. What is 19.8 inches a measurement of?

_____

_____

24. What three colors compose a pixel triad on a CRT monitor?

_____

_____

_____

25. Suppose a monitor has a dot pitch of 0.20 mm.

A. What is that a measurement of?

_____

_____

_____

_____

B. Would a monitor that has a dot pitch of 0.26 mm be better or worse than one with a 0.20 mm dot pitch?

_____

26. Suppose a monitor's specs report that it has a refresh rate of 120 Hz at 1,024 x 768 resolution.

A. Is the refresh rate good enough to avoid eyestrain at that resolution?

_____

B. Would a refresh rate of 60 Hz be better or worse than a rate of 120 Hz?

_____

C. At a resolution of 1,600 x 1,200, would you expect the best available refresh rate to be higher, lower, or the same as at 1,024 x 768 resolution?

_____

Adjusting Display Settings in Windows

Often, an end-user thinks there's a problem with his or her display when actually it just isn't adjusted correctly. By changing the display resolution, color depth, and refresh rate and by making sure the latest updates are installed for the display drivers, you can easily optimize the display.

Display settings differ between Windows versions, of course, in terms of the exact steps for changing them, but the concepts remain the same between versions. Generally speaking, you right-click the desktop, choose Properties, and then use the Settings tab in the Display Properties dialog box to make changes. For dpi and refresh rate settings, click Advanced.

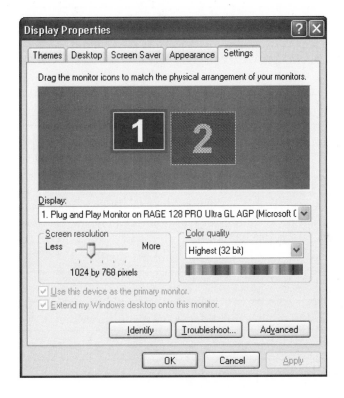

In Windows Vista (not covered on the 2006 A+ objectives, but still useful to know about), you right-click the desktop, choose Personalize, and then click Display Settings.

Test your knowledge of Windows display settings.

27. A user complains that text appears very fuzzy on his new LCD monitor. He knows it isn't the display adapter malfunctioning because his old CRT monitor looked very crisp. What is likely the problem?

_____

_____

_____

_____

28. A user complains that on his new laptop PC, the icons on the Windows desktop are extremely small and hard to see. He wants to avoid the problem with fuzzy text from Question 26, though. What can you suggest?

_____

_____

_____

_____

29. A user complains that every time he tries to set his Windows display to a very high resolution, the color depth setting decreases and can't be increased until he switches to a lower resolution. Why is this happening?

_____

_____

_____

_____

30. A user complains that after installing a new version of Windows, his display is limited to 640 x 480 resolution and 16 colors. He cannot change those settings in his Display Properties dialog box. What's wrong, and how can it be fixed?

_____

_____

_____

_____

31. A user complains that his CRT display is hurting his eyes with its flickering. What setting should you change, and should that setting be increased or decreased?

_____

_____

_____

_____

32. A user wants to adjust the refresh rate on his monitor (a CRT), but Windows detects it as a generic monitor and doesn't have any information about its maximum refresh rate capability. The user is asking you what refresh rate to use.

A. Is there any danger in the user choosing a refresh rate that's too high?

_____

_____

B. Is there any danger in the user choosing a refresh rate that's too low?

_____

_____

C. How can you get Windows to identify the monitor so that it will display appropriate refresh rate options for that model?

_____

_____

_____

_____

D. If you cannot get Windows to identify the monitor, how else can you find out what refresh rates the monitor supports?

_____

_____

_____

_____

Exercise 7-3: Using the Display Properties Dialog Box

Access the Display Properties dialog box as I describe at the beginning of this section and then follow these steps:

1. Change your display to a lower resolution; then change it back again.

2. Change your display to a lower color depth; then change it back again.

3. Change your display to a lower refresh rate; then change it back again.

4. Experiment with different dpi settings and note the effect on the desktop icons and text.

5. If Windows doesn't correctly detect your monitor, visit your monitor manufacturer's Web site and see whether an `.inf` file is available for your monitor. If you find one, download it and install it.

Cleaning and Adjusting a Monitor

You don't have to be a PC technician to clean and adjust a monitor, of course — end-users do it all the time. However, as a technician, you'll be expected to know how to do those things and to advise others on the proper way to do them.

The monitor itself probably has separate adjustment controls on it that have no relationship to your PC or to Windows. They adjust the picture on the monitor itself, regardless of the source of that picture. It usually has a button that activates some sort of menu system and buttons that move you up/down or left/right within that menu system. You can figure out the menu system by trial and error or break down and go to the monitor manufacturer's Web site to find a manual with some directions.

Although the menu systems differ widely among models, the adjustments themselves are fairly standard. The A+ exam tests your knowledge of the types of adjustments you can make, but it doesn't test you on the specific steps for working with monitor menu systems.

Test your knowledge of the settings available for cleaning and adjusting a monitor:

33. Is ordinary glass cleaner suitable for cleaning a monitor? Why or why not?

_____

_____

_____

34. How can you remove accumulated lint and dust from the ventilation holes in the top of a CRT monitor?

_____

_____

_____

35. If a CRT monitor has a faint green tinge on one side of the display when viewing a pure white page, what setting should you adjust?

_____

_____

36. If a CRT monitor seems to be entirely missing one of its three triad colors (red, green, or blue), what should you check?

_____

_____

37. If the image on a CRT is slightly bowed on the sides, what setting should you adjust?

_____

_____

38. What does the *phase* setting control?

_____

_____

39. What does degaussing to do a CRT monitor?

_____

_____

_____

Answers to Questions in This Chapter

The following are the answers to the practice questions presented earlier in this chapter:

1. **How much video RAM would a display adapter need to have in order to support a 32-bit color depth at 1,600 x 1,200 resolution, with no 3D acceleration? How do you calculate this?**

   7,680,000 bytes, or approximately 8MB

   This is calculated by multiplying 1,600 x 1,200 to derive the total number of pixels and then multiplying by the color depth (32), and then dividing by 8 to convert from bits to bytes.

2. **How much video RAM would you need for the color depth and resolution from Question 1 with triple-buffered 3D acceleration? How do you calculate this?**

   23,040,000, or approximately 24MB. Because that is not a common amount of RAM for a display adapter to have, you would round up to the next likely amount, which is 32MB.

   This is calculated by multiplying the standard 2D resolution by 3 to account for the buffers.

3. **List at least two ways of determining how much video RAM a display adapter has.**

   As the PC starts up from a cold boot, the display adapter make, model, and memory amount flashes briefly onscreen. You can also get this information from the Display Properties dialog box in Windows, or from the System Information utility in Windows.

4. HDMi

5. Component/RGB

6. DVI

7. VGA

8. S-Video

9. **Rank the following in order of preference for a display adapter interface, based on maximum speed from most to least preferable: Vesa Local Bus (VLB), 8x AGP, ISA, 16x PCIe, and PCI.**

   16x PCIe, 8x AGP, PCI, VLB, ISA

10. **If an LCD monitor is reported to be 19 inches, exactly what dimension is that a measurement of?**

    It's a measurement of the monitor's diagonal length.

11. **What type of connector(s) would a high-end LCD monitor most likely have: VGA, DVI, or both?**

A high-end LCD monitor would have both. A low-end monitor would likely have only VGA (analog).

12. **What is native resolution?**

Native resolution is the highest resolution at which an LCD monitor can operate.

13. **Is a higher native resolution always better? Why or why not?**

Not necessarily. At the highest resolution, icons and text on-screen are very small; some people might prefer an easier-to-read display. And because most LCD monitors look their sharpest only at their native resolution, a lower native resolution might be preferable.

14. **What is response time a measurement of?**

Response time measures the amount of time it takes for a pixel to go from fully on to fully off.

15. **What unit of measurement describes response time?**

Response time is measured in milliseconds (ms).

16. **When evaluating response time, is a higher or a lower number better?**

Lower

17. **How is contrast measured on an LCD monitor?**

Contrast is measured as a ratio, such as 500:1.

18. **When evaluating contrast, is a higher or a lower number better?**

Higher

19. **How is brightness measured on an LCD monitor?**

Brightness is measured in candela, or in candela per square meter.

20. **When evaluating brightness, is a higher or a lower number better?**

Generally, higher numbers are better. However, higher brightness also increases power consumption, which may be an issue on a computer running on batteries.

21. **Are CRTs usually analog or digital?**

CRTs are usually analog.

22. **What is the most common connector type on a CRT monitor?**

VGA

23. **Suppose a CRT's size is reported in its specs as 21/19.8 inches.**

    A. **What is 21 inches a measurement of?**

    It's a measurement of the monitor glass, including the portion hidden underneath the plastic bezel.

    B. **What is 19.8 inches a measurement of?**

    It's a measurement of the maximum viewable image size.

24. **What three colors compose a pixel triad on a CRT monitor?**

    Red, green, and blue

25. **Suppose a monitor has a dot pitch of 0.20 mm.**

    A. **What is that a measurement of?**

    It's the distance diagonally between two pixels of the same color.

    B. **Would a monitor that has a dot pitch of 0.26 mm be better or worse than one with a 0.20 mm dot pitch?**

    It would be worse because lower dot pitch is better.

26. **Suppose a monitor's specs report that it has a refresh rate of 120 Hz at 1,024 x 768 resolution.**

    A. **Is the refresh rate good enough to avoid eyestrain at that resolution?**

    Yes, anything over 85 Hz will usually avoid eyestrain.

    B. **Would a refresh rate of 60 Hz be better or worse than a rate of 120 Hz?**

    Worse

    C. **At a resolution of 1,600 x 1,200, would you expect the best available refresh rate to be higher, lower, or the same as at 1,024 x 768 resolution?**

    It would be lower because refresh rate becomes more difficult to maintain as the resolution increases.

27. **A user complains that text appears very fuzzy on his new LCD monitor. He knows it isn't the display adapter malfunctioning because his old CRT monitor looked very crisp. What is likely the problem?**

    LCD monitors look crisp only in their maximum (native) resolution. The user should increase the resolution to clear up this problem.

28. **A user complains that on his new laptop PC, the icons on the Windows desktop are extremely small and hard to see. He wants to avoid the problem with fuzzy text from Question 26, though. What can you suggest?**

    If you need to increase the icon size without decreasing the resolution, you can change the dpi setting in the Display Properties dialog box. From the Settings tab, click Advanced to access the dpi setting.

29. **A user complains that every time he tries to set his Windows display to a very high resolution, the color depth setting decreases and can't be increased until he switches to a lower resolution. Why is this happening?**

    This happens when the amount of video RAM is insufficient to support the higher combination of resolution and color depth. The user needs a display adapter with more memory.

30. **A user complains that after installing a new version of Windows, his display is limited to 640 x 480 resolution and 16 colors. He cannot change those settings in his Display Properties dialog box. What's wrong, and how can it be fixed?**

    This is probably being caused by Windows' failure to detect the display adapter and install a driver for it. The user should acquire the driver for the display adapter for the new version of Windows and install that.

31. **A user complains that his CRT display is hurting his eyes with its flickering. What setting should you change, and should that setting be increased or decreased?**

    The refresh rate should be increased.

32. **A user wants to adjust the refresh rate on his monitor (a CRT), but Windows detects it as a generic monitor and doesn't have any information about its maximum refresh rate capability. The user is asking you what refresh rate to use.**

    A. **Is there any danger in the user choosing a refresh rate that's too high?**

       Yes, a too-high refresh rate will damage a CRT.

    B. **Is there any danger in the user choosing a refresh rate that's too low?**

       No, there is no danger in this, other than the annoyance of the flickering.

    C. **How can you get Windows to identify the monitor so that it will display appropriate refresh rate options for that model?**

       You can download an `.inf` file from the monitor manufacturer and then install it from Device Manager as you would a driver.

    D. **If you cannot get Windows to identify the monitor, how else can you find out what refresh rates the monitor supports?**

       You can find out the specs for the monitor at the manufacturer's Web site and then install a driver (actually an `.inf` file) for a similar model of monitor with similar capabilities if Windows doesn't contain settings for the exact model you have. Then you can choose a refresh rate setting that the monitor will work with.

33. **Is ordinary glass cleaner suitable for cleaning a monitor? Why or why not?**

    No, it isn't. It contains ammonia, which can damage the antiglare coating.

34. **How can you remove accumulated lint and dust from the ventilation holes in the top of a CRT monitor?**

    Use a vacuum that is designed for electronics.

35. **If a CRT monitor has a faint green tinge on one side of the display when viewing a pure white page, what setting should you adjust?**

    Convergence

36. **If a CRT monitor seems to be entirely missing one of its three triad colors (red, green, or blue), what should you check?**

    If one color is missing entirely, check whether a pin on the monitor cable is bent or broken.

37. **If the image on a CRT is slightly bowed on the sides, what setting should you adjust?**

    This setting is sometimes generically called *geometry,* but the more specific name for the amount of bow in the sides is *pincushioning*.

38. **What does the *phase* setting control?**

    Side-to-side positioning of the image.

39. **What does degaussing to do a CRT monitor?**

    It removes any residual magnetic charge that might be distorting the colors on the display.

Chapter 8

Printers

· ·

In This Chapter

▶ Identifying types of printers

▶ Understanding the laser printing process

▶ Selecting a printer connection type

▶ Setting up a printer in Windows

▶ Setting printer options

▶ Managing a Windows print queue

▶ Troubleshooting printing problems

· ·

You can find many types of printers out there, but they all work on basically the same principle: They take data from a PC, process it, and turn it into a printed page. As a PC technician, you need to understand how the various technologies work, how to select the best printer for a particular usage, how to install and configure it in Windows, and how to troubleshoot any problems that might occur with it.

In this chapter, you test your knowledge of printer technologies, processes, connections, and troubleshooting.

Identifying Types of Printers

The A+ exam has several questions about how the various printer technologies work. You need to know the basics of each printer type, including how it takes data from the PC and converts it to printed output and how it handles paper and consumables (ink, toner, and so on).

When classifying printers, here are several ways of looking at them:

✔ **Ink type:** Some printers use powdered ink (toner). Other printers use a solid block of wax that gets melted and turned into a liquid for application, liquid ink that's liquid all the time, inked ribbon, or marking pens. (Actually, a device that uses marking pens is called a *plotter,* not a printer, but that's splitting hairs.)

✔ **Impact versus nonimpact:** Impact printers strike an inked ribbon with some type of hammer; these printers can make multiple carbon copies. Nonimpact printers gently lay the ink down on the page in a nonviolent fashion, and they can make only one copy at a time.

✔ **Sheet-fed versus tractor-fed:** Some printers pull through continuous-feed paper using a tractor-feed sprocket system, whereas others pull individual sheets of paper from a tray.

✔ **Page printer versus line printer:** Some printers hold the entire page in their memory at once and then spit it out onto the paper in one pass. Other printers print one line at a time, which means that the bottom of the page can still be transferring to the printer when the top of the page begins printing.

1. Test your knowledge of printer types by filling in the following table:

	Laser	Inkjet (Solid Ink)	Thermal	Dot Matrix
Impact or Nonimpact?				
Ink Type?				
Sheet-Fed or Tractor-Fed?				
Page Printer or Line Printer?				

2. What type of printer measures its quality as 9-pin (near letter quality) or 24-pin (letter quality)?

3. What type of printer places ink on the paper by using either bubble or piezoelectric technology?

4. What type of printer, used in high-end graphic arts, converts a solid ink (on a film roll) into a gas, which is then applied in a continuous tone to the paper?

5. What type of printer changes the electrical charge on a drum to produce an image?

Understanding the Laser Printing Process

Laser printers are the workhorses of the business world. The A+ exams have always been very heavy on the theory behind how these printers work — some would say more than they deserve — but that heavy focus on laser theory does help technicians understand what's going on inside that box so that they can more easily identify a problem when it occurs. You should also know the names of the parts inside the printer so that you can associate them with each of the steps.

Match the following parts of a laser printer to their descriptions:

A. Paper feed mechanism

B. Paper transport path

C. Toner cartridge

D. Drum

E. Power supply

F. Primary corona

G. Laser

H. Transfer corona

I. Static charge eliminator

J. Fuser

6. _____ The surface on which the picture of the page is drawn with an electromagnetic charge

7. _____ The heating unit that melts the plastic particles in the toner so that they stick to the paper

8. _____ A plastic container that holds the toner

9. _____ A set of rollers that move the paper through the printer

10. _____ A set of rollers that grab the paper from the tray and feed it into the printer

11. _____ The roller or wire that applies the initial negative charge to the drum

12. _____ A row of teeth that reduce the positive charge on the paper as it exits from the printer

13. _____ The unit that reduces the negative charge on the drum in certain spots so that the toner will stick to it

14. _____ Converts AC power to DC power and steps down the voltage to provide power to the printer

15. _____ The roller or wire that positively charges the paper so that the negatively charged toner will stick to it

16. Fill in the name of each step of the laser printing process and number them in the correct order:

Description	Name	Order (1 through 6)
Laser reduces the charge on certain areas of the drum to –100V.		
Primary corona applies a –600V charge to the drum.		
Excess toner is cleaned off the drum.		

Description	Name	Order (1 through 6)
Transfer corona applies +600V to the paper, and the paper picks up toner from the drum.		
Toner is melted onto the paper, and the paper is ejected from the printer.		
Drum picks up toner on areas the laser has touched.		

Selecting a Printer Connection Type

You can hook up a printer to a computer in a lot of ways, either directly or indirectly. It's useful to know as many of them as possible because that knowledge increases the likelihood that you'll be able to hook up the printer successfully when things start going wrong — bad cables, bad connectors, disabled ports, and so on.

For the A+ exam, you need to know how to configure and connect these printer port types:

- **Parallel:** The traditional DB-25 legacy parallel port interface, also known as LPT.
- **Network:** This refers to a printer with its own NIC and its own IP address on the network. (Printers can also be shared on a network, but they use some other type of port to get there.)
- **USB:** The ubiquitous Universal Serial Bus port, found on nearly every system — simple, Plug and Play, and hot-pluggable.
- **Serial:** The traditional legacy serial port interface, also known as COM.

  Note that for a printer you have to have a 25-pin serial port, not the more common and modern 9-pin variety. Printing is virtually the only thing that requires the 25-pin serial port; for all other serial port functionality, either a 9-pin or a 25-pin will work equally well.
- **FireWire (IEEE 1394):** The main competitor to USB, less common for printers but still seen occasionally.
- **Bluetooth:** A short-range radio frequency (RF) wireless technology, requiring only that the printer and the PC both have Bluetooth adapters.

- ✓ **802.11:** Any of several Wi-Fi variants, including 802.11 a/b/g/n; has a longer range than Bluetooth.

- ✓ **Infrared:** A wireless technology that's suitable for short ranges in which there is a clear line of sight between the two points.

- ✓ **SCSI:** Primarily a parallel disk drive interface, but also used for some printers and scanners.

Test how much you know about the various printer connectors:

17. Place these printer interfaces in order from slowest to fastest: Legacy Parallel, USB, Legacy Serial.

_____

18. Suppose you need to change the legacy parallel port mode on a PC. Where would you go to do it?

_____

19. SPP (Standard Parallel Port) is one of the legacy parallel port modes; bidirectional is another. Name the other two.

_____

20. Of the port modes you listed in Question 19, which one requires a DMA channel?

_____

21. Place these printer interfaces in order from slowest to fastest: Infrared, 802.11b, Bluetooth 2.0.

_____

Exercise 8-1: Comparing Printer Interfaces

For this exercise, you need a printer with two different interfaces on it (parallel, network, USB, and so on).

_1._ Connect the printer to your PC by using one interface.

_2._ Print a graphics-heavy multipage document and time the print process from start to finish.

_3._ Connect the printer by using the other interface.

_4._ Reprint the same document and time the print process.

_5._ Compare the two printing times. Did the interface make any difference in the speed?

Do Steps 6–10 only if you have a printer with a legacy parallel interface available:

_6._ Enter BIOS Setup and set the parallel port mode to Bidirectional.

**Note:** To enter BIOS Setup, press the key specified on the screen at startup, such as `Press F2 to Enter Setup.`

7. Enter Windows and print the same document as in Step 2. Time the print process.

8. Enter BIOS Setup and set the parallel port mode to ECP.

9. Enter Windows and print the same document again. Time the print process.

10. Compare the printing times. Did the parallel port mode make any difference?

Setting Up a Printer in Windows

Connecting a printer is as simple as running a cable between the PC and the printer. Some interfaces are hot-pluggable, meaning you can connect them without shutting down the PC; others aren't. (You need to know which are hot-pluggable, of course.)

To print from Windows, you need to install a driver for the printer. When Windows detects a new printer, a Found New Hardware dialog box opens, prompting you to insert the driver disk for the printer. You can do so and follow the remaining prompts, or you can click Cancel and then run the Setup software that came with the printer.

Windows comes with a fairly large library of printer drivers, so if you don't have the driver disk, it might install anyway. If not, you can click Cancel when Windows detects the printer and then download the necessary driver from the printer manufacturer's Web site.

Test your knowledge of setting up a printer on a Windows PC:

22. In the Control Panel, in which applet can you find the Add Printer Wizard?

_____

23. Are each of these printer interfaces hot-pluggable? Circle Yes or No.

    A. Legacy Parallel   Yes / No

    B. Legacy Serial   Yes / No

    C. USB   Yes / No

    D. FireWire   Yes / No

    E. Ethernet (RJ-45)   Yes / No

    F. SCSI   Yes / No

24. Answer the following questions about this image:

A. What does the check mark signify?

_____

B. What does the hand signify?

_____

25. In the following image, what does the line underneath the printer signify?

_____

_____

Exercise 8-2: Working with Printer Drivers

1. Locate the driver disk for your printer or download the latest version of the driver.

2. Remove the printer's driver from Windows and disconnect the printer from the PC.

3. Reconnect the printer/reinstall the printer driver by using any method (Found New Hardware or the printer's own Setup utility).

4. Set up a second copy of the driver for the printer by using the Add Printer Wizard and manually choosing the port and the printer make/model.

Setting Printer Options

After you install a printer's driver in Windows, you can configure the printer's settings by using its Properties dialog box. To get to the Properties dialog box for a printer, right-click its icon in the Printers and Faxes folder (or the Printers folder, in Vista) and choose Properties.

The tabs available in the printer's Properties dialog box depend on what's specified in the printer driver, but you can nearly always find a General tab where you can set the printer's name, location (useful in a corporate setting), and comment (useful when shared on a network).

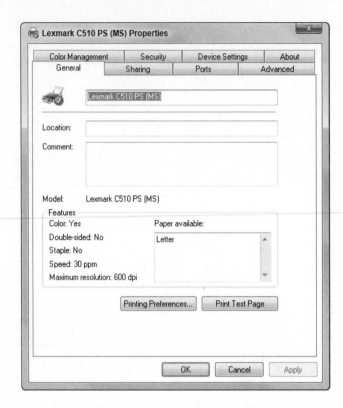

You can access additional settings, also printer-dependent, by clicking the Printing Preferences button on the General tab. These settings might include paper tray selection, color/black-and-white mode selection, paper quality, print resolution, and so on.

Be careful not to set Printing Preferences that conflict with the settings you might want in an individual application. For example, if you set the page orientation to Landscape in the Printing Preferences, your word-processing program might suddenly start printing all documents in that orientation.

Test your knowledge of printer options and settings:

26. Which of the following are settings you can control from the Advanced tab of a printer's Properties dialog box? Circle as many as apply.

A. Change the port assignment (LPT1, USB1, and so on).

B. Set a priority.

C. Turn the print spooler on or off.

D. Set up a separator page.

E. Share the printer on the network.

F. Assign permission for the printer to a user or group of users.

G. Change the printer's network name.

H. Print a test page.

27. Suppose you want to have two sets of saved settings/options for a single printer, and you want to switch back and forth between them. How can you do this in Windows without having to change the settings manually each time?

_____

_____

_____

_____

28. Suppose you want a printer driver to print to the first available printer in a bank of networked laser printers. How would you set the ports on the Ports tab of the Properties dialog box?

_____

_____

_____

_____

29. Suppose you want to print to a network printer by specifying its IP address, but that IP address isn't listed on the Ports tab. How would you create a standard TCP/IP port for this use?

_____

_____

_____

_____

30. Suppose your printer has a built-in Helvetica Narrow font that you want to be used whenever it prints a document that calls for Helvetica font, even though you have a TrueType Helvetica font installed. What feature in the printer's Properties dialog box enables you to do this?

_____

Exercise 8-3: Changing Printer Properties

1. Right-click a printer's icon and choose Properties. Examine each of the available tabs for that printer.

2. On the General tab, change the printer's name and add a comment for it.

3. Print a test page.

4. Click Printing Preferences and examine the available settings in the Printing Preferences dialog box. Then click OK to return to the Properties dialog box.

5. If you have more than one printer, repeat Step 1 for each of them and compare the availability of the various settings.

   For example, a fax driver won't have a Ports tab, and an inkjet printer might have a Utility or Tools tab containing controls for cleaning the print heads.

6. Close all open dialog boxes.

Managing a Windows Print Queue

By default, Windows spools (queues) print jobs for each printer. In other words, it holds print jobs in a storage area while it waits for the printer to accept them. This frees up the application from which you're printing and allows the print job to finish in the background.

You can view a printer's queue by double-clicking its icon in the Printers and Faxes folder. From there, you can reprioritize waiting jobs, cancel individual jobs, pause the entire queue, clear the entire queue, and more.

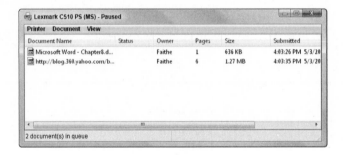

See how much you know about working with print queues in Windows:

31. The print queue in the preceding image is paused. What command would you use to unpause it?

_____

_____

32. Suppose you wanted to delete the second print job in the queue but not the first one. What command would do this?

_____

_____

33. Suppose you wanted to clear both jobs from the queue with a single command. What command would do this?

_____

_____

34. Suppose you wanted to allow the second print job to print before the first one. One way is to pause the first job until the second one has printed. What is the other way?

_____

_____

35. Suppose a very large print job is in the queue, and you want to force it to wait until after 5:00 p.m. to print so that it doesn't interfere with smaller print jobs needed while the business is open to customers. You won't be in the building at 5:00 p.m., though, so you won't be able to release a paused print job at that time. How could you do this?

_____

_____

_____

_____

Exercise 8-4: Working with Print Queues

1. Open the queue for your default printer. Pause it.

2. Print at least three items from different programs. To save paper, make them all short, one-page print jobs.

3. In the queue, reprioritize the last job so that it will print before the others.

4. Pause one of the other print jobs.

5. Release the queue and note in which order the jobs print.

6. Cancel the remaining print job (the paused one).

Troubleshooting Printing Problems

Selecting the right printer and hooking it up correctly are important tasks, but most PC technicians' interactions with printers also involve troubleshooting. Printers have more mechanical parts than most other pieces of computer equipment, and that means they break down more frequently and in various ways.

Even though printers are more prone to hardware failure than some components, the majority of printing problems aren't the hardware's fault. The operating system, the printer's driver, and even the application from which the user is printing can all be sources of problems and bottlenecks.

Test your knowledge of printer troubleshooting by identifying the likely cause of each of the following problems:

36. The printer is producing garbled or corrupted output.

_____

_____

_____

37. The application freezes until the print job is mostly completed.

_____

_____

_____

38. The job in the print queue won't print and can't be deleted.

_____

_____

_____

39. The printing is faint (dot matrix printer).

_____

_____

_____

40. One color doesn't print (inkjet printer).

_____

_____

_____

41. The printout has horizontal color stripes (inkjet printer).

_____

_____

_____

42. The printer has frequent paper jams.

_____

_____

_____

43. White stripes appear (laser printer).

_____

_____

_____

44. Some pages come out blank (laser printer).

_____

_____

_____

45. A vertical black line appears on each page (laser printer).

_____

_____

_____

46. Toner is smeared on pages (laser printer).

_____

_____

_____

Answers to Questions in This Chapter

The following are the answers to the practice questions presented earlier in this chapter:

1. **Test your knowledge of printer types by filling in the following table:**

	Laser	*Inkjet*	*Thermal (Solid Ink)*	*Dot Matrix*
Impact or Nonimpact?	Nonimpact	Nonimpact	Nonimpact	Impact
Ink Type?	Toner	Liquid	Wax	Ribbon
Sheet-Fed or Tractor-Fed?	Sheet	Sheet	Sheet	Tractor
Page Printer or Line Printer?	Page	Line	Page	Line

2. **What type of printer measures its quality as 9-pin (near letter quality) or 24-pin (letter quality)?**

   Dot matrix

3. **What type of printer places ink on the paper by using either bubble or piezoelectric technology?**

   Ink jet

4. **What type of printer, used in high-end graphic arts, converts a solid ink (on a film roll) into a gas, which is then applied in a continuous tone to the paper?**

   Dye sublimation

5. **What type of printer changes the electrical charge on a drum to produce an image?**

   Laser

6. D

7. J

8. C

9. B

10. A

11. F

12. I

13. G

14. E

15. H

16. **Fill in the name of each step of the laser printing process and number them in the correct order:**

Description	Name	Order (1 through 6)
Laser reduces the charge on certain areas of the drum to −100V.	Writing	2
Primary corona applies a −600V charge to the drum.	Charging	1
Excess toner is cleaned off the drum.	Cleaning	6
Transfer corona applies +600V to the paper, and the paper picks up toner from the drum.	Developing	3
Toner is melted onto the paper, and the paper is ejected from the printer.	Fusing	5
Drum picks up toner on areas laser has touched	Transferring	4

17. **Place these printer interfaces in order from slowest to fastest: Legacy Parallel, USB, Legacy Serial.**

Legacy Serial, Legacy Parallel, USB

18. **Suppose you need to change the legacy parallel port mode on a PC. Where would you go to do it?**

BIOS Setup

19. **SPP (Standard Parallel Port) is one of the legacy parallel port modes; bidirectional is another. Name the other two.**

Enhanced Capabilities Port (ECP)

Enhanced Parallel Port (EPP)

20. **Of the port modes you listed in Question 19, which one requires a DMA channel?**

ECP

21. **Place these printer interfaces in order from slowest to fastest: Infrared, 802.11b, Bluetooth 2.0.**

Infrared: 115.2 Kbps

Bluetooth: 2.1 Mbps

802.11B: 11 Mbps

22. **In the Control Panel, in which applet can you find the Add Printer Wizard?**

Printers and Faxes (Windows XP) or Printers (Windows Vista)

23. **Are each of these printer interfaces hot-pluggable? Circle Yes or No.**

    A. Legacy Parallel: <u>No</u>

    B. Legacy Serial: <u>No</u>

    C. USB: <u>Yes</u>

    D. FireWire: <u>Yes</u>

    E. Ethernet (RJ-45): <u>Yes</u>

    F. SCSI: <u>No</u>

24. **Answer the following questions about this image:**

    A. What does the check mark signify?

      The default printer

    B. What does the hand signify?

      Shared

25. **In the following image, what does the line underneath the printer signify?**

    Network printer

26. **Which of the following are settings you can control from the Advanced tab of a printer's Properties dialog box? Circle as many as apply.**

    A. Change the port assignment (LPT1, USB1, and so on): <u>No</u>

    B. Set a priority: <u>Yes</u>

    C. Turn the print spooler on or off: <u>Yes</u>

    D. Set up a separator page: <u>Yes</u>

    E. Share the printer on the network: <u>No</u>

    F. Assign permission for the printer to a user or group of users: <u>No</u>

    G. Change the printer's network name: <u>No</u>

    H. Print a test page: <u>No</u>

27. **Suppose you want to have two sets of saved settings/options for a single printer, and you want switch back and forth between them. How can you do this in Windows without having to change the settings manually each time?**

You can create a second instance of the printer by copying the printer's icon or by using the Add Printer Wizard, and assign different properties to each copy. Then you can print to one copy or the other depending on the desired settings for that job.

28. **Suppose you want a printer driver to print to the first available printer in a bank of networked laser printers. How would you set the ports on the Ports tab of the Properties dialog box?**

On the Ports tab, place a check mark next to each port you want to use. The printer driver will then print the job each time to the first available port from among that list.

29. **Suppose you want to print to a network printer by specifying its IP address, but that IP address isn't listed on the Ports tab. How would you create a standard TCP/IP port for this use?**

    On the Ports tab, click Add Port and follow the prompts to create a Standard TCP/IP Port.

30. **Suppose your printer has a built-in Helvetica Narrow font that you want to be used whenever it prints a document that calls for Helvetica font, even though you have a TrueType Helvetica font installed. What feature in the printer's Properties dialog box enables you to do this?**

    Use the Font Substitution Table.

31. **The print queue shown in the preceding image is paused. What command would you use to unpause it?**

    Printer⇨Pause Printing

32. **Suppose you wanted to delete the second print job in the queue but not the first one. What command would do this?**

    Select the print job and press the Delete key, or choose Document⇨Cancel.

33. **Suppose you wanted to clear both jobs from the queue with a single command. What command would do this?**

    Printer⇨Cancel All Documents

34. **Suppose you wanted to allow the second print job to print before the first one. One way is to pause the first job until the second one has printed. What is the other way?**

    Select the print job and choose Document⇨Properties and then adjust the Priority slider.

35. **Suppose a very large print job is in the queue, and you want to force it to wait until after 5:00 p.m. to print so that it doesn't interfere with smaller print jobs needed while the business is open to customers. You won't be in the building at 5:00 p.m., though, so you won't be able to release a paused print job at that time. How could you do this?**

    Select the print job and choose Document⇨Properties and set the Schedule setting to print only from 5:00 p.m. to whatever time the business opens in the morning.

36. **The printer is producing garbled or corrupted output.**

    Delete and reinstall printer driver.

37. **The application freezes until the print job is mostly completed.**

    Turn on print spooler in printer's Properties dialog box.

38. **The job in print queue won't print and can't be deleted.**

    Stop and restart the print spooler service (Control Panel⇨Performance and Maintenance⇨Administrative Tools).

39. **The printing is faint (dot matrix printer).**

    Replace the ribbon.

40. **One color doesn't print (inkjet printer).**

    Try cleaning the print heads; if that doesn't help, replace ink cartridge.

41. **The printout has horizontal color stripes (inkjet printer).**

    Clean the print heads.

42. **The printer has frequent paper jams.**

    Use a different type of paper or check feed rollers to make sure they are picking up the paper correctly.

43. **White stripes appear (laser printer).**

    Clean coronas, check to make sure there is adequate toner, and shake toner cartridge to redistribute remaining toner evenly.

44. **Some pages come out blank (laser printer).**

    Check that there is toner available; check that coronas are working.

45. **A vertical black line appears on each page (laser printer).**

    The drum is scratched; replace the drum.

46. **Toner is smeared on pages (laser printer).**

    The fuser isn't working.

Chapter 9

Multimedia and Input Devices

*T*echnicians often support a wide variety of input and output devices that are either installed in a PC (like a sound card) or attached to a PC externally (like a keyboard or mouse). Many types of these devices exist, each with their own tricks for installing, configuring, and troubleshooting. In this chapter, you test your knowledge of scanners, sound cards, keyboards, mice, and other devices.

Working with Scanners

Most scanners are closed systems hardware-wise; you typically won't be disassembling one and messing with its innards. A technician's primary interactions with scanners consist of selecting the right scanner in the first place and then hooking it up to the PC and installing its driver correctly. You might also need to do some basic interface troubleshooting if the scanner isn't recognized in Windows or if it causes problems with another device.

Test your knowledge of scanner types, technologies, configuration, and troubleshooting:

1. Which type of scanner uses a technology called Photomultiplier Tube (PMT), which involves wrapping the photo around a glass tube?

_____

2. What type of scanner has a stationary scan head, which the paper feeds past, like a fax machine?

_____

3. What does CCD stand for, and what does it do inside a scanner?

_____

_____

_____

_____

4. Name three interfaces that scanners use to connect to a PC.

_____

_____

5. When scanning a picture, suppose your scanning software gives you the choice of JPEG or TIF format.

   A. Which file format is more suitable for Web use?

_____

   B. Why is it more suitable?

_____

_____

_____

6. What utility included with Windows XP can you use to scan a picture?

_____

7. Some cheaper scanners have a CIS instead of a CCD. What does CIS stand for?

_____

8. What does the Y direction sampling rate represent in a scanner's specifications?

_____

_____

_____

_____

9. What is an interpolated resolution, and why isn't it a reliable measurement of a scanner's hardware capability?

_____

_____

_____

_____

10. What is dynamic range in a scanner, and what scale is used to measure it?

_____

_____

_____

_____

11. Suppose you set up a new flatbed scanner. The first time you try to use it, you hear a grinding sound, and the light bar doesn't move. What's wrong, and how would you fix it?

_____

_____

_____

_____

12. On a system with a single legacy parallel port, suppose you want to hook up a parallel interface scanner. How can you do this if you already have a parallel printer connected to that port?

_____

_____

_____

_____

13. What is TWAIN, and what is the Windows XP alternative to it?

_____

_____

_____

_____

14. Suppose you're sharing a parallel port between a scanner and a printer. Either device works when it's the only device connected to that port, but when the port is shared, neither one works. What setting in BIOS Setup can you change to try to solve the problem?

_____

_____

Exercise 9-1: Evaluating Scanners

For this exercise, you need a scanner attached to a Windows PC.

1. Examine the scanner physically, looking for a locking mechanism. Make sure the scanner is unlocked.

2. Connect the scanner to the PC and install a driver or utility software if needed.

3. Scan a small photo using the Scanner and Camera Wizard in Windows if possible.

   Not all scanners will work with that wizard; if yours doesn't, use the proprietary software that came with the scanner.

4. Save the photo to your hard drive as a JPEG file.

5. Look up the scanner's specifications (using its make and model) on the Internet, and determine the following information about it:

   • Color depth: _____

   • Dynamic range: _____

   • Speed (based on what size image?):

   _____

   • Interface type: _____

6. Go to www.microsoft.com/hcl and find out which versions of Windows this scanner is compatible with.

Understanding Sound Cards

A sound card (or a built-in equivalent on the motherboard) performs a variety of sound-related input and output functions.

Sound cards typically have a series of externally accessible ports on them, including these common ports:

✔ **Microphone:** Analog input gets converted to digital and stored on disk.

✔ **Speakers:** Digital output gets converted to analog and fed to speakers.

✔ **MIDI devices:** Digital musical instruments send data to the PC to be stored on disk. For example, you can use a digital keyboard to compose music.

✔ **Line In:** You can connect any generic analog device here to convert analog data to digital and store it on disk. For example, you can connect a stereo system here to bring in music from a cassette or LP.

✔ **Line Out:** You can connect any generic analog device here to receive analog output. For example, you can connect a cassette tape recorder here to record digital music to a cassette.

Some sound cards also have a row of internal ports across the top edge of the card for connecting internal devices to the card, such as:

✔ **Telephone answering device (TAD):** A cable runs between this port and an internal modem so that you can hear messages from answering machine software through your PC speakers

✔ **CD In (Audio in):** On some older systems, it's necessary to run an analog cable from the CD drive to this port to be able to hear audio CDs play through the speakers.

✔ **Aux In:** This is an all-purpose input port; you can use it for a second CD drive's audio cable or some other internal device that generates sound that you want to hear through the speakers.

✔ **Sony/Philips Digital Interface (S/PDIF):** This interface would typically connect via cable to an external backplate with several S/PDIF ports on it. These ports might be useful for exporting sound to a portable digital audio player, for example.

✔ **TV tuner:** If a TV tuner card is installed in the PC, you can connect it to the sound card via this port so that you can hear the TV through the speakers.

✔ **Mic Con:** If the computer has an internal microphone, it connects here. Most mics are external, however.

Test your knowledge of sound card ports and specifications:

15. On many sound cards, external ports are color-coded. List the most common color for each of the following:

A. Line Out: _____

B. Speaker Out: _____

C. Microphone: _____

D. Line In: _____

E. Digital Out: _____

16. Suppose a sound card has a 15-pin D-sub connector on it with pins arranged in two rows (8 and 7). Name two different devices you could potentially connect to such a port.

_____

17. Sound cards generate analog output for MIDI music via either wavetable synthesis or FM synthesis.

A. Which is better?

_____

B. Why is it better?

_____

_____

_____

18. Is it better to have a higher or a lower number for a card's signal-to-noise ratio?

_____

19. Is it better to have a higher or a lower number for a card's analog-to-digital sampling rate?

_____

Exercise 9-2: Determining Sound Card Specifications

1. Examine your sound card physically and make a list of its external and internal ports. Compare this list with the lists presented earlier in this section.

2. Look up your sound card make and model online. Determine its specifications in the following areas:

- Number of MIDI voices that can play simultaneously: _____
- ROM size: _____
- RAM size: _____
- MIDI channels for recording and playback: _____
- Recording depth: _____
- Maximum recording rate: _____
- Playback depth: _____
- Maximum playback rate: _____
- Signal-to-noise ratio: _____

Installing and Configuring a Sound Card

Most sound cards are fully Plug and Play and easy to install. You just shut down the PC and pop them into an available slot, the same as any other expansion card. Then run the Setup software that came with the card to complete the installation. (Running the Setup software isn't always necessary, but sound cards seem to be more likely than other device types to not be automatically recognized in Windows without their setup software.)

After you install the card, if it doesn't automatically start generating sound out of the attached speakers, you need to troubleshoot. Here's a basic outline of that process:

1. Confirm that Windows recognizes the sound card in Device Manager. If it doesn't, rerun the Setup software for the sound card and check resource assignments. Make sure the device hasn't been disabled there.

2. Make sure the speakers are turned on, plugged in, and connected to the Speaker jack on the sound card (and not some other jack).

3. Make sure the speaker volume is turned up on the speakers themselves and in the Windows Volume Control. Make sure sound in Windows is not set to Mute.

Test your skills in installing and configuring sound cards:

20. What type of motherboard slot is most commonly used for sound cards?

_____

21. If you have built-in sound on the motherboard and you want to add a newer, better sound card to the system, must you disable the built-in sound first?

_____

22. Are sound cards hot-pluggable?

   _____

23. In Device Manager, what does it signify if a question mark appears next to the sound card
   (in Windows XP)?

   _____

24. In Device Manager, what does it signify if a red X appears next to the sound card
   (in Windows XP)?

   _____

25. In Device Manager, what does it signify if an exclamation point appears next to the sound
   card (in Windows XP)?

   _____

26. In the notification area of the taskbar, what does it mean if a red X appears next to the
   volume icon?

   _____

27. In Windows XP, if no volume icon appears in the notification area, where in the Control
   Panel can you potentially enable it?

   _____

   _____

28. In Windows XP, in the Sounds and Audio Devices Properties box, what does it mean if no
   device is listed as the default device on the Audio tab in the Sound Playback section?

   _____

   _____

Exercise 9-3: Working with Sound Cards

For this exercise, you need a PC with sound support running under Windows XP.

1. Open the Device Manager and locate the sound card. View its properties and make
   sure it's working correctly.

2. Open the Sounds and Audio Devices Properties from the Control Panel.

3. On the Sounds tab, make sure a sound scheme has been chosen. Test a couple of
   the sounds.

4. On the Audio tab, check that the sound card is set as the default device for sound
   playback.

5. On the Voice tab, check that the sound card is set as the default device for voice recording.

6. On the Hardware tab, examine the list of sound devices, drivers, and codecs. View the properties for a couple of the items.

7. Display the volume controls (from the speaker icon in the taskbar's notification area).

8. Adjust the volume sliders for a few of the sound types.

9. From the volume control window, choose Options➪Properties. Click Recording and click OK. The volume controls change to those for recording (input) devices.

10. Adjust the volume for the microphone port.

11. Close the volume control window.

Selecting a Keyboard or Mouse

Managing to get the correct interface is the first concern when selecting input devices such as keyboards and mice. You want to make sure that the connector matches up with what's available on the PC, whether that's an AT plug, a PS/2, a USB, or some proprietary interface.

After interface, selection is largely a matter of personal preference. Does the user want wired or wireless? some special shape or size of device? some special buttons, keys, or features? It's all out there.

Test your knowledge of keyboard, mouse, and trackball features:

29. How many function keys are there on a modern keyboard?

_____

30. What two keys are present on a Windows keyboard that other keyboards lack, and what do they do?

_____

_____

31. What is different about a Dvorak keyboard compared to other keyboards?

_____

_____

32. What type of motherboard uses a 5-pin DIN connector for a keyboard?

_____

33. What type of motherboard uses a 6-pin mini-DIN (PS/2) style connector for a keyboard?

_____

34. If a mouse has a wheel, what does it do?

_____

35. True or False: An optical mouse is the same thing as a cordless mouse.

_____

Adjusting Input Device Settings in Windows

Input devices connect easily to most systems, and they start working automatically without any fanfare. Whether they work exactly as expected, however, is another thing entirely.

You can adjust most input devices via their properties in the Control Panel to make them more or less sensitive to your input. In the case of devices that control the cursor, such as a mouse or trackball, you can also adjust the cursor appearance.

See how much you know about adjusting keyboard and mouse settings in Windows XP:

36. Which input device has a blink rate setting?

_____

37. What does the keyboard repeat delay control?

_____

38. What feature enables you to highlight or drag without holding the mouse button down?

_____

39. Suppose a user is having trouble double-clicking; she can't click twice in a row fast enough for it to register as a double-click. Would you change her double-click speed to be Faster or Slower?

_____

40. Suppose the cursor on-screen looks like it has copies of itself trailing along behind it as you move the mouse.

A. What feature has been turned on (possibly inadvertently)?

_____

B. From which tab in the Mouse Properties would you turn it off?

_____

41. From which Control Panel applet would you set up StickyKeys, FilterKeys, and ToggleKeys?

_____

Exercise 9-4: Changing Mouse and Keyboard Settings

1. Open the Control Panel and display the Keyboard Properties dialog box.

2. Adjust the keyboard repeat rate, repeat delay, and cursor blink rate. Experiment with several settings by using the text box in the center of the dialog box to test them.

3. Close the Keyboard Properties dialog box and open the Mouse Properties dialog box.

4. Change the pointer scheme.

5. Adjust the pointer speed.

6. Turn on pointer trails; then try them out and turn them back off again.

7. Switch the primary and secondary mouse buttons; try them out, and then switch them back again.

8. Close the Mouse Properties dialog box.

Answers to Questions in This Chapter

The following are the answers to the practice questions presented earlier in this chapter:

1. **Which type of scanner uses a technology called Photomultiplier Tube (PMT), which involves wrapping the photo around a glass tube?**

    Drum

2. **What type of scanner has a stationary scan head, which the paper feeds past, like a fax machine?**

    Sheet-fed

3. **What does CCD stand for, and what does it do inside a scanner?**

    Charge coupled device. It's the unit that measures the amount of light bounced back off each spot on the page and converts it to a numeric value representing each pixel.

4. **Name three interfaces that scanners use to connect to a PC.**

    Parallel, SCSI, and USB

5. **When scanning a picture, suppose your scanning software gives you the choice of JPEG or TIF format.**

    A. Which file format is more suitable for Web use?

    JPEG

    B. Why is it more suitable?

    It is a smaller, more compact format, and because Web display does not require a high resolution, it is most appropriate for that usage.

6. **What utility included with Windows XP can you use to scan a picture?**

    Windows Image Acquisition (Scanner and Camera Wizard)

7. **Some cheaper scanners have a CIS instead of a CCD. What does CIS stand for?**

    Contact Image Sensor

8. **What does the Y direction sampling rate represent in a scanner's specifications?**

    It's the number of positions that the CCD stops and takes readings as it moves vertically down the page.

9. **What is an interpolated resolution, and why isn't it a reliable measurement of a scanner's hardware capability?**

    Interpolation simulates extra pixels by averaging the values of two pixels and inserting a new one in-between them. It is not a good measurement of a scanner's hardware because it is software-generated.

10. **What is dynamic range in a scanner, and what scale is used to measure it?**

Dynamic range measures the scanner's ability to distinguish between light and dark. It is measured on a four-point scale, with 4 being the best.

11. **Suppose you set up a new flatbed scanner. The first time you try to use it, you hear a grinding sound, and the light bar doesn't move. What's wrong, and how would you fix it?**

It's locked. Look for a locking mechanism on the bottom of the scanner that you can release.

12. **On a system with a single legacy parallel port, suppose you want to hook up a parallel interface scanner. How can you do this if you already have a parallel printer connected to that port?**

You can set up a passthrough. The scanner itself might have an in and an out port for a parallel interface, or you can use a splitter box.

13. **What is TWAIN, and what is the Windows XP alternative to it?**

TWAIN is the driver interface for connecting Windows to a scanning device in Windows versions prior to XP. Although it appears in all-caps as an acronym, it actually isn't an acronym. (Techies joke that it stands for Technology Without an Interesting Name.) The Windows XP alternative is known as Windows Image Acquisition (WIA).

14. **Suppose you're sharing a parallel port between a scanner and a printer. Either device works when it's the only device connected to that port, but when the port is shared, neither one works. What setting in BIOS Setup can you change to try to solve the problem?**

You can change the parallel port mode setting in BIOS Setup. Experiment with SPP, Bidirectional, ECP, and EPP, and find which mode works best with the sharing.

15. **On many sound cards, external ports are color-coded. List the most common color for each of the following:**

A. Line Out: Green

B. Speaker Out: Black

C. Microphone: Red or pink

D. Line In: Blue

E. Digital Out: Yellow

16. **Suppose a sound card has a 15-pin D-sub connector on it with pins arranged in two rows (8 and 7). Name two different devices you could potentially connect to such a port.**

MIDI instrument

Joystick

17. **Sound cards generate analog output for MIDI music via either wavetable synthesis or FM synthesis.**

    A. Which is better?

    Wavetable synthesis is better.

    B. Why is it better?

    It uses actual sound clips of the instruments rather than simulated sounds for a more realistic sound.

18. **Is it better to have a higher or a lower number for a card's signal-to-noise ratio?**

    Higher

19. **Is it better to have a higher or a lower number for a card's analog-to-digital sampling rate?**

    Higher

20. **What type of motherboard slot is most commonly used for sound cards?**

    PCI

21. **If you have built-in sound on the motherboard and you want to add a newer, better sound card to the system, must you disable the built-in sound first?**

    No

22. **Are sound cards hot-pluggable?**

    No

23. **In Device Manager, what does it signify if a question mark appears next to the sound card (in Windows XP)?**

    Windows cannot identify the device.

24. **In Device Manager, what does it signify if a red X appears next to the sound card (in Windows XP)?**

    The device has been disabled.

25. **In Device Manager, what does it signify if an exclamation point appears next to the sound card (in Windows XP)?**

    There is a problem with the device, such as a resource conflict.

26. **In the notification area of the taskbar, what does it mean if a red X appears next to the volume icon?**

    The volume has been muted.

27. **In Windows XP, if no volume icon appears in the notification area, where in the Control Panel can you potentially enable it?**

In Sounds and Audio Devices, on the Volume tab, mark the Place Volume icon in the Taskbar check box.

28. **In Windows XP, in the Sounds and Audio Devices Properties box, what does it mean if no device is listed as the default device on the Audio tab in the Sound Playback section?**

Windows doesn't recognize that you have any devices for audio playback.

29. **How many function keys are there on a modern keyboard?**

12

30. **What two keys are present on a Windows keyboard that other keyboards lack, and what do they do?**

Windows key: opens the Start menu

Menu key: same as right-clicking

31. **What is different about a Dvorak keyboard compared to other keyboards?**

The letters are arranged differently from the standard QWERTY keyboard.

32. **What type of motherboard uses a 5-pin DIN connector for a keyboard?**

AT

33. **What type of motherboard uses a 6-pin mini-DIN (PS/2) style connector for a keyboard?**

ATX

34. **If a mouse has a wheel, what does it do?**

Scrolls and zooms

35. **True or False: An optical mouse is the same thing as a cordless mouse.**

False. An optical mouse lacks a ball; it may or may not be cordless.

36. **Which input device has a blink rate setting?**

Keyboard

37. **What does the keyboard repeat delay control?**

The amount of time between holding down a key and having it start to repeat

38. **What feature enables you to highlight or drag without holding the mouse button down?**

ClickLock

39. **Suppose a user is having trouble double-clicking; she can't click twice in a row fast enough for it to register as a double-click. Would you change her double-click speed to be Faster or Slower?**

Slower

40. **Suppose the cursor on-screen looks like it has copies of itself trailing along behind it as you move the mouse.**

A. What feature has been turned on (possibly inadvertently)?

Pointer trails

B. From which tab in the Mouse Properties dialog box would you turn it off?

Pointer options

41. **From which Control Panel applet would you set up StickyKeys, FilterKeys, and ToggleKeys?**

Accessibility

Part III
Operating System Basics

In this part . . .

*H*ere you review operating system facts and figures. You practice installing and upgrading Windows, working with command-line interfaces to manage files and folders, run and configure applications, and manage hardware device drivers and their resource assignments.

Chapter 10

Installing and Upgrading Windows

· ·

In This Chapter

▶ Identifying Windows system requirements

▶ Identifying valid upgrade paths

▶ Performing an installation

▶ Setting up multibooting

▶ Transferring user data files

· ·

*E*very PC needs an operating system, of course, and Windows is by far the most pop-ular one. Much of the A+ exam's software portion deals with Windows XP, with sec-ondary emphasis on Windows 2000 and Windows 9x (that is, 95, 98, and Me). The next several chapters deal with Windows work, starting with this chapter, in which you review the procedures for installing and upgrading.

Identifying Windows System Requirements

The latest and greatest operating system isn't always appropriate for every PC. A PC with a meager amount of RAM and an older CPU will actually run more slowly and poorly under a newer OS in many cases. Therefore good technicians must know the system requirements for each operating system so that they're in a position to choose one that will run well on the available hardware.

When determining whether an operating system can run on a certain PC, ask yourself these three questions:

✔ Does the PC meet the minimum requirements for that OS in terms of CPU, memory, and disk drives?

✔ Are there any compatibility issues between any specific devices installed and the new operating system? (For example, is a driver available for a certain device?)

✔ Are there any compatibility issues between any software the user needs to run and the new operating system?

Evaluate each of these factors before installing any operating system. In some cases, the upgrade process performs some of these checks automatically, but for the A+ exam and for on-the-job proficiency, a technician should be familiar with the minimum require-ments for each OS that he or she will be called upon to install.

1. Test your knowledge of Windows system requirements for each version by filling in the following table of specifications:

Version	CPU	Memory	Hard Drive
Windows NT Workstation 4			
Windows 95			
Windows 98			
Windows Me			
Windows 2000 Professional			
Windows XP			
Windows Vista Home Basic*			
Windows Vista Home Premium, Business, or Ultimate*			

* Vista isn't covered in the current A+ exams, but you should know the requirements anyway.

2. What is the minimum display resolution required for Windows XP?

_____

3. How do you determine a computer's CPU and RAM if it doesn't already have an operating system installed on it?

_____

_____

4. How do you determine a computer's CPU and RAM if Windows is currently running on the PC?

_____

_____

Exercise 10-1: Cataloguing Your Hardware

1. Take an inventory of the following makes and models of hardware in your system:

- CPU: _____
- Amount of RAM: _____
- Hard drive capacity: _____
- Amount of free space on hard drive: _____
- Sound card make and model: _____

- Network card make and model: _____
- Modem make and model (if present): _____
- Display adapter make and model: _____

2. Visit the Windows Vista Hardware Compatibility List at `http://winqual.` `microsoft.com/hcl/default.aspx` and look up your sound, network, modem, and display adapters to see whether they're Vista-compatible.

Identifying Valid Upgrade Paths

When you're considering a Windows upgrade on a system, it's important to know whether the old version can be directly upgraded to the new one. If it can, it's said to be a valid _upgrade path_. If it can't, you need to do a full install of the new Windows version, preferably with a clean wipe of the drive.

TIP

Even if a valid upgrade path exists between the old version and the new, you might still want to do a clean install if the old version is giving you problems in any way. Those problems could potentially transfer to the new version; a clean install ensures they're wiped away.

Here are some of your options when deciding between a clean install and an upgrade:

- ✔ **Upgrade:** With Windows running, insert the CD for the new version. If needed, double-click its icon in the My Computer window. When asked whether you want to upgrade, click Yes and follow the prompts.

- ✔ **Clean install, full disk wipe (9x versions):** Boot from a startup floppy disk. If you need to redo the partitions, use FDISK. Use FORMAT to reformat the hard disk. Then install from the Windows CD.

- ✔ **Clean install, full disk wipe (2000/XP/Vista):** Boot from the Windows Setup CD, and when prompted, choose to reformat the disk. While you're there, if you need to change the partitioning, delete the existing partitions and create new ones.

- ✔ **Clean install, keep old files on disk (9x versions):** Boot from a startup floppy, and rename the Windows folder (Winback is a good name) and the Program Files folder (Progback is a good name). Then do a clean install from the Windows CD using the default folder names, which creates new versions of the Windows and Program Files folders.

PRACTICE

5. Test your knowledge of Windows upgrade paths by filling out the following table, writing Yes or No in the appropriate places.

	To Win95	To Win98	To WinMe	To Win2000	To WinXP
From Win95	N/A				
From Win98		N/A			
From WinMe			N/A		
From Win2000				N/A	
From WinXP					N/A

6. (Optional) Windows Vista isn't covered on the current A+ exams, but you still might find it useful to know the upgrade paths for various versions of it from Windows 2000 or Windows XP. (There is no upgrade path from any other Windows versions to Vista.)

   Fill in the following table cells with Yes and No to indicate which versions of XP are upgradable to which versions of Vista:

	To Vista Home Basic	To Vista Home Premium	To Vista Business	To Vista Ultimate
From XP Pro				
From XP Home				
From XP Media Center Edition				
From XP Tablet PC Edition				
From XP x64				

Performing an Installation

The process of performing a Windows installation is actually pretty simple and smooth, thanks to the Windows Setup utility. Just follow the prompts.

Before you get to that point, though, you have some important decisions to make. Where will you run Setup from — a network? A bootable CD? What computer name will you assign? What workgroup will the PC join? How will you set up the disk's partitions? What file system will you use? Do you have a valid product key for installation? Sure, there are defaults for most of those settings, but a good technician knows how and when to discard those defaults and go a different way.

Test your knowledge of Windows installation:

7. Which Setup CDs are bootable? Write Yes or No next to each of the following:

   A. Windows 95_____

   B. Windows 98_____

   C. Windows Me_____

   D. Windows 2000_____

   E. Windows XP_____

   F. Windows Vista_____

8. When doing a clean network install (that is, an install on a PC that has no previous OS on it), how would you get network access, given that an operating system is usually required to load a network driver?

_____

_____

_____

_____

9. Suppose you have four PCs, and they are all running Windows 2000. You want to upgrade them all to Windows XP.

A. Is it legal to upgrade all four PCs to Windows XP using a single retail copy of Windows XP?

_____

B. What barriers or problems might you encounter when attempting to do this?

_____

_____

_____

_____

C. How is it that some corporations are able to install Windows XP on hundreds of PCs via drive imaging without encountering any technical problems or breaking any laws?

_____

_____

_____

_____

10. When specifying a computer name for a PC during Windows Setup:

A. How many characters can a name be?

_____

B. Can a name include spaces?

_____

11. When setting up a PC to be part of a large corporate network, which should you indicate that the PC is part of: a workgroup or a domain?

_____

12. When installing Windows 2000 on a PC that will dual-boot with Windows 98, if you need to be able to access all drives from within both operating systems, which file system should you use on the Windows 2000 drive?

_____

13. When installing Windows XP on a system where it will be the only OS, which file system should you use?

_____

14. What is the executable file that starts the 32-bit Windows 2000/XP Setup process, used on a system that already has a 32-bit OS installed?

_____

15. What switch would you use with the command from Question 14 to do an unattended install?

_____

16. What switch would you use with the command from Question 14 to install the Recovery Console on the system?

_____

17. What does the Setup Manager (setupmgr.exe) do?

_____

Exercise 10-2: Working with Setup Manager

This exercise requires a system with an empty hard drive and a Windows XP Setup CD.

1. Use Setup Manager (setupmgr.exe) to create an unattended installation file.

setupmgr.exe is located in deploy.cab on the Windows CD, and you can extract it with the Extract command or browse for it by browsing the .cab file from any existing Windows PC.

2. Perform an unattended install on the PC using the file you created in Step 1.

Setting Up Multibooting

Sometimes a user needs to have two or more operating systems available on the same PC. When this is set up, a boot menu appears each time the PC starts up, prompting the user to select the OS desired. This is called *multibooting,* or you can call it *dual-booting* if only two OSes are involved.

On a multiboot system, you can control which OS is the default and how long the boot menu remains on the screen before it goes ahead with loading the default OS. (Normally this is 30 seconds but can be easily changed.)

 Some Windows versions are multiboot-aware, and some are not. When you install a multiboot-aware version of Windows on a system that already contains another OS, it automatically sets up the boot menu to appear at startup. Therefore, when configuring systems for more than one OS, you should install the OS that is not multiboot-aware *first.*

Test your knowledge of multiboot systems:

18. Which Windows versions are multiboot-aware? Write Yes or No next to each of the following:

A. Windows 95_____

B. Windows 98_____

C. Windows Me_____

D. Windows 2000_____

E. Windows XP_____

F. Windows Vista_____

19. What file controls the content of the boot menu where the installed OSes are listed at startup?

_____

20. With what program can you edit that file?

_____

21. In Windows XP, via what Control Panel applet could you access and edit the file you listed in Question 19?

_____

22. Suppose you have installed Windows 98 on the C drive and now you want to set up Windows XP as a second OS on the same PC.

A. Must Windows XP be placed on a different physical drive?

_____

B. Must Windows XP be placed on a different logical drive?

_____

C. What file system would be best to use for the Windows XP partition if you want to be able to access it from Windows 98?

_____

Exercise 10-3: Setting Up Dual-Boot Systems

This exercise requires a system with at least two logical drives and the Setup files for two versions of Windows.

1. If either of your Windows versions is not multiboot-aware, install it first. Otherwise choose either of the versions to install first.

2. Install the second version of Windows on a different logical drive.

3. In Windows, open `boot.ini` from the root directory of the main hard drive and examine its settings.

4. (Optional) Change the wording in the name that will appear on the boot menu for one of the copies of Windows, and save your work.

5. Restart the system and confirm that the wording change appears on the boot menu. Select one of the OSes and boot into it.

6. Modify `boot.ini` to change the amount of time it waits before selecting the default OS to five seconds.

7. Restart the system and confirm that after five seconds, the default OS loads.

Transferring User Data Files

Upgrading to a new version of Windows leaves the users' data in place. However, if you decide you want to do a clean Windows install, you must back up the user's data before wiping the drive and then restore it after you get the new OS installed.

Here are three ways to transfer user data from one PC to another or from one Windows install to another:

   ✔ Some versions of Windows (notably XP and Vista) have a wizard that handles file and settings transfer. You can use this to create a special backup set that transfers only what you need.

✔ You can use Microsoft Backup to create a backup set consisting of the files to be saved, and then use Backup again on the new install to restore them.

✔ You can manually copy the needed files to a removable disk or to a network location, and then you can copy them back again after the install.

Test your ability to back up and restore user data files between Windows installations.

23. In Windows XP, what is the name of the wizard that you can use to transfer files and settings?

_____

24. How would you back up the address book from Outlook Express?

_____

_____

_____

_____

25. How would you restore the address book in Outlook Express on the new installation?

_____

26. To back up a user's Outlook data file, what file would you back up?

_____

27. In Windows XP, where is the file from Question 26 stored?

_____

28. To back up a user's Internet Explorer favorites, what folder would you back up?

_____

29. In Windows XP, where is the file from Question 28 stored?

_____

30. When files from an encrypted folder are backed up to a removable drive, what happens to the encryption?

_____

Exercise 10-4: Transferring Files

1. Back up all the e-mail, addresses, and favorites from your PC using any method.

2. Transfer them to another PC and confirm that they work there.

Answers to Questions in This Chapter

The following are the answers to the practice questions presented earlier in this chapter:

1. **Test your knowledge of Windows system requirements for each version by filling in the following table of specifications:**

Version	*CPU*	*Memory*	*Hard Drive*
Windows NT Workstation 4	Pentium	16MB (32MB recommended)	110MB
Windows 95	386DX (486 recommended)	4MB (8MB recommended)	50 to 55MB
Windows 98	486DX 66 (Pentium recommended)	16MB (24MB recommended)	165 to 355MB
Windows Me	150 MHz Pentium	32MB	480 to 645MB
Windows 2000 Professional	133 MHz Pentium	64MB	2GB with at least 650MB free
Windows XP	233 MHz	64MB (128MB recommended)	1.5GB
Windows Vista Home Basic	1 GHz	512MB	20GB with at least 15GB free
Windows Vista Premium, Business, or Ultimate	1 GHz	1GB	40GB with at least 15GB free

2. **What is the minimum display resolution required for Windows XP?**

800 x 600

3. **How do you determine a computer's CPU and RAM if it doesn't already have an operating system installed on it?**

Look at the screen as the PC is booting or look in BIOS Setup.

4. **How do you determine a computer's CPU and RAM if Windows is currently running on the PC?**

Look at System Information or at the System Properties dialog box.

5. **Test your knowledge of Windows upgrade paths by filling out the following table, writing Yes or No in the appropriate places.**

	To Win95	To Win98	To WinMe	To Win2000	To WinXP
From Win95	N/A	Yes	Yes	Yes	Yes
From Win98	No	N/A	Yes	Yes	Yes
From WinMe	No	No	N/A	Yes	Yes
From Win2000	No	No	No	N/A	Yes
From WinXP	No	No	No	No	N/A

6. **(Optional) Windows Vista isn't covered on the current A+ exams, but you still might find it useful to know the upgrade paths for various versions of it from Windows 2000 or Windows XP. (There is no upgrade path from any other Windows versions to Vista.)**

   Fill in the following table cells with Yes and No to indicate which versions of XP are upgradable to which versions of Vista:

	To Vista Home Basic	To Vista Home Premium	To Vista Business	To Vista Ultimate
From XP Pro	No	No	Yes	Yes
From XP Home	Yes	Yes	Yes	Yes
From XP Media Center Edition	No	Yes	No	Yes
From XP Tablet PC Edition	No	No	Yes	Yes
From XP x64	No	No	No	No

7. **Which Setup CDs are bootable? Write Yes or No next to each of the following:**

   A. Windows 95: <u>No</u>

   B. Windows 98: <u>No</u>

   C. Windows Me: <u>No</u>

   D. Windows 2000: <u>Yes</u>

   E. Windows XP: <u>Yes</u>

   F. Windows Vista: <u>Yes</u>

8. **When doing a clean network install (that is, an install on a PC that has no previous OS on it), how would you get network access, given that an operating system is usually required to load a network driver?**

   You can boot from a startup floppy that contains a real-mode network driver.

9. **Suppose you have four PCs, and they are all running Windows 2000. You want to upgrade them all to Windows XP.**

A. Is it legal to upgrade all four PCs to Windows XP using a single retail copy of Windows XP?

No

B. What barriers or problems might you encounter when attempting to do this?

Windows can be activated on only one PC (or sometimes two, depending on the version). Activating a copy of Windows locks it to that particular hardware configuration.

C. How is it that some corporations are able to install Windows XP on hundreds of PCs via drive imaging without encountering any technical problems or breaking any laws?

They buy site licenses, which allows them to use copies of Windows that are not subject to activation.

10. When specifying a computer name for a PC during Windows Setup:

A. How many characters can a name be?

15

B. Can a name include spaces?

No

11. When setting up a PC to be part of a large corporate network, which should you indicate that the PC is part of: a workgroup or a domain?

Domain

12. When installing Windows 2000 on a PC that will dual-boot with Windows 98, if you need to be able to access all drives from within both operating systems, which file system should you use on the Windows 2000 drive?

FAT32

13. When installing Windows XP on a system where it will be the only OS, which file system should you use?

NTFS

14. What is the executable file that starts the 32-bit Windows 2000/XP Setup process, used on a system that already has a 32-bit OS installed?

WINNT32.EXE

15. What switch would you use with the command from Question 14 to do an unattended install?

/unattend:<filename>

16. What switch would you use with the command from Question 14 to install the Recovery Console on the system?

/cmdcons

17. **What does the Setup Manager (`setupmgr.exe`) do?**

It launches a wizard that will help you create a file for an unattended install.

18. **Which Windows versions are multiboot-aware? Write Yes or No next to each of the following:**

   A. Windows 95: <u>No</u>

   B. Windows 98: <u>No</u>

   C. Windows Me: <u>No</u>

   D. Windows 2000: <u>Yes</u>

   E. Windows XP: <u>Yes</u>

   F. Windows Vista: <u>Yes</u>

19. **What file controls the content of the boot menu where the installed OSes are listed at startup?**

`boot.ini`

20. **With what program can you edit that file?**

Notepad or EDIT, or with MSCONFIG or the `bootcfg` file.

21. **In Windows XP, via what Control Panel applet could you access and edit the file you listed in Question 19?**

System

22. **Suppose you have installed Windows 98 on the C drive and now you want to set up Windows XP as a second OS on the same PC.**

   A. Must Windows XP be placed on a different physical drive?

   No

   B. Must Windows XP be placed on a different logical drive?

   Yes

   C. What file system would be best to use for the Windows XP partition if you want to be able to access it from Windows 98?

   `FAT32`

23. **In Windows XP, what is the name of the wizard that you can use to transfer files and settings?**

Files and Settings Transfer Wizard

24. **How would you back up the address book from Outlook Express?**

From Outlook Express, choose File⇨Export⇨Address Book.

25. **How would you restore the address book in Outlook Express on the new installation?**

From Outlook Express, choose File⇨Import⇨Address Book.

26. **To back up a user's Outlook data file, what file would you back up?**

`Outlook.pst`

27. **In Windows XP, where is the file from Question 26 stored?**

`Documents and Settings\`*`user name`*`\Local Settings\Application Data\Microsoft\Outlook`

28. **To back up a user's Internet Explorer favorites, what folder would you back up?**

The Favorites folder

29. **In Windows XP, where is the file from Question 28 stored?**

`Documents and Settings\`*`user name`*`\Favorites`

30. **When files from an encrypted folder are backed up to a removable drive, what happens to the encryption?**

Encryption is removed.

Chapter 11

Files, Folders, and Command Prompts

· ·

In This Chapter

▶ Understanding file-naming rules

▶ Changing file attributes

▶ Using command-line file management

▶ Running command-line system diagnostics

▶ Managing disks from the command prompt

▶ Changing text files with EDIT

· ·

*E*ven though Windows is a GUI environment, there are still plenty of techie-level activities that involve working with a command prompt. A technician needs to know his or her way around the command-line interface, including using switches and optional parameters, getting help with command syntax, and working with a DOS-based text editor like EDIT. In this chapter, you review these skills, as well as test your ability to name files properly and set their attributes.

Understanding File-Naming Rules

Different operating systems and disk types have restrictions on the names you can assign to files and folders. If you violate the rules for naming, the OS generally tells you so, but it's easier to avoid the mistakes in the first place by keeping the rules in mind.

Another reason to think about file naming is to prepare for sharing files between operating systems and platforms. For example, if you plan to share a file created in Windows 98 with someone who uses an MS-DOS system, you should confine the filename to the stricter MS-DOS limits, and if you're sharing files with a UNIX system, you should watch the capitalization, because UNIX is case-sensitive.

Test your knowledge of file-naming conventions under various operating systems:

1. List the maximum length of characters for a filename in each of the following operating systems:

A. MS-DOS: _____

B. Windows 3.1: _____

C. Windows 95: _____

        D. Windows XP: _____

        E. Mac OS: _____

        F. UNIX (modern versions): _____

2.   For each operating system, write Yes or No to indicate whether it is case-sensitive:

        A. MS-DOS: _____

        B. Windows 3.1: _____

        C. Windows 95: _____

        D. Windows XP: _____

        E. Mac OS: _____

        F. UNIX (modern versions): _____

3.   For each operating system, write Yes or No to indicate whether you can use spaces in file-names:

        A. MS-DOS: _____

        B. Windows 3.1: _____

        C. Windows 95: _____

        D. Windows XP: _____

        E. Mac OS: _____

        F. UNIX (modern versions): _____

4.   For Windows XP, for each symbol, write Yes or No to indicate whether it is allowed to be used in filenames:

        A. ! _____

        B. @ _____

        C. # _____

        D. $ _____

        E. % _____

        F. ^ _____

        G. & _____

H. * _____

I. (_____

J. \ _____

K. - _____

L. + _____

M. { _____

N. } _____

O. [_____

P. ~ _____

Q. | _____

R. : _____

S. ; _____

T. " _____

U. ' _____

V. < _____

W. > _____

X. , _____

Y. ? _____

Z. / _____

5. List three reserved words that cannot be used as filenames in Windows XP.

_____

_____

_____

6. What type of discs are the ISO 9660 and Joliet file systems associated with?

_____

7. For compatibility with MS-DOS, each file that uses a long filename in Windows has an MS-DOS alternative name that conforms to the MS-DOS 8-3 limitation. For the following filenames in Windows, what would be the MS-DOS equivalent name, assuming it was the only file in that location?

A. `Microsoft.txt`

_____

B. `My Windows.txt`

_____

C. `Files.txt`

_____

D. `Microsoft Windows.txt`

_____

Exercise 11-1: Finding Equivalent MS-DOS Filenames

Do the following to see the MS-DOS 8-3 equivalent filenames for files on your system:

1. Open a command prompt window.

2. Display the Windows folder.

3. Type **DIR /X** and press Enter to see a file listing with an extra column showing the MS-DOS equivalent filenames for any files that are longer than eight characters or that contain spaces or disallowed characters under MS-DOS.

4. For more information on file naming under different operating systems, see the article at `http://en.wikipedia.org/wiki/File_name`.

Changing File Attributes

File attributes are on/off status flags you can set for a file, such as Read-Only. You can view and change file attributes either from a command prompt or from the file's Properties dialog box in Windows.

Don't confuse file attributes with *metadata,* which is additional information appended to a data file's header to help describe its content. For example, metadata associated with a Word document might include the author's name and the number of minutes that have been spent editing it.

See how much you know about viewing and modifying file attributes:

8. What command displays attributes at a command prompt?

_____

9. What are the four attributes that you can turn on/off with the command from Question 8?

_____

_____

_____

_____

10. What is the syntax for using the command from Question 8 to set the Read-Only attribute for a file named `Readme.txt` to On?

_____

11. What is the syntax for using the command from Question 8 to set the hidden attribute for all files in the current directory to Off?

_____

12. What two attributes are available only on files and folders on NTFS volumes?

_____

_____

13. On which tab of a file's Properties dialog box in Windows do you set the Hidden attribute?

_____

14. Suppose a user is trying to open a Word document that a co-worker created, but Word won't open it. Which attribute might need to be turned off?

_____

15. Suppose a user is trying to locate a Word document in C:\Books, but it doesn't appear in the file listing. He needs to turn off the Hidden attribute for the file, but how can he do that if he can't see the file in the file listing to select it? List two ways.

_____

_____

_____

_____

16. What does the Archive attribute indicate about a file?

_____

_____

_____

Exercise 11-2: Working with File Attributes

Follow these steps to practice setting file attributes, both at a command line and within the Windows GUI.

1. Open a command prompt window and go to the root directory of your C: drive.

2. Type **ATTRIB** and press Enter to see the file attributes.

3. Remove the Archive attribute from all the files at the root directory level using the ATTRIB command:

```
ATTRIB -A *.*
```

4. Identify a file that is set to Read-Only and then remove the Read-Only attribute.

5. Do another ATTRIB listing to confirm that the Read-Only attribute has been removed.

6. Use ATTRIB to turn the Read-Only attribute back on again for that file.

7. From the Windows GUI, display the properties for a file (any file), and turn on its Hidden attribute.

8. If Windows isn't set up to show hidden files, do the following to turn on their display:

 a. From Windows Explorer, choose Tools⇨Folder Options.

 b. Click the View tab.

 c. Click the Show Hidden Files and Folders check box.

 d. Click OK.

9. Redisplay the properties for the file you set as Hidden and then turn that attribute back off.

Using Command-Line File Management

Old-time MS-DOS users scoff at the friendly Windows GUI interface, preferring to "go commando" whenever possible and work with the command prompt. In most cases, this is nothing more than recalcitrance; there's not much you can do with a command prompt that you can't do more easily with a GUI.

That rule has a few exceptions, and one of them is that it's much easier to rename a group of files from a command prompt than it is in a GUI. At a command prompt, you can use wildcards. For example, if you have 100 files named FILE001 through FILE100, you can rename them all to DOCX001 through DOCX100 with the command REN FILE??? DOCX???.

Sometimes, however, you *have* to use the command prompt. For example, if the system doesn't boot into the GUI, you might need to work from a startup floppy (Windows 9x) or the Recovery Console (2000/XP/Vista). So in addition to gaining "geek cred" by learning about command-line file management, you prepare for those disastrous times when you need the actual skill.

Check your skills for managing files at a command prompt:

17. In Windows 9x, what command can you type at the Run prompt to open a command window?

_____

18. In Windows XP, what command can you type at the Run prompt to open a command window?

_____

19. What command displays a listing of files in the current location?

_____

20. What switch, when used with the command from Question 19, displays the listing in a wide multicolumn format?

_____

21. What command opens the MS-DOS Editor, which is the DOS equivalent of Notepad?

_____

22. What syntax would you use to open the editor from Question 21 and open the file Myfile.txt in it at the same time?

_____

23. What command copies files from one location to another?

_____

24. What syntax would you use with the command from Question 23 to copy . . .

A. Myfile.txt from the current folder onto the A:\ drive?

_____

B. Myfile.txt from the A:\ drive to the current folder?

_____

C. Myfile.txt within the current folder, but with the copy named Yourfile.txt?

_____

D. All the files in the current folder to the A:\ drive?

_____

E. All the files with a .txt extension from the current folder to the A:\ drive?

_____

F. All the files that begin with the letter *C* from the current folder to the A:\ drive?

_____

G. All the files that have exactly five letters in their names from the current folder to the A:\ drive?

_____

H. All the files that have six letters and have names ending in JET from the A:\ drive to the C:\Books folder?

_____

25. What command changes directories (folders)?

_____

26. What command would change from the C: drive to the root directory of the A: drive?

_____

27. What command works like the COPY command except that it copies subfolders too?

_____

28. What command and syntax would you use to create a new subfolder named Books within the current folder?

_____

29. What command renames files and folders?

_____

30. What is the syntax for renaming the file `Myfile.txt` to be called `Yourfile.txt`?

_____

31. What command and syntax would you use to remove a subfolder named `Books` within the current folder?

_____

32. The command in Question 31 will remove a subfolder only if it is empty. Some versions of MS-DOS and Windows 9x, however, have a command that removes subfolders that aren't empty and deletes their contents with a single operation. What is this command?

_____

Exercise 11-3: Using MS-DOS Commands, Part I

In this exercise, you'll use a variety of common commands at a command prompt to perform file management tasks.

1. Open a command prompt window.
2. Set the current location to `C:\Windows\System32`.
3. Display a list of all files that begin with *O* and have an `.exe` extension.
4. Create a new folder named Testing off the root directory of `C:` (`C:\Testing`).
5. Copy all the files from Step 3 into that folder.
6. Set the current location to `C:\Testing`.
7. Rename the first file on the list `Check.exe`.
8. Rename all remaining files to change the first letter of each filename to *P*. (For example, `osk.exe` becomes `psk.exe`.)
9. Delete all files that begin with a *C*.
10. Delete all remaining files in the Testing folder.
11. Delete the Testing folder.

Using Command-Line System Utilities

Even though Windows is one of the GUI-iest GUIs around, it still has command-line utilities available. In some cases, a command-line utility serves as an alternative or substitute for a Windows-based utility (for example, to be used in cases where you can't load the GUI for some reason). In other cases, the command-line utility provides unique functionality that's not available in the Windows graphical environment.

In addition to true command-line utilities, Windows also offers many utilities that do have a GUI interface but don't have a menu command associated with them from within the Windows Start menu. To run these utilities, you must use the Run command (off the Start menu), but then when you get into them, they function as any other Windows utility would.

See how much you know about the utilities that come with various Windows versions:

33. What Windows application does the MSCONFIG command open?

_____

34. What Windows application does the REGEDIT command open?

_____

35. What command-line utility checks the PC's IP address?

_____

36. What switch, when used with the command from Question 35, flushes the DNS cache?

_____

37. What command-line utility checks for network connectivity between the local PC and a specified IP address or URL?

_____

38. What command-line utility traces the route between the local PC and a specified IP address or URL?

_____

39. What is the command-line equivalent to Scan Disk?

_____

40. What switch must you use with the command from Question 39 in order to fix any errors found?

_____

41. What command closes the command prompt window?

_____

42. What command displays all currently running tasks, including services?

_____

Exercise 11-4: Using MS-DOS Commands, Part II

From a command prompt, do the following:

1. Determine your IP address.
2. Flush the DNS cache.
3. Ping www.wiley.com.
4. Trace the route to www.wiley.com.
5. Display a list of all currently running tasks.
6. Check the C: drive for errors and fix any errors found.
7. Close the command prompt window using a command (not the X in the corner of the window).

Managing Disks from the Command Prompt

In Windows 2000, XP, and Vista, a Disk Management utility provides GUI access to disk management tasks such as disk partitioning, formatting, and checking, but you might not always be able to get into the GUI environment. Therefore you need to know the commands for partitioning, formatting, and otherwise manipulating disks from a prompt.

In Windows 9x versions, you can format and check disks from within the GUI, but to partition them you must use an MS-DOS type of partitioning utility; disks cannot be partitioned from within Windows 9x.

Test your knowledge of command-line disk management:

43. What command and syntax would you use to format a floppy disk in the A: drive?

_____

44. What command converts FAT volumes to NTFS?

_____

45. What command opens a disk-partitioning utility in MS-DOS and Windows 9x?

_____

46. What command opens a command-line disk-partitioning utility in Windows XP/Vista?

_____

47. What command for partitioning drives is available from within the Recovery Console?

_____

48. What command and syntax would you use to assign a volume label of BACKUP to the D: drive?

_____

49. What command and syntax would you use to display the F: drive's volume label and serial number?

_____

50. What command controls the settings that specify whether to check a disk at boot time on Windows XP/Vista systems?

_____

51. Suppose you have only one floppy disk drive and you want to copy a floppy disk. What command and syntax would you use to do this?

_____

52. Suppose you have only one floppy disk drive and you want to compare two floppy disks. What command and syntax would you use to do this?

_____

Exercise 11-5: Using MS-DOS Commands, Part III

Do the following on a Windows 9x system, if you have one available:

1. Create a startup floppy.
2. Boot the system from it.
3. Use FDISK to examine the partitions.
4. Exit to a command prompt.
5. Insert another floppy disk and format it.
6. Copy the startup floppy to the blank floppy disk.
7. Compare the contents of the two floppy disks.
8. View the volume labels and serial numbers for each disk. Are they the same? Why or why not?

Changing Text Files with EDIT

Notepad is the standard text editor in Windows, but if you can't get into Windows, you need an alternative. The MS-DOS Editor, also known as EDIT, is just such an alternative. It's an old program — originating in MS-DOS — but still valuable in a pinch.

In EDIT, depending on the version, the mouse might or might not be available, so you need to know how to get things done via keystrokes. (If it turns out that the mouse is available, that's a bonus.)

As in Windows, the Alt key activates the menu system, and the highlighted letter in a menu name opens that menu. For example, pressing Alt makes the *F* in the word File bold, and then typing **F** opens the File menu, which contains a list of commands, each with one bold letter. Typing that letter issues that command.

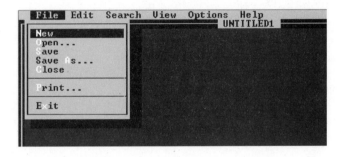

Exercise 11-6: Working with EDIT

1. Open a command prompt window.

2. Change to a folder you'll use to store the example file you'll create.

3. Type **EDIT test.txt** and press Enter.

4. Type your name and address.

5. Press Alt+F, then press S. This saves your work.

6. Press Alt+F, then press A. This opens a Save As dialog box.

7. The current filename, `test.txt`, is already selected. Type **test2.txt**, replacing it.

8. Press Tab three times, so an underline flashes on the OK button.

9. Press Enter.

10. Press Alt+O and then type **C**. The Colors dialog box opens.

11. Using Tab to move between sections, and using the Up and Down arrow keys to select colors, change the background color of the Edit window to Red. Then close the dialog box.

12. Exit from Notepad (Alt+F, X).

Answers to Questions in This Chapter

The following are the answers to the practice questions presented earlier in this chapter:

1. **List the maximum length of characters for a filename in each of the following operating systems:**

   A. MS-DOS: <u>8</u>

   B. Windows 3.1: <u>8</u>

   C. Windows 95: <u>255</u>

   D. Windows XP: <u>255</u>

   E. Mac OS: <u>255</u>

   F. UNIX (modern versions): <u>255</u>

2. **For each operating system, write Yes or No to indicate whether it is case-sensitive:**

   A. MS-DOS: <u>No</u>

   B. Windows 3.1: <u>No</u>

   C. Windows 95: <u>No</u>

   D. Windows XP: <u>No</u>

   E. Mac OS: <u>No</u>

   F. UNIX (modern versions): <u>Yes</u>

3. **For each operating system, write Yes or No to indicate whether you can use spaces in filenames:**

   A. MS-DOS: <u>No</u>

   B. Windows 3.1: <u>No</u>

   C. Windows 95: <u>Yes</u>

   D. Windows XP: <u>Yes</u>

   E. Mac OS: <u>Yes</u>

   F. UNIX (modern versions): <u>Yes</u>

4. **For Windows XP, for each symbol, write Yes or No to indicate whether it is allowed to be used in filenames:**

   A. ! <u>Yes</u>

   B. @ <u>Yes</u>

   C. # <u>Yes</u>

   D. $ <u>Yes</u>

   E. % <u>Yes</u>

   F. ^ <u>Yes</u>

   G. & <u>Yes</u>

H. * <u>No</u>

I. (<u>Yes</u>

J. \ <u>No</u>

K. - <u>Yes</u>

L. + <u>Yes</u>

M. { <u>Yes</u>

N. } <u>Yes</u>

O. [<u>No</u>

P. ~ <u>Yes</u>

Q. | <u>No</u>

R. : <u>No</u>

S. ; <u>Yes</u>

T. " <u>No</u>

U. ' <u>Yes</u>

V. < <u>No</u>

W. > <u>No</u>

X. , <u>Yes</u>

Y. ? <u>No</u>

Z. / <u>No</u>

5. **List three reserved words that cannot be used as filenames in Windows XP.**

   aux, con, prn, lpt1 through lpt9, com1 through com10

6. **What type of discs are the ISO 9660 and Joliet file systems associated with?**

   CDs

7. **For compatibility with MS-DOS, each file that uses a long filename in Windows has an MS-DOS alternative name that conforms to the MS-DOS 8-3 limitation. For the following filenames in Windows, what would be the MS-DOS equivalent name, assuming it was the only file in that location?**

   A. `Microsoft.txt`

   `Micros~1.txt`

   B. `My Windows.txt`

   `mywind~1.txt`

   C. `Files.txt`

   `Files.txt`

   D. `Microsoft Windows.txt`

   `Microso~1.txt`

8. **What command displays attributes at a command prompt?**

   ATTRIB

9. **What are the four attributes that you can turn on/off with the command from Question 8?**

   Read-Only, Hidden, System, and Archive

10. **What is the syntax for using the command from Question 8 to set the Read-Only attribute for a file named** Readme.txt **to On?**

    ATTRIB +R Readme.txt

11. **What is the syntax for using the command from Question 8 to set the hidden attribute for all files in the current directory to Off?**

    ATTRIB -h *.*

12. **What two attributes are available only on files and folders on NTFS volumes?**

    Compression and encryption

13. **On which tab of a file's Properties dialog box in Windows do you set the Hidden attribute?**

    General

14. **Suppose a user is trying to open a Word document that a co-worker created, but Word won't open it. Which attribute might need to be turned off?**

    Encryption

15. **Suppose a user is trying to locate a Word document in** C:\Books, **but it doesn't appear in the file listing. He needs to turn off the Hidden attribute for the file, but how can he do that if he can't see the file in the file listing to select it? List two ways.**

    One way is to use the ATTRIB command at a prompt. Another is to turn on the display of hidden files and folders in Windows and then select the file from the GUI.

16. **What does the Archive attribute indicate about a file?**

    It has changed since it was last backed up by a Backup program that uses the Archive flag to determine which files need to be backed up in an incremental or differential backup.

17. **In Windows 9x, what command can you type at the Run prompt to open a command window?**

    COMMAND

18. **In Windows XP, what command can you type at the Run prompt to open a command window?**

    CMD

19. **What command displays a listing of files in the current location?**

    DIR

20. What switch, when used with the command from Question 19, displays the listing in a wide multicolumn format?

/W

21. What command opens the MS-DOS Editor, which is the DOS equivalent of Notepad?

EDIT

22. What syntax would you use to open the editor from Question 21 and open the file **Myfile.txt** in it at the same time?

EDIT Myfile.txt

23. What command copies files from one location to another?

COPY

24. What syntax would you use with the command from Question 23 to copy . . .

A. **Myfile.txt** from the current folder onto the **A:** drive?

COPY Myfile.txt A:\

B. **Myfile.txt** from the **A:** drive to the current folder?

COPY A:\Myfile.txt

C. **Myfile.txt** within the current folder, but with the copy named **Yourfile.txt**?

COPY Myfile.txt Yourfile.txt

D. All the files in the current folder to the **A:** drive?

COPY *.* A:\

E. All the files with a **.txt** extension from the current folder to the **A:** drive?

COPY *.txt A:\

F. All the files that begin with the letter *C* from the current folder to the **A:** drive?

COPY C*.* A:\

G. All the files that have exactly five letters in their names from the current folder to the **A:** drive?

COPY ?????.* A:\

H. All the files that have six letters and have names ending in JET from the A:\ drive to the C:\Books folder?

COPY A:\???JET.* C:\Books

25. What command changes directories (folders)?

CD

26. What command would change from the **C:** drive to the root directory of the **A:** drive?

CD A:\

27. What command works like the COPY command except that it copies subfolders too?

XCOPY

28. **What command and syntax would you use to create a new subfolder named `Books` within the current folder?**

    MD Books

29. **What command renames files and folders?**

    REN

30. **What is the syntax for renaming the file `Myfile.txt` to be called `Yourfile.txt`?**

    REN Myfile.txt Yourfile.txt

31. **What command and syntax would you use to remove a subfolder named `Books` within the current folder?**

    RD Books

32. **The command in Question 31 will remove a subfolder only if it is empty. Some versions of MS-DOS and Windows 9x, however, have a command that removes subfolders that aren't empty and deletes their contents with a single operation. What is this command?**

    DELTREE

33. **What Windows application does the MSCONFIG command open?**

    System Configuration Utility

34. **What Windows application does the REGEDIT command open?**

    Registry Editor

35. **What command-line utility checks the PC's IP address?**

    IPCONFIG

36. **What switch, when used with the command from Question 35, flushes the DNS cache?**

    IPCONFIG /flushdns

37. **What command-line utility checks for network connectivity between the local PC and a specified IP address or URL?**

    PING

38. **What command-line utility traces the route between the local PC and a specified IP address or URL?**

    TRACERT

39. **What is the command-line equivalent to Scan Disk?**

    CHKDSK

40. **What switch must you use with the command from Question 39 in order to fix any errors found?**

    /F

41. **What command closes the command prompt window?**

EXIT

42. **What command displays all currently running tasks, including services?**

TASKLIST

43. **What command and syntax would you use to format a floppy disk in the A: drive?**

FORMAT A:

44. **What command converts FAT volumes to NTFS?**

CONVERT

45. **What command opens a disk-partitioning utility in MS-DOS and Windows 9x?**

FDISK

46. **What command opens a command-line disk-partitioning utility in Windows XP/Vista?**

DISKPART

47. **What command for partitioning drives is available from within the Recovery Console?**

DISKPART

48. **What command and syntax would you use to assign a volume label of BACKUP to the D: drive?**

LABEL D: BACKUP

49. **What command and syntax would you use to display the F: drive's volume label and serial number?**

VOL F:

50. **What command controls the settings that specify whether to check a disk at boot time on Windows XP/Vista systems?**

CHKNTFS

51. **Suppose you have only one floppy disk drive and you want to copy a floppy disk. What command and syntax would you use to do this?**

DISKCOPY A: A:

52. **Suppose you have only one floppy disk drive and you want to compare two floppy disks. What command and syntax would you use to do this?**

DISKCOMP A: A:

Chapter 12

Installing and Configuring Applications

In This Chapter

▶ Troubleshooting application installation and removal

▶ Identifying background-running programs

▶ Configuring legacy applications in Windows

*T*he A+ exam objectives don't emphasize applications heavily, but don't let that fool you — as a technician, you'll spend a huge amount of time troubleshooting why some application or another doesn't work on a user's system. Applications are what users *have* PCs for in the first place, after all, and that's what they complain about most bitterly when problems occur.

In this chapter, you test your knowledge of procedures for installing and removing applications, figuring out what applications are running at any given moment, and coaxing stubborn old applications into running in newer Windows versions.

Troubleshooting Application Installation and Removal

Anyone can install and remove applications from the Control Panel in Windows. It's a pretty painless follow-the-prompts process:

✔ **In Windows 9x, 2000, and XP:** From the Control Panel, choose Add or Remove Programs. Then select the program to remove and click its Uninstall button.

✔ **In Windows Vista:** From the Control Panel, choose Programs⇨Programs and Features. Then select the program to remove and click Uninstall on the toolbar at the top of the listing.

But what happens when things don't go quite as planned? Installation files go missing, uninstall routines don't work, installed programs don't work as advertised, and so on. Those are the cases that separate the true techies from the rest of the pack. You should know not only how to install and remove applications, but what's happening behind the scenes and at what points the process can break down.

Test your knowledge of application installation and removal:

1. Windows Installer uses installation packages that have what extension?

_____

2. Suppose an application won't uninstall from Add or Remove Programs because it claims that the installation package is missing. How can you restore the installation package so that you can uninstall the program?

_____

_____

_____

3. From what Registry key can you manually remove a dead entry (that is, an entry that refers to a program that has already been removed) from the Add or Remove Programs listing?

_____

_____

4. Suppose Windows XP tells you that the currently logged-in user doesn't have sufficient permission to install or remove an application. How can you get around this issue without having to log off and log on as a different user?

_____

5. Suppose the application you're trying to install was written for an earlier version of Windows and won't install correctly in Windows XP. How can you get around this?

_____

_____

6. Before installing a new program you aren't sure about, it's smart to back up the Registry. What utility provides an easy way of doing this in Windows XP?

_____

Exercise 12-1: Practicing Safe Installation Techniques

1. Set a System Restore point.

2. Go to www.download.com and download a program designed for an earlier version of Windows. Install it, troubleshooting as needed if the installation file won't run using default settings.

3. Remove the program you just installed.

4. Restore the System Restore point you created in Step 1.

5. Go through the Add or Remove Programs list in Windows and remove any unwanted applications. Deal with any problems you encounter as needed.

Identifying Background Running Programs

Most applications run only when you specifically start them, but a few insist on being "always on" in the background. They say it's for your convenience, and in some cases that's true, but having a lot of programs running full-time that you use only infrequently is a waste of system resources. And although a single program running in the background might take up very little space, the combined effect of dozens of them can bog down a system.

When troubleshooting a system that's performing sluggishly, a good first step is to see what's running in the background, and if you see anything unusual, determine how it got there. Many times, programs that run unexpectedly in the background are actually being loaded at startup, so you can fix any performance problems they're having by modifying the list of startup applications.

The tricky part to all this is that often the running processes — and the list of startup applications — contain long lists of cryptically named files, and you have to know from experience what they are or find a good resource reference. Do a Web search on "Windows task list" or check out www.answersthatwork.com, which has a decent reference for this purpose.

See how much you know about Windows background and startup processes:

7. How can you open the Windows Task Manager in Windows XP/Vista?

_____

8. How can you open the Windows Task Manager in Windows 95/98/Me?

_____

9. What tab in the Windows Task Manager displays the currently running processes?

_____

10. To find the processes that are consuming the most processor time, you should sort the list of running processes by which column?

_____

11. Do most background running programs display on the Applications tab of the Windows Task Manager? Why or why not?

_____

_____

_____

_____

12. Why is it usually not a good idea to shut down individual running processes via Windows Task Manager?

_____

_____

_____

_____

13. For each of the following processes you might find in the Windows Task Manager, tell whether it is (E) Essential for proper Windows operation, (O) Optional but okay, or (H) Harmful and indicative of a problem.

    A. absr.exe_____

    B. aexplore.exe_____

    C. bbeagle.exe_____

    D. billmind.exe_____

    E. csrss.exe_____

    F. explorer.exe_____

14. Is having multiple copies of svchost.exe running indicative of a problem?

_____

15. In what folder on the Start/All Programs menu system should you place an application if you want the application to load at startup?

_____

16. What command (used with Run) opens the System Configuration utility?

_____

17. Which tab in the System Configuration utility contains the list of programs that are set to load at startup?

_____

18. From the tab in Question 17, how do you disable a program from loading at startup?

_____

19. Disabling a program from loading at startup via the System Configuration utility is actually just a stopgap measure to use while troubleshooting. Name two ways that are better (that is, tidier and more permanent) for preventing a program from loading at startup.

_____

_____

_____

_____

Exercise 12-2: Trimming the Number of Processes Running

A system might be running background processes that you don't need right now, and those processes can slow down your system. Here's how you trim back those processes:

1. Open the Windows Task Manager and sort the list of running processes by name.

2. There are so many different processes that you might encounter that the best way to decipher them is to use a Web reference. Open a Web browser and go to www. answersthatwork.com and look up each of the processes in the Task List database there.

3. If you find any processes on your system that should not be running, do the following troubleshooting procedure for each one:

   a. Look in Add or Remove Programs and see whether you can find an application listed there that could be completely removed to solve this problem. If there is, remove it.

   b. If you don't want to remove the entire application, look in the application's configuration options to see whether it can be set to not load at startup.

   c. If the application cannot be prevented via its settings from loading at startup, open the System Configuration Utility and disable it from loading at startup.

4. Reboot the system and check the running processes again. Repeat the procedure if needed.

Configuring Legacy Applications in Windows

Legacy applications are designed for earlier versions of Windows or for MS-DOS. In theory, most of them should work in newer Windows versions, but in practice, they often do not. You can either accept this or try poking and prodding to coax the application into working. Sometimes it's the Setup program for the application that won't run in the newer Windows version, so if you can convince it to run, the application itself works fine after installation. Other times it's the reverse: The Setup program seems to install the application just fine, but then the application bombs out when you try to use it.

Windows XP and Vista both offer compatibility settings that enable older Windows programs to run in many cases. In Windows XP, you can use the Compatibility tab in the application file's Properties dialog box, or you can use the Program Compatibility Wizard. In Windows Vista, there is no wizard; you use the Compatibility tab.

Although it's rare to encounter an MS-DOS program these days, it's also likely that if you do encounter one, it won't work correctly in Windows XP unless you tweak the settings a bit. The compatibility settings for MS-DOS programs aren't part of the Compatibility Wizard. Instead, they're set directly within the application's Properties dialog box. The Properties dialog box for an MS-DOS application is very different from that of a Windows application; extra tabs appear, including Program, Font, Memory, and Screen.

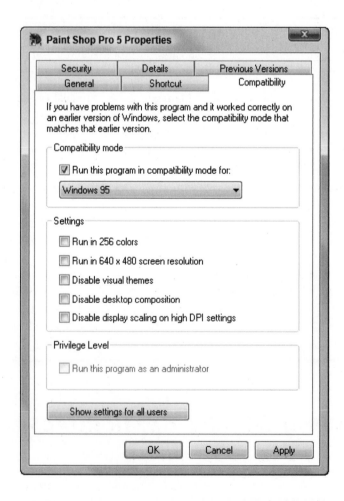

Check your understanding of Compatibility modes for legacy applications:

20. What operating systems can the Compatibility Mode in Windows XP emulate?

_____

_____

_____

_____

21. If an application needs to be run in Super VGA mode, what resolution is that?

_____

22. How can you access the Program Compatibility Wizard from Windows XP?

_____

23. Answer the following questions about the Properties dialog box for an MS-DOS application:

A. What does the Advanced button on the Program tab enable you to specify?

_____

B. Suppose you need to add a switch such as /X to be used when running the application. On what tab and in what text box would you add this?

_____

_____

C. If an MS-DOS application requires expanded memory, on what tab and in what text box would you set this up?

_____

_____

D. If the MS-DOS application crashes frequently, you might need to turn off Fast ROM emulation. From which tab would you disable that feature?

_____

E. Suppose the application uses Alt+spacebar as a keyboard shortcut. That is a reserved Windows keyboard shortcut, and conflicts occur. From which tab can you disable Windows from claiming that key combination?

_____

F. Suppose that when the user switches from the DOS program to Windows, the mouse no longer works in the DOS program when he returns to it. What setting on what tab might be useful in fixing this problem?

_____

G. Suppose that when the Windows screen saver kicks in, the MS-DOS program crashes. What setting on what tab might be useful in fixing this problem?

_____

H. Suppose that the user wants the MS-DOS program to continue running in the background even when it is not the foreground application. What setting on what tab will allow this?

_____

Exercise 12-3: Configuring MS-DOS Applications

1. Acquire an MS-DOS program to experiment with.

   Check out www.dosgames.com for some amusing MS-DOS games that will fit the bill.

2. Try running the program with default settings and make notes about any problems you have.

3. Use the program file's Properties dialog box to change any settings needed to make it work better.

4. Acquire an old Windows 95 program to experiment with.

   Check out www.download.com for some free programs.

5. Try running the program with default settings and make notes about any problems you have.

6. Use the Program Compatibility Wizard or the Compatibility tab in the program file's Properties dialog box to set the program to run as a Windows 95 application.

Answers to Questions in This Chapter

The following are the answers to the practice questions presented earlier in this chapter:

1. **Windows Installer uses installation packages that have what extension?**

   `.msi` (stands for Microsoft Installer)

2. **Suppose an application won't uninstall from Add or Remove Programs because it claims that the installation package is missing. How can you restore the installation package so that you can uninstall the program?**

   Reinstall the application and then remove it. Reinstalling it re-creates the missing installer files.

3. **From what Registry key can you manually remove a dead entry (that is, an entry that refers to a program that has already been removed) from the Add or Remove Programs listing?**

   `HKEY_LOCAL_MACHINE\SOFTWARE\Microsoft\Windows\CurrentVersion\Uninstall`. Each application has its own application key entry in there. Just delete the entire application key to remove the program from the Add or Remove Programs listing.

4. **Suppose Windows XP tells you that the currently logged-in user doesn't have sufficient permission to install or remove an application. How can you get around this issue without having to log off and log on as a different user?**

   Right-click the installer file, choose Run As, and then log in as an administrator.

5. **Suppose the application you're trying to install was written for an earlier version of Windows and won't install correctly in Windows XP. How can you get around this?**

   Right-click the installer file and choose Properties, and on the Compatibility tab, set the installer up to run as in the earlier version.

6. **Before installing a new program you aren't sure about, it's smart to back up the Registry. What utility provides an easy way of doing this in Windows XP?**

   System Restore

7. **How can you open the Windows Task Manager in Windows XP/Vista?**

   Right-click the taskbar and choose Task Manager.

8. **How can you open the Windows Task Manager in Windows 95/98/Me?**

   Press Ctrl+Alt+Delete

9. **What tab in the Windows Task Manager displays the currently running processes?**

   The Processes tab

10. **To find the processes that are consuming the most processor time, you should sort the list of running processes by which column?**

    CPU

11. **Do most background running programs display on the Applications tab of the Windows Task Manager? Why or why not?**

No, because only applications that have an open window appear on the Applications tab.

12. **Why is it usually not a good idea to shut down individual running processes via Windows Task Manager?**

Because individual processes are often part of a larger application that is being run, and shutting down an individual process might crash the application.

13. **For each of the following processes you might find in the Windows Task Manager, tell whether it is (E) Essential for proper Windows operation, (O) Optional but okay, or (H) Harmful and indicative of a problem.**

A. absr.exe: <u>H</u>

B. aexplore.exe: <u>O</u>

C. bbeagle.exe: <u>H</u>

D. billmind.exe: <u>O</u>

E. csrss.exe: <u>E</u>

F. explorer.exe: <u>E</u>

14. **Is having multiple copies of svchost.exe running indicative of a problem?**

No, it is normal.

15. **In what folder on the Start/All Programs menu system should you place an application if you want the application to load at startup?**

StartUp

16. **What command (used with Run) opens the System Configuration utility?**

MSCONFIG

17. **Which tab in the System Configuration utility contains the list of programs that are set to load at startup?**

The Startup tab

18. **From the tab in Question 17, how do you disable a program from loading at startup?**

Clear its check box.

19. **Disabling a program from loading at startup via the System Configuration utility is actually just a stopgap measure to use while troubleshooting. Name two ways that are better (that is, tidier and more permanent) for preventing a program from loading at startup.**

You can remove the program entirely (Add or Remove Programs), or you can explore the program's options to see whether it can be configured to not load at startup.

20. **What operating systems can the Compatibility Mode in Windows XP emulate?**

Windows 95

Windows 98/Windows Me

Windows NT 4 (Service Pack 5)

Windows 2000

21. **If an application needs to be run in Super VGA mode, what resolution is that?**

800 x 600

22. **How can you access the Program Compatibility Wizard from Windows XP?**

Choose Start⇨All Programs⇨Accessories⇨Program Compatibility Wizard, or you can run it from the Help and Support Center.

23. **Answer the following questions about the Properties dialog box for an MS-DOS application:**

A. What does the Advanced button on the Program tab enable you to specify?

It enables you to specify custom `autoexec` and `config` files for the application.

B. Suppose you need to add a switch such as /X to be used when running the application. On what tab and in what text box would you add this?

The Program tab. Add it to the end of the string in the Cmd Line text box.

C. If an MS-DOS application requires expanded memory, on what tab and in what text box would you set this up?

The Memory tab, Expanded (EMS) Memory text box

D. If the MS-DOS application crashes frequently, you might need to turn off Fast ROM emulation. From which tab would you disable that feature?

The Screen tab

E. Suppose the application uses Alt+spacebar as a keyboard shortcut. That is a reserved Windows keyboard shortcut, and conflicts occur. From which tab can you disable Windows from claiming that key combination?

The Misc tab

F. Suppose that when the user switches from the DOS program to Windows, the mouse no longer works in the DOS program when he returns to it. What setting on what tab might be useful in fixing this problem?

The Misc tab, Exclusive Mode check box

G. Suppose that when the Windows screen saver kicks in, the MS-DOS program crashes. What setting on what tab might be useful in fixing this problem?

The Misc tab, Allow Screen Saver check box

H. Suppose that the user wants the MS-DOS program to continue running in the background even when it is not the foreground application. What setting on what tab will allow this?

The Misc tab, Always Suspend check box

Chapter 13

System Resources and Device Drivers

· ·

In This Chapter

▶ Understanding system resources

▶ Viewing and changing device resource assignments

▶ Viewing device driver details

▶ Updating and rolling back a device driver

· ·

*V*ery often, when a device isn't working properly, it's not the device's fault. It's much more often a problem with system resources or the device driver. This chapter checks your understanding of these important pieces of the hardware-software interface puzzle.

Understanding System Resources

To interface with the rest of the system, a device needs access to system resources. In the olden days prior to Plug and Play, assigning resources was an arduous task, involving fiddling with jumper caps and switches on circuit boards and running setup utilities. With Windows 95 and higher, Plug and Play does most of the resource assignments automatically, but with varying degrees of success. (Generally, the earlier versions of Windows do the poorer job of it.) That's why you need to know about what system resources devices require.

The A+ exam contains several questions about default resource assignments, especially those for COM and LPT ports, so be prepared to memorize them as part of your study.

Test your knowledge of system resource types and assignments:

1. List the four types of system resources that a device can require. (Not all devices require all types.)

_____

_____

2. Of the types you listed in Question 1 . . .

A. Which type does a system have either 16 or 24 of, depending on the age of the system?

_____

B. Which two types are typically expressed as hexadecimal ranges, such as EFBF0000-EFBFFFFF or CCB8-CCBF?

_____

C. Which type enables the device to bypass the CPU and access RAM directly?

_____

D. Which type provides a signaling pathway by which the device can tell the CPU it needs attention?

_____

E. Which type is sometimes in short supply on an older system with many ISA devices because each ISA device must have its own unique assignment?

_____

3. Fill in the following chart with the default resource assignments:

Port	Standard I/O Address Range	Standard IRQ Assignment
COM1		
COM2		
COM3		
COM4		
LPT1		
LPT2		

4. Suppose you have a notebook with a built-in infrared port. What IRQ is it likely to use?

_____

5. What IRQ is a cascade link to IRQ9?

_____

6. What IRQ does a primary IDE controller use by default?

_____

7. What IRQ is reserved for the use of the real-time clock?

_____

8. What IRQ is reserved for the use of the system timer?

_____

9. What is the relationship between the IRQ number of a device and its priority with the CPU?

_____

_____

10. Name two devices that are likely to use a DMA channel.

_____

Viewing and Changing Device Resource Assignments

You might need to change a resource assignment when Plug and Play has let you down in some way — that is, when it has been unable to juggle the resource assignments so that every device has what it needs. When situations like that occur, resource assignments conflict, and one or both of the devices involved in the conflict don't work. This problem used to be quite common on older systems, due to four factors:

✔ The systems had more components that needed their own unique IRQ assignments to work properly (for example, ISA cards), so it was more common to run out of available IRQs.

✔ The systems had only 16 IRQs, rather than the 24 that are common in today's systems that have an Advanced Programmable Interrupt Controller (APIC)

✔ The systems lacked Advanced Configuration and Power Interface (ACPI) support, which manages resource assignments much more deftly than Windows does on its own.

✔ Earlier versions of Windows generally did a poorer job at Plug and Play resource assignment.

As a result, the newer the system, the less likely it is that resources will be a concern. Older systems are still out there aplenty, though, so that's why the A+ exam still hits resource troubleshooting and reallocation fairly hard.

Test your knowledge of viewing and changing resource assignments in Windows:

11. What Windows utility is shown here, providing a list of all resource conflicts and sharing?

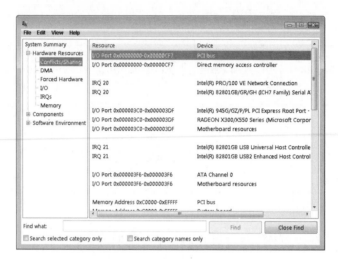

12. What Windows utility is shown here, providing a list of the hardware installed on the system?

13. From Device Manager, how do you display the Properties dialog box for a particular device?

_____

_____

14. In Device Manager . . .

A. What does a yellow circle with an exclamation point next to a device mean?

_____

_____

B. What does a question mark next to a device mean?

_____

_____

C. What does a red X next to a device mean?

_____

_____

15. Can a device have more than one I/O range assigned to it?

_____

16. In a device's Properties dialog box from Device Manager, what check box do you clear to be able to reassign resources manually for it?

_____

17. Write Yes next to those devices likely to have a Resources tab in their Properties dialog box in Device Manager, from which you can view and change resource assignments. Next to those devices unlikely to have a tab, write No.

A. Network adapter: _____

B. Floppy drive controller: _____

C. Floppy disk drive: _____

D. Modem: _____

E. USB keyboard: _____

F. Display adapter: _____

G. Monitor: _____

Exercise 13-1: Working with Resource Assignments

1. Open System Information and view the Conflicts/Sharing section of Hardware Resources.

   Keep in mind that sharing doesn't always indicate a conflict; some devices can share without a problem.

2. In System Information, view the IRQs list and check the status in the Status column. Make a note of any IRQ assignments that don't have a status of OK.

3. Select Forced Hardware and make a note of any devices that appear there.

   These devices aren't being used as Plug and Play; they have resources hard-assigned to them with jumpers or by other hardware means. This should be avoided as much as possible, but is sometimes necessary on very old equipment.

4. Close System Information and open Device Manager.

5. In the list of hardware categories, note whether any categories are expanded.

   Typically, a category is expanded if a device in that category has a problem.

6. If any devices have symbols next to them (such as an exclamation point, a question mark, or a red X), double-click that device to view its Properties dialog box to see what's wrong with it.

7. View the Properties dialog box for several different devices (even if they don't have a problem), and examine the Resources tab. (Not all devices have that tab.) Notice what types of resources each device uses.

   Very few devices use all four types (memory, I/O, IRQ, and DMA).

8. Find a device for which the Use Automatic Settings check box is not grayed out (try the floppy disk controller, for example), and clear that check box.

9. Select a different setting from the Setting Based On drop-down list. This is how you would manually change the settings to resolve a conflict.

10. Click an individual resource, such as the IRQ, in the Resource Settings list above the Settings Based On list. Then click Change Setting.

    A message probably appears saying you cannot change that setting; this is because ACPI is managing that setting for you. That's okay.

11. Click OK to clear the message box. Then click Cancel to close the device's Properties dialog box without making the change.

12. Close all the Properties dialog boxes for the devices, and in Device Manager, choose View, Resources by Type. Then expand the Interrupt Request (IRQ) category and note what IRQs are in use.

On some newer systems and in Windows Vista, you'll find dozens of ISA-based virtual IRQs, numbered in the 100s, on this list. Ignore them; the only ones you would ever work with would be the ones numbered 0 to 23.

Viewing Device Driver Details

In addition to needing system resources, a device also needs a *driver,* which is a translator between the device's language and the operating system's language. All devices need drivers, but some of them might not obviously appear to need one because Windows provides it automatically. (For example, Windows automatically provides a driver for most types of mice.)

Driver files usually have a .sys extension, but the driver might also have some helper files that work with it. It also might have more than one .sys file.

When evaluating whether a driver should be updated, you need to determine the current driver's version number and date and perhaps other details about it, such as where it came from. (For example, did it come from Windows itself, from the company that made the device, or from an outside party?) You can get this information from System Information or the Device Manager.

Check your ability to get driver information:

18. From System Information, under System Summary, what category can you expand to find driver information for each individual device?

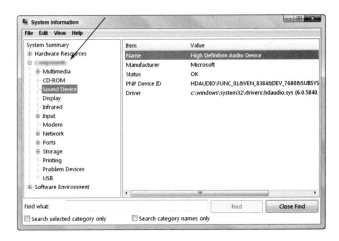

19. In Device Manager, after you double-click a device, what tab do you click to see driver information?

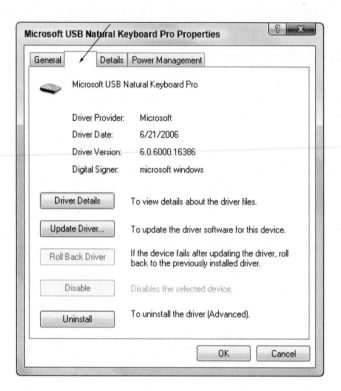

20. In the preceding figure, what extra information could you get by clicking Driver Details?

Exercise 13-2: Obtaining Driver Information

Follow these steps to practice getting driver information from Windows:

1. Open System Information. Expand the Components category and click Display. Information about your display adapter appears.

2. Expand the Input category and click the Keyboard entry.

3. Locate the driver information in the right pane. This information might include the following:

- Driver shows the complete path to the main driver file, the version number, and the file size.

- Installed Drivers lists all the files involved in running the display adapter.

- Driver Version provides the version number.

4. Close System Information and open Device Manager.

5. Expand the Keyboards category and double-click your keyboard.

6. On the Driver tab, examine the details provided. Then click the Driver Details button to see the individual filenames.

7. Click OK when you're finished looking at that information.

Updating or Rolling Back a Device Driver

Drivers can cause a lot of trouble and grief because they have such an intimate friendship with your operating system and hardware. If they're dysfunctional, they can throw the whole relationship into turmoil. So it pays to have the very best drivers you can get.

What constitutes a "good" driver for a piece of hardware? The best driver is

✔ Written for the exact piece of hardware you have

✔ Written for the exact version of Windows you have

✔ Digitally signed

✔ The most up-to-date version available that meets the preceding criteria

What does *digitally signed* mean? Well, back in the Windows 9x days, all kinds of problems occurred with drivers because hardware companies were free to let their programmers write whatever drivers they wanted and slip them into people's Windows systems via the device's Setup program. Some of these drivers replaced the standard Windows versions, and they started causing system problems that were very tough to troubleshoot. To fix this, Microsoft came up with the signed drivers system. To get a signature, a driver must pass Microsoft-regulated testing to prove that it will cause no harm and will work correctly. Then the driver's digital signature certifies that it has passed the testing and hasn't been modified since its release. (The latter prevents malware and viruses from tampering with drivers.) Windows XP and Vista all but insist on signed drivers; you can install a driver that isn't digitally signed, but not without a fight (or at least a few dialog boxes displaying dire warnings).

When a newer driver is available, it's not critical that you upgrade to it immediately. However, if the device is having problems, such as a display adapter failing to run a certain game without crashing, a driver update might be what you need to solve the problem.

Installing a new driver doesn't usually hurt anything, but it can be a scary prospect nonetheless because if the new driver doesn't work, the device doesn't work. That's not such a big deal for optional items like sound cards, but when it's a critical device like the display adapter, it's enough to give pause. Fortunately, you can use the Roll Back Driver feature in Windows to return to the earlier driver if the new one acts up in a bad way.

Windows Update can provide updates for some device drivers. Any drivers you receive via Windows Update should, in theory anyway, work flawlessly with your version of Windows because Microsoft has tested them thoroughly enough to stand behind their distribution.

Check your knowledge of driver updates and rollbacks:

21. How do you start the Hardware Update Wizard (Windows XP) for a device?

_____

_____

_____

22. How do you roll back a previous installed driver update?

_____

_____

_____

23. Suppose there is no driver available for Windows XP for your specific model of network interface card. Which would be better — to use a driver for Windows XP for a different model of card, or to use a driver for Windows 2000 for that specific model you have?

_____

_____

24. Suppose an unsigned display adapter driver is available at a third-party Web site, and it appears to have a more recent date than the one you have installed. Should you install it? Why or why not?

_____

_____

_____

_____

25. Suppose Windows cannot automatically detect your monitor, but a driver file for it is available at the monitor manufacturer's Web site. Windows warns that the driver is unsigned when you try to install it. Is it okay to install it anyway? Why or why not?

_____

_____

_____

_____

26. Suppose the new driver you just installed makes Windows crash every time it starts up. How can you get into Windows to roll back the driver?

_____

Exercise 13-3: Updating and Rolling Back Device Drivers

1. Open Device Manager. Pick one of the nonessential devices and display its Properties dialog box.

2. On the Device tab, click Update Driver.

3. Allow the wizard to access the Internet to look for a better driver. If it finds one, allow the wizard to install it. If not, try another device.

   You might have to try a few devices before you find one that might need an update.

4. After installing the update, reboot and check the device for any problems.

5. Pretend that the new driver had a problem that prevented Windows from starting up normally. Reboot in Safe Mode and roll back the driver.

6. Reboot normally.

Answers to Questions in This Chapter

The following are the answers to the practice questions presented earlier in this chapter:

1. **List the four types of system resources that a device can require. (Not all devices require all types.)**

   Memory address, I/O address, DMA channel, and Interrupt Request (IRQ)

2. **Of the types you listed in Question 1 . . .**

   A. **Which type does a system have either 16 or 24 of, depending on the age of the system?**

   IRQ

   B. **Which two types are typically expressed as hexadecimal ranges, such as EFBF0000-EFBFFFFF or CCB8-CCBF?**

   Memory address and I/O address

   C. **Which type enables the device to bypass the CPU and access RAM directly?**

   DMA channel

   D. **Which type provides a signaling pathway by which the device can tell the CPU it needs attention?**

   IRQ

   E. **Which type is sometimes in short supply on an older system with many ISA devices because each ISA device must have its own unique assignment?**

   IRQ

3. **Fill in the following chart with the default resource assignments:**

Port	Standard I/O Address Range	Standard IRQ Assignment
COM1	4	3F8-3FF
COM2	3	2F8-2FF
COM3	4	3E8-3EF
COM4	3	2E8-2EF
LPT1	7	378-37F
LPT2	5	278-27F

4. **Suppose you have a notebook with a built-in infrared port. What IRQ is it likely to use?**

   It would be IRQ3 or IRQ4 because infrared ports are virtual COM ports, and COM ports 3 and 4 use IRQs 4 and 3 respectively.

5. **What IRQ is a cascade link to IRQ9?**

   2

6. **What IRQ does a primary IDE controller use by default?**

   14

7. **What IRQ is reserved for the use of the real-time clock?**

   8

8. **What IRQ is reserved for the use of the system timer?**

   0

9. **What is the relationship between the IRQ number of a device and its priority with the CPU?**

   The lower the IRQ number, the higher the priority.

10. **Name two devices that are likely to use a DMA channel.**

    Floppy drive and sound card

11. **What Windows utility is shown here, providing a list of all resource conflicts and sharing?**

    System Information

12. **What Windows utility is shown here, providing a list of the hardware installed on the system?**

    Device Manager

13. **From Device Manager, how do you display the Properties dialog box for a particular device?**

    Double-click the device, or click it and then click Properties, or right-click it and click Properties.

14. **In Device Manager . . .**

    A. What does a yellow circle with an exclamation point next to a device mean?

    There is a problem with the device, such as a resource conflict. View the device's Properties dialog box and check for resource problems.

    B. What does a question mark next to a device mean?

    Windows can't identify the device. Use the Setup utility that came with the device to fix this.

    C. What does a red X next to a device mean?

    The device has been disabled. View the device's Properties dialog box and enable the device from there.

15. **Can a device have more than one I/O range assigned to it?**

    Yes. For example, the floppy disk drive controller may have more than one I/O range.

16. **In a device's Properties dialog box from Device Manager, what checkbox do you clear to be able to reassign resources manually for it?**

    Use Automatic Settings

17. **Write Yes next to those devices likely to have a Resources tab in their Properties dialog box in Device Manager, from which you can view and change resource assignments. Next to those devices unlikely to have a tab, write No.**

A. Network adapter: <u>Yes</u>

B. Floppy drive controller: <u>Yes</u>

C. Floppy disk drive: <u>No</u>

D. Modem: <u>Yes</u>

E. USB keyboard: <u>No</u>

F. Display adapter: <u>Yes</u>

G. Monitor: <u>No</u>

18. **From System Information, under System Summary, what category can you expand to find driver information for each individual device?**

The Components category

19. **In Device Manager, after you double-click a device, what tab do you click to see driver information?**

The Driver tab

20. **In the preceding figure, what extra information could you get by clicking Driver Details?**

The names and locations of the driver files, and also the copyright information for the driver (although of course the latter is of limited usefulness in troubleshooting)

21. **How do you start the Hardware Update Wizard (Windows XP) for a device?**

From Device Manager, double-click the device. Click its Driver tab and click Update Driver.

22. **How do you roll back a previous installed driver update?**

From Device Manager, double-click the device. Click its Driver tab and click Roll Back Driver.

23. **Suppose there is no driver available for Windows XP for your specific model of network interface card. Which would be better — to use a driver for Windows XP for a different model of card, or to use a driver for Windows 2000 for that specific model you have?**

It would be better to use the Windows 2000 driver. Windows 2000 and Windows XP are based on the same basic platform, so drivers often work between them. On the other hand, a driver for a different model of hardware wouldn't work very well because there would be different features available and possibly incompatibilities with the commands the driver sends to the device.

24. **Suppose an unsigned display adapter driver is available at a third-party Web site, and it appears to have a more recent date than the one you have installed. Should you install it? Why or why not?**

It wouldn't be a good idea to use this driver unless there was some serious problem with the current driver. Third-party sites often contain untested, mislabeled, or incomplete drivers. On a noncritical device, it might be worth taking the chance, but the display adapter is such a critical part of Windows that an unsigned driver is a bad investment.

25. **Suppose Windows cannot automatically detect your monitor, but a driver file for it is available at the monitor manufacturer's Web site. Windows warns that the driver is unsigned when you try to install it. Is it okay to install it anyway? Why or why not?**

    It is okay to install it anyway. One reason is that the monitor manufacturer is a reliable source for a driver, but a more important reason is that monitor drivers aren't like other drivers. Monitors are (usually) analog, so there is no real driver per se for them. What's called a driver is actually just an information file (`.inf`) containing data about the monitor's capabilities, such as the maximum refresh rate for a CRT.

26. **Suppose the new driver you just installed makes Windows crash every time it starts up. How can you get into Windows to roll back the driver?**

    Use Safe Mode.

Part IV

Maintaining and Troubleshooting the Operating System

"Well, here's your problem. You only have half the ram you need."

In this part . . .

*T*he chapters in this part help you review and practice
maintenance and troubleshooting tasks related to the
operating system. You also find exercises related to monitoring and optimizing Windows systems with the Task
Manager and other tools, reviewing the boot sequences
and system files for various Windows versions, and
troubleshooting problems related to hardware, booting,
and recovery.

Chapter 14

Monitoring and Optimizing Windows

In This Chapter

▶ Monitoring system performance with Task Manager

▶ Monitoring system performance with Performance Monitor

▶ Monitoring system performance with Event Viewer

▶ Optimizing virtual memory usage

▶ Running Disk Cleanup

▶ Running the Disk Defragmenter

*A*re you ready to soup up that hotrod of a system you've got there and make it really roar? (Or, more likely, are you ready to tune up that old clunker so that it performs more decently?) Improving the performance of a Windows system involves two basic activities: monitoring the system as it operates to look for potential bottlenecks, and running optimization utilities to fix up any system problems or dead weight that might be preventing top performance. In this chapter, you test your knowledge of performing Windows-based tune-ups.

Monitoring System Performance with Task Manager

When the system doesn't seem to be performing up to par, Task Manager can often tell you what the problem is. It lists all running applications, processes, and services, and it provides some basic performance information about the CPU, memory, and networking usage.

The Windows Vista and Windows 2000/XP versions of the Task Manager show slightly different information. Windows XP is shown here. The Vista version isn't covered on the current A+ exam.

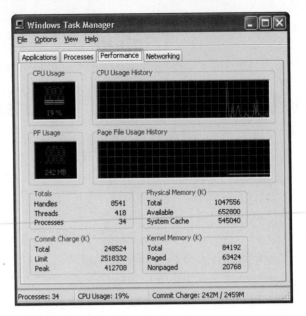

Test your knowledge of using the Task Manager to monitor system performance:

1. How can you open the Task Manager in Windows 95/98/Me?

_____

_____

2. How can you open the Task Manager in Windows 2000/XP?

_____

_____

3. Which of these things can you find out from Task Manager (on any tab)? Place a check mark next to each one that is available there.

A. _____ Which process is using the most RAM?

B. _____ What applications are open?

C. _____ Which application is using the most RAM?

D. _____ How many threads is a particular process using?

E. _____ How much physical memory does the computer have?

F. _____ What is the size of the page file?

G. _____ What is the hard drive access speed/rate?

H. _____ Which applications, if any, are not responding (crashed)?

I. _____ What percentage of network resources is being consumed?

Exercise 14-1: Working with the Task Manager

Follow these steps to practice using Task Manager to explore the system:

1. Open the Task Manager in Windows XP.

2. On the Applications tab, note the running applications.

3. On the Applications tab, click New Task. In the Open dialog box, type **CMD** and click OK.

   A new command window opens.

   This step illustrates how you can start applications from the Task Manager. It's useful to know about because if Windows is crashing, sometimes you might not be able to access the Start menu, but you can still access the Task Manager.

4. On the Processes tab, sort the list of tasks by name (by clicking the Image Name column heading) and locate cmd.exe. Note how much memory it's using.

5. Sort by the Memory column and find the process that is using the most memory. Check the value in the User Name column for it.

   If the username is SYSTEM, it's a Windows-generated process. If the username is your logged-in name, it's from an application you're running.

6. Sort by the CPU column and find the process that is using the most CPU time.

   It's probably System Idle Process, which means the CPU is available for whatever commands you issue. If some other task is consistently taking more of the CPU than System Idle Process is, you might have a problem with a runaway application.

7. On the Applications tab, note the statuses of each task in the Status column. They should all be Running. Select the command prompt window (cmd.exe) and end it using the End Task button.

   This is how you would end a task if its status were Not Responding.

8. On the Performance tab, take a look at the Commit Charge section. (If you don't have that section, you probably aren't using Windows XP, so skip this part.)

   The Total is the available physical memory and virtual memory. The Limit is the maximum combined total possible. The Peak is the highest combined total that the system has actually used since boot-up. If the Peak value comes close to the Limit value or to the Total value, the system needs more physical RAM because it is relying too much on the page file.

9. On the Networking tab, examine the network utilization percentage.

   For a client PC, it will probably be very low. A high network utilization on a client PC might mean that someone unauthorized is accessing the PC or that a network application is malfunctioning.

10. Close Task Manager.

Monitoring System Performance with Performance Monitor

The Performance Monitor utility provides detailed information about how the system is performing by using various detailed measurements of the memory, CPU, and hard drive performance. It is actually a preconfigured Microsoft Management Console (MMC) with the following two snap-ins installed:

- ✔ **System Monitor:** Consists of a set of overlaid line graphs, with each colored line representing a different counter. You can customize the display by adding and removing counters to the graph area. System Monitor graphs are useful for short-term, real-time monitoring, such as when you're troubleshooting.

- ✔ **Performance Logs and Alerts:** Consists of categories within which might be one or more log files that are tracking your system's performance. You can enable the default Counter Log, and/or you can create your own logging instructions to track performance. This monitoring is useful for record keeping and extended monitoring.

The Performance Monitor utility in Windows Vista is very different. It doesn't use graphs at all; instead, it provides text-based information in expandable categories. It isn't covered on the current A+ exam.

Test your knowledge of working with the Performance Monitor in Windows XP:

4. From the Control Panel, how do you start the Performance Monitor?

_____

_____

5. From the Run dialog box, how do you start the Performance Monitor?

_____

_____

6. What button in the System Monitor adds another counter to the graph? Draw an arrow pointing to it here:

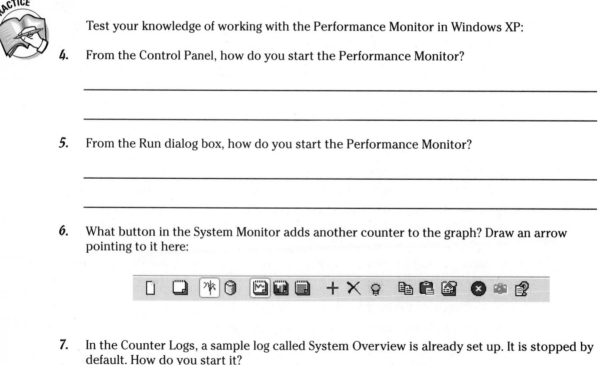

7. In the Counter Logs, a sample log called System Overview is already set up. It is stopped by default. How do you start it?

_____

_____

8. How do you stop the System Overview sample log from running after it has been started?

   _____

   _____

9. Suppose you want to set up a new Counter Log. How do you begin creating a new one from the Performance window?

   _____

   _____

Exercise 14-2: Setting Up a Counter Log

Use the following steps to practice using the Performance Monitor to set up a counter log.

1. Open the Performance Monitor window in Windows XP.

2. Click the System Monitor entry in the left pane and watch the graph recording system usage information for a minute or two.

3. Click the Add button to open the Add Counters dialog box. Then under Performance Object, choose Paging File.

4. Select % Usage and click Explain. This opens a window that describes the setting. Close that window after reading the information.

5. Click Add to add the counter. Then click Close.

6. Right-click % Usage in the list at the bottom of the window and then choose Properties. On the Data tab, select % Usage and change the Color setting to bright pink.

7. On the Graph tab, change the Maximum value for Vertical Scale to 20. Then click OK.

   This option isn't something you would change permanently, but it's useful if the values are so small that you're having a hard time seeing and interpreting them.

8. Right-click any of the counters in the list and choose Properties. Go back to the Graph tab and reset the Maximum value to 100. Then click OK.

9. Select the % Usage entry in the list and click the Delete button (X) on the toolbar to remove it from the graph.

10. Expand the Performance Logs and Alerts section in the left pane and click the Counter Logs entry.

11. Right-click System Overview and click Start.

12. Double-click System Overview and look on the General tab, under Current log file name, to see where the log file is being stored.

13. Allow the log file to run for one hour or so. Then browse to the location you noted in Step 4 and double-click the log file to examine what has been recorded.

14. (Optional) Create your own set of Counter Log settings and set them up to be saved to a tab-delimited text file. Then let them run for a few hours and view the results.

Monitoring System Performance with Event Viewer

An *event* is something that happens with the system or an application, such as startup, shutdown, a device being added or removed, a warning message appearing, an application crashing, and so on. Not every event is significant, and even error events are sometimes one-time flukes that never recur. However, by examining the event logs, you can get a sense of what has been happening and how the system has been responding to it. This is especially useful when you suspect that a recurring problem is affecting system performance.

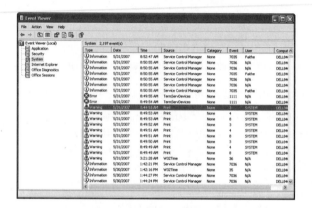

The Event Viewer has a different interface style in Windows Vista, but many of the categories of events are still the same. The Vista version isn't covered on the current A+ exams.

Test your knowledge using Event Viewer in Windows XP:

10. From the Control Panel, how do you open the Event Viewer?

_____

Match the following types of information-gathering to the area of Event Viewer where you would find the needed information.

A. Application

B. Security

C. System

11. _____ You're wondering whether your paging file might be corrupt, and you're looking for evidence of any errors that might confirm your suspicion.

12. _____ An instant messaging program is crashing frequently, and you want to find out how many times it has crashed in the last few days and what executable file is involved.

13. _____ The print spooler is stalled for a particular printer, and you can't seem to get it working. You want to find out when the problem with the print spooler first occurred.

14. _____ Outlook consistently crashes as it's trying to load its data file. You want to get more information about any error message it might have generated, to get an idea of what might be the problem.

15. _____ The date/time clock in Windows doesn't seem to be updating automatically as it should from the Internet, and you're looking for errors that might indicate why.

16. _____ Your antivirus program has lately been failing to start when you boot up, and you want to see whether there's any information in the log about why it's failing.

17. _____ You want to see who has been logging into your PC while you've been away from your desk.

Exercise 14-3: Working with the Event Viewer

In Windows XP:

1. Open the Event Viewer from the Control Panel.

2. Take a look at the categories in the left pane.

   The three fixed categories are Application, Security, and System. You might also have other categories, depending on how your system is set up. For example, you might have one for Internet Explorer and one or more for Office.

3. Click Application.

4. Click the Type column heading to sort by event type.

   The Information items represent normally occurring events, such as applications starting up and shutting down. You can usually ignore them unless you have some reason to need their information, such as wondering whether a particular application has been run by someone in your absence or finding out how often users are employing a certain utility or tool.

5. Scroll down the list to the Warning events and double-click one of the events to open its properties.

6. Read the description of the event. If you see a hyperlink for more information, click that hyperlink and read the additional information. When you're finished, close the event's Properties dialog box.

7. Scroll down to the Error events and double-click one of those events to open its properties.

8. Read the description, and if desired, follow the hyperlink for more information. Then close the Properties dialog box.

9. In the left pane, click Security. Scroll through the security events, and if you see any abnormal events (that is, events other than Success Audit), double-click them to examine them.

10. In the left pane, click System. Browse several examples of Information, Warning, and Error events.

11. In the left pane, click any remaining categories and browse their events.

12. Close the Event Viewer window.

Optimizing Virtual Memory Usage

Virtual memory is just what the name implies — memory that isn't real. It's a feature wherein Windows sets aside a portion of the hard drive to be an overflow holding tank for the physical RAM installed in the system. As physical RAM gets full, Windows starts swapping data out of it and onto this reserved area of the hard drive, for temporary storage. Then when an application or the system calls for that data out of RAM, Windows swaps that data back into physical RAM and moves whatever was in its place out to the hard drive. The area of the hard drive set aside for this purpose is called the *paging file* or *swap file*.

Windows manages the paging file automatically, and in many cases, it's best to leave it at that. However, you can make a few adjustments to the paging file that can slightly improve system performance. For example, you might change the maximum size allotted for the paging file, or you might relocate it to a better, faster, or more reliable disk drive.

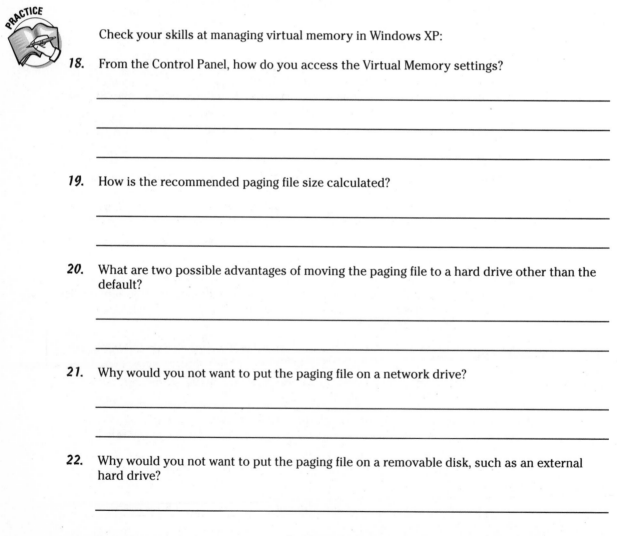

Check your skills at managing virtual memory in Windows XP:

18. From the Control Panel, how do you access the Virtual Memory settings?

_____

_____

_____

19. How is the recommended paging file size calculated?

_____

_____

20. What are two possible advantages of moving the paging file to a hard drive other than the default?

_____

_____

21. Why would you not want to put the paging file on a network drive?

_____

_____

22. Why would you not want to put the paging file on a removable disk, such as an external hard drive?

_____

_____

Exercise 14-4: Managing Virtual Memory

Check your skills at managing virtual memory in Windows XP:

1. Open the Virtual Memory window and turn off automatic Windows management of the paging file.

   Hint: Do this from the System Properties dialog box, from the Advanced tab.

2. Check the current setting. Choose Custom Size if it isn't already chosen.

3. If you find more than one hard drive listed on the Drive list and an unselected drive is a faster drive or one that isn't being used much (so there's less competition for its bandwidth), choose it.

4. Set the initial size to the amount listed under Recommended.

5. Set the maximum size to twice the amount from Step 4. Then click Set and click OK.

6. Reboot the PC, timing how long it takes for the PC to start up, and return to the Virtual Memory window.

7. Turn off virtual memory altogether by choosing the No Paging File option.

8. Click Set and then click OK. Reboot the computer. Time how long it takes to start up.

   It will probably be slower than usual.

9. Return to the Virtual Memory window and choose the System Managed Size option. Return the paging file to the original drive it was on at the beginning of the exercise.

10. Reboot the PC and time how long it takes to start up.

Running Disk Cleanup

The Disk Cleanup utility can tidy up a system by removing unneeded files. Who decides what "unneeded" is? Well, Windows gives you its recommendations, and then you can go through and say yay or nay. The files it finds might include cached Web pages, temporary files left behind when a program crashed, Setup files left behind when you upgraded to a new version of Windows, files in the Recycle Bin, and so on.

The More Options tab has shortcuts to some other utilities that can free up hard drive space on the PC, such as adding and removing Windows components and installed programs. These are just shortcuts to other features, though, and not part of Disk Cleanup itself.

23. List two different ways of starting Disk Cleanup in Windows XP.

_____

_____

_____

_____

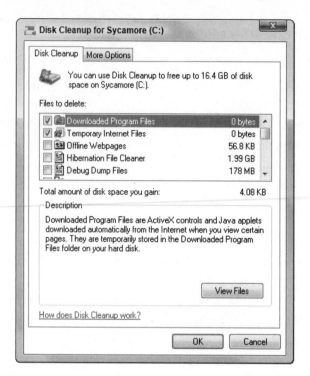

Exercise 14-5: Cleaning Up the Hard Drive

Follow these steps to tidy up a hard drive with the Disk Cleanup utility:

1. Start Disk Cleanup.

2. Review the types of files that Windows has selected by default in the Files to Delete list, and mark or clear any check boxes as needed. Here are some tips:

   • Anything that is selected by default is usually safe to delete; anything that isn't selected, you should look at critically before selecting.

   • If you delete temporary Internet files, some Web pages will load more slowly.

   • If you delete Office Setup files, you will need the Office CD to make changes to your Microsoft Office installation.

   • When you choose temporary files to delete, Disk Cleanup removes only the ones that haven't been modified in over a week. Therefore you might still have some left after Disk Cleanup; this is normal.

   • Debug dump files can nearly always be eliminated without incident because they're for programmer use only.

3. Click OK. At the confirmation box, click Delete Files (Vista) or Yes (all other Windows versions).

Running the Disk Defragmenter

When a file is stored on a drive, if there's room, the file is placed in contiguous clusters on the drive surface. This makes the file easily accessible to the hard drive's read/write head because it is all in one place, and it makes the hard drive access time as fast as it can be. Over time, however, as the file is modified, the additional pieces are written to nonadjacent areas, and the file becomes *fragmented*. The hard drive's read/write heads must move around more to pick up the pieces, so the disk access time suffers. *Defragmenting* a hard drive can improve its performance by rewriting as many files as possible to contiguous clusters.

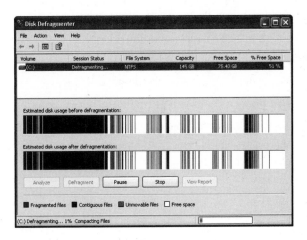

24. List two different ways of starting the Disk Defragmenter in Windows XP.

_____

_____

_____

_____

Exercise 14-6: Defragmenting a Hard Drive

Follow these steps to defragment your hard drive.

1. Start the Disk Defragmenter utility in Windows XP.

2. Click Analyze to check the hard drive's current fragmentation status.

It takes a few minutes to complete its analysis.

3. Even if the analysis reports that you don't need to defragment, click Defragment anyway.

4. Wait for the defragmentation to complete.

You can minimize the window and do other things while you're waiting.

Answers to Questions in This Chapter

The following are the answers to the practice questions presented earlier in this chapter:

1. **How can you open the Task Manager in Windows 95/98/Me?**

   Ctrl+Alt+Delete

2. **How can you open the Task Manager in Windows 2000/XP?**

   Right-click the Taskbar and click Task Manager.

3. **Which of these things can you find out from Task Manager (on any tab)? Place a check mark next to each one that is available there.**

   A. _Yes_ Which process is using the most RAM?

   B. _Yes_ What applications are open?

   C. _No_ Which application is using the most RAM?

   D. _No_ How many threads is a particular process using?

   E. _Yes_ How much physical memory does the computer have?

   F. _Yes_ What is the size of the page file?

   G. _No_ What is the hard drive access speed/rate?

   H. _Yes_ Which applications, if any, are not responding (crashed)?

   I. _Yes_ What percentage of network resources is being consumed?

4. **From the Control Panel, how do you start the Performance Monitor?**

   Choose Control Panel⇨Administrative Tools⇨Performance.

5. **From the Run dialog box, how do you start the Performance Monitor?**

   Choose Start⇨Run, type **perfmon**, and click OK.

6. **What button in the System Monitor adds another counter to the graph? Draw an arrow pointing to it here:**

7. **In the Counter Logs, a sample log called System Overview is already set up. It is stopped by default. How do you start it?**

   You can right-click it and choose Start, or you can click the Start button (right-pointing arrow) on the toolbar.

8. **How to you stop the System Overview sample log from running after it has been started?**

   You can right-click it and choose Stop, or you can click the Stop button (square) on the toolbar.

9. **Suppose you want to set up a new Counter Log. How do you begin creating a new one from the Performance window?**

   Right-click an empty area of the window and choose New Log Settings.

10. **From the Control Panel, how to you open the Event Viewer?**

    Control Panel⇨Administrative Tools⇨Event Viewer

11. C

12. A

13. C

14. A

15. C

16. A

17. B

18. **From the Control Panel, how do you access the Virtual Memory settings?**

    1. From Classic view, choose System. From Category view, choose Performance and Maintenance and then choose System.

    2. Click the Advanced tab and, under Performance, click Settings.

    3. Click the Advanced tab and click the Change button.

19. **How is the recommended paging file size calculated?**

    It is 1.5 times the amount of physical RAM installed.

20. **What are two possible advantages of moving the paging file to a hard drive other than the default?**

    You could move it to a faster drive for faster access. You could also move it to a less-used drive, so there is less competition for bandwidth.

21. **Why would you not want to put the paging file on a network drive?**

    Because it might not always be available (for example, because the network is down).

22. **Why would you not want to put the paging file on a removable disk, such as an external hard drive?**

    Because it might not always be available and because someone might disconnect it as Windows is running, causing Windows to crash.

23. **List two different ways of starting Disk Cleanup in Windows XP.**

You can choose Start➪All Programs➪Accessories➪System Tools➪Disk Cleanup.

You can open My Computer, right-click a drive, choose Properties, and click Disk Cleanup on the General tab.

24. **List two different ways of starting the Disk Defragmenter in Windows XP.**

You can choose Start➪All Programs➪Accessories➪System Tools➪Disk Defragmenter.

You can open My Computer, right-click a drive, choose Properties, click the Tools tab, and click Defragment Now.

Chapter 15

Understanding the System Files and Boot Sequences

. . . .

In This Chapter

▶ Understanding the major system files

▶ Reviewing the Windows 98 boot sequence

▶ Reviewing the Windows XP boot sequence

. . . .

*T*he A+ exams hit system files and boot sequences very hard, and so must you when studying. For each of the operating systems covered on the test, you need to know what loads at startup, and in what order, and what each of those files accomplishes. You also should be able to identify the files that various versions of Windows need to function, such as Registry and initialization files. This chapter helps you study all that.

Understanding the Major System Files

When an operating system isn't working, sometimes one or more system files has gotten corrupted or deleted. It pays, therefore, to know what system files are essential for a particular OS and to understand how they fit into the big picture.

The current version of the A+ exam covers Windows 2000 and XP specifically, but you should also know a bit about Windows 9x system files, just in case you need to work on an older system. Also, you should study older OS versions to get a sense of how one version has built on the next, adding capabilities and maintaining backward compatibility.

Test your knowledge of operating system files:

1. In the following list, place the appropriate letter (or letters) next to the system files required for running each operating system.

A. MS-DOS   B. Windows 95/98/Me   C. Windows 2000/XP

I. _____ NTOSKRNL.EXE

II. _____ EMM386.EXE

III. _____ NTDETECT.COM

          A. MS-DOS   B. Windows 95/98/Me   C. Windows 2000/XP

IV. _____ WINNT32.EXE

V. _____ COMMAND.COM

VI. _____ SYSTEM.DAT

VII. _____ USER.DAT

VIII. _____ IO.SYS

IX. _____ KERNEL32.DLL

X. _____ SYSTEM

XI. _____ USER32.DLL

XII. _____ NTUSER.DAT

XIII. _____ USER.EXE

XIV. _____ GDI32.DLL

XV. _____ SAM

XVI. _____ VMM386.VXD

XVII. _____ GDI.EXE

XVIII. _____ SECURITY

XIX. _____ NTLDR.EXE

XX. _____ BOOT.INI

XXI. _____ MSDOS.SYS

XXII. _____ NTBOOTDD.SYS

XXIII. _____ HIMEM.SYS

XXIV. _____ HAL.DLL

XXV. _____ SOFTWARE

XXVI. _____ DEFAULT

Referring to the list of filenames in Question 1, fill in the following filenames to match the descriptions given:

2. The three files that a bootable floppy disk for MS-DOS or Windows 9x must have in order to be bootable:

   _____

   _____

3. The two files that make up the registry for Windows 9x:

   _____

4. The six files that make up the Registry for Windows 2000/XP:

   _____

   _____

   _____

5. The command interpreter under Windows 9x:

   _____

6. The main executable program file for Windows 9x:

   _____

7. The extended memory manager for both DOS and Windows:

   _____

8. The 32-bit memory manager for Windows 9x:

   _____

9. The 32-bit device driver manager for Windows 9x:

   _____

10. The 32-bit memory manager for Windows XP:

    _____

11. The expanded memory manager for MS-DOS and Windows 9x:

    _____

12. The hardware detection program that runs at Windows XP startup:

    _____

13. The initialization file for multibooting under Windows 2000/XP:

    _____

14. The main executable file for Windows XP:

    _____

15. The GUI manager for Windows 9x:

    _____

16. The I/O manager for Windows 9x:

    _____

17. The interface between the hardware and the OS under Windows 2000/XP:

    _____

Exercise 15-1: Locating System Files

Follow these steps to explore the locations of the system files on your PC:

1. In Windows 2000 or XP, open the Search window.

2. Search for the following files and note their locations:

    - NTLDR.EXE: _____
    - NTDETECT.COM: _____
    - BOOT.INI: _____
    - WINNT32.EXE: _____
    - NTBOOTDD.SYS: _____
    - HAL.DLL: _____
    - NTOSKRNL.EXE: _____
    - GDI.EXE: _____
    - USER.EXE: _____
    - SAM: _____
    - SECURITY: _____
    - SYSTEM: _____
    - DEFAULT: _____
    - NTUSER.DAT: _____

Reviewing the Windows 9x Boot Sequence

When people say that Windows 9x is built on the "DOS platform," what they mean is that MS-DOS and Windows 9x share similar boot sequences and system files. Windows 9x starts out with the same boot sequence as MS-DOS, and then additional files load on top of those. That's why Windows 9x can use an MS-DOS boot disk to provide command-line access to the PC in the event that Windows won't start normally.

The following questions test your knowledge of the Windows 9x boot sequence:

18. Put the following steps of the Windows 9x boot process into the correct sequence by numbering them from 1 to 15:

A. _____ IO.SYS looks for LOGO.SYS and displays it as the Windows splash screen.

B. _____ IO.SYS loads HIMEM.SYS if it was not loaded in CONFIG.SYS.

C. _____ The BIOS performs a POST.

D. _____ WIN.COM loads the GUI by loading three files: KRNL32.DLL, GDI.EXE, and USER.EXE.

E. _____ The master boot record takes control and locates IO/SYS.

F. _____ IO.SYS loads SYSTEM.DAT.

G. _____ The BIOS searches the drives for the master boot record.

H. _____ WIN.COM reads SYSTEM.INI if present and executes its instructions.

I. _____ IO.SYS looks for MSDOS.SYS and processes its instructions.

J. _____ VMM386.VXD loads 32-bit device drivers into memory.

K. _____ IO.SYS looks for the Registry files, SYSTEM.DAT and USER.DAT.

L. _____ WIN.COM loads the virtual memory manager, VMM386.VXD.

M. _____ WIN.COM checks the content of the StartUp folder on the Start menu and executes any shortcuts found there.

N. _____ IO.SYS loads WIN.COM and then hands off control to it.

O. _____ IO.SYS looks for CONFIG.SYS and AUTOEXEC.BAT and executes them if found.

Exercise 15-2: Monitoring the Windows 9x Boot Process

Windows 9x versions have a very handy Step-by-Step Confirmation feature that enables you to observe the boot process interactively, saying Yes or No to each item. It's a good troubleshooting tool, and it's a good learning tool for slowing down the boot process so that you can really understand what's going on.

In a Windows 95, 98, or Me system, do the following:

1. As the PC is booting, press F8 to display the Startup Menu.

2. Select the Step-by-Step Confirmation option.

3. For each line that appears, make a note of what file is being loaded and then press Y to allow it to load. Identify as many of the files mentioned in the previous section as possible. Jot down notes here:

_____

_____

_____

_____

_____

_____

_____

_____

_____

_____

_____

_____

4. After Windows has started up, restart it again normally.

Theoretically, this step shouldn't be necessary if you answered Y to every prompt in Step 3, but it doesn't hurt, and it ensures that you didn't accidentally disallow anything during the boot process before.

Reviewing the Windows XP Boot Sequence

If you have time to memorize only one boot sequence, the Windows 2000/XP sequence is the one to focus on because it's covered more heavily on the A+ exams. People refer to the sequences as if they were the same thing because, basically, they are — the same major system files load in the same order for both.

19. Put the following steps of the Windows 9x boot process into the correct sequence by numbering them from 1 to 10:

A. _____ NTOSKRNL.EXE loads the device drivers and the GUI.

B. _____ NTLDR runs NTDETECT.COM, which detects the installed hardware and sends information to the Registry.

C. _____ The BIOS performs a POST.

D. _____ NTLDR hands over control to NTOSKRNL.EXE.

E. _____ NTLDR finds and reads BOOT.INI. If there are multiple operating systems, it displays a menu for user choice.

F. _____ NTLDR switches the CPU into 32-bit protected mode.

G. _____ NTLDR reads NTOSKRNL.EXE into memory.

H. _____ The BIOS searches the drives for the MBR.

I. _____ NTLDR locates the drivers for the hardware that the Registry reports is installed (but does not install them yet).

J. _____ The MBR takes control and locates NTLDR.

Exercise 15-3: Bootlogging in Windows XP

In Windows XP, you can't use Step-by-Step Confirmation, but you can enable boot logging, which saves a record of what files have loaded, and in what order, to a text file.

1. Enable boot logging by doing either of the following:

   a. Choose Start⇨Run. Type MSCONFIG and click OK.

   b. On the BOOT.INI tab, select the Boot Log check box.

   c. Click OK.

   d. Reboot the PC.

OR

   a. Click Start, right-click My Computer, and choose Properties.

   b. Click the Advanced tab in the Properties dialog box, and under Startup and Recovery, click Settings.

   c. Click Edit to open `Boot.ini` in Notepad.

   d. Add the `/bootlog` switch to the end of the line that loads Windows XP. For example:

```
multi(0)disk(0)rdisk(0)partition(1)\Windows="Microsoft Windows
        XP Professional" /fastdetect /NoExecute=OptIn /bootlog
```

   e. Save the changes, close Notepad, and reboot the PC.

2. Open the file `C:\Windows\Ntbtlog.txt` in Notepad and see what files are loading at startup, and in what order. Compare this with the sequence you specified in the previous Practice section. Make notes here:

_____

_____

_____

_____

_____

_____

_____

_____

_____

_____

Answers to Questions in This Chapter

The following are the answers to the practice questions presented earlier in this chapter:

1. **In the following list, place the appropriate letter (or letters) next to the system files required for running each operating system.**

   A. MS-DOS   B. Windows 95/98/Me   C. Windows 2000/XP

   I.   __C__   NTOSKRNL.EXE

   II. __B__   EMM386.EXE

   III. __C__   NTDETECT.COM

   IV. __C__   WINNT32.EXE

   V.   __A, B__ COMMAND.COM

   VI. __B__   SYSTEM.DAT

   VII. __B__   USER.DAT

   VIII. __A, B__ IO.SYS

   IX. __B__   KERNEL32.DLL

   X.   __C__   SYSTEM

   XI. __B__   USER32.DLL

   XII. __C__   NTUSER.DAT

   XIII. __B__   USER.EXE

   XIV. __B__   GDI32.DLL

   XV. __C__   SAM

   XVI. __B__   VMM386.VXD

   XVII. __B__   GDI.EXE

   XVIII. __C__   SECURITY

   IXX. __C__   NTLDR.EXE

   XX. __C__   BOOT.INI

   XXI. __A, B__ MSDOS.SYS

   XXII. __C__   NTBOOTDD.SYS

   XXIII. __B, C__ HIMEM.SYS

   XXIV. __C__   HAL.DLL

   XXV. __C__   SOFTWARE

   XXVI. __C__   DEFAULT

2. **The three files that a bootable floppy disk for MS-DOS or Windows 9x must have in order to be bootable:**

   IO.SYS, MSDOS.SYS, and COMMAND.COM

3. **The two files that make up the registry for Windows 9x:**

   SYSTEM.DAT and USER.DAT

4. **The six files that make up the Registry for Windows 2000/XP:**

   SAM, SECURITY, SOFTWARE, SYSTEM, DEFAULT, and NTUSER.DAT

5. **The command interpreter under Windows 9x:**

   COMMAND.COM

6. **The main executable program file for Windows 9x:**

   WIN.COM

7. **The extended memory manager for both DOS and Windows:**

   HIMEM.SYS

8. **The 32-bit memory manager for Windows 9x:**

   KERNEL32.DLL

9. **The 32-bit device driver manager for Windows 9x:**

   VMM386.VXD

10. **The 32-bit memory manager for Windows XP:**

    NTOSKRNL.EXE

11. **The expanded memory manager for MS-DOS and Windows 9x:**

    EMM386.EXE

12. **The hardware detection program that runs at Windows XP startup:**

    NTDETECT.COM

13. **The initialization file for multibooting under Windows 2000/XP:**

    BOOT.INI

14. **The main executable file for Windows XP:**

    WINNT32.EXE

15. **The GUI manager for Windows 9x:**

    GDI.EXE

16. **The I/O manager for Windows 9x**

    USER.EXE

17. **The interface between the hardware and the OS under Windows 2000/XP:**

    HAL.DLL

18. **Put the following steps of the Windows 9x boot process into the correct sequence by numbering them from 1 to 15:**

    A. __5__ IO.SYS looks for LOGO.SYS and displays it as the Windows splash screen.

    B. __9__ IO.SYS loads HIMEM.SYS if it was not loaded in CONFIG.SYS.

    C. __1__ The BIOS performs a POST.

    D. __14__ WIN.COM loads the GUI by loading three files: KRNL32.DLL, GDI.EXE, and USER.EXE.

    E. __3__ The master boot record takes control and locates IO/SYS.

    F. __7__ IO.SYS loads SYSTEM.DAT.

    G. __2__ The BIOS searches the drives for the master boot record.

    H. __13__ WIN.COM reads SYSTEM.INI if present and executes its instructions.

    I. __4__ IO.SYS looks for MSDOS.SYS and processes its instructions.

    J. __12__ VMM386.VXD loads 32-bit device drivers into memory.

    K. __6__ IO.SYS looks for the Registry files, SYSTEM.DAT and USER.DAT.

    L. __11__ WIN.COM loads the virtual memory manager, VMM386.VXD.

    M. __15__ WIN.COM checks the content of the StartUp folder on the Start menu and executes any shortcuts found there.

    N. __10__ IO.SYS loads WIN.COM, and then hands off control to it.

    O. __8__ IO.SYS looks for CONFIG.SYS and AUTOEXEC.BAT and executes them if found.

19. **Put the following steps of the Windows 9x boot process into the correct sequence by numbering them from 1 to 10:**

    A. __10__ NTOSKRNL.EXE loads the device drivers and the GUI.

    B. __6__ NTLDR runs NTDETECT.COM, which detects the installed hardware and sends information to the Registry.

    C. __1__ The BIOS performs a POST.

    D. __9__ NTLDR hands over control to NTOSKRNL.EXE.

    E. __5__ NTLDR finds and reads BOOT.INI. If there are multiple operating systems, it displays a menu for user choice.

    F. __4__ NTLDR switches the CPU into 32-bit protected mode.

    G. __7__ NTLDR reads NTOSKRNL.EXE into memory.

    H. __2__ The BIOS searches the drives for the MBR.

    I. __8__ NTLDR locates the drivers for the hardware that the Registry reports is installed (but does not install them yet).

    J. __3__ The MBR takes control and locates NTLDR.

Chapter 16

Troubleshooting Hardware Problems

Troubleshooting is one of the most difficult skills to master for a technician because there are so many specific little rules and "gotchas" that experienced people learn on the job over time. General logic, though, can usually get you somewhere in the ballpark of a solution.

If you watch medical TV shows like *House,* you've probably heard the term "differential diagnosis." In a nutshell, it means that if you don't know whether the problem is A or B, you figure out how A and B differ in their symptoms, and then you perform a test that will create that distinction. For example, if you don't know whether a blank-screen problem is with the monitor or the display adapter, you swap out the monitor and observe the result. If the problem remains, you know it's the display adapter. It sounds like just plain old common sense — and in most cases, it is, but the tricky part is being able to formulate tests that distinguish between the problems. You have to know how a PC behaves when it's under one kind of duress versus another.

In this chapter, you review various problem scenarios and test your ability to identify the most likely root causes and solutions.

Troubleshooting No-Power Problems

You push the power button on the PC, and nothing happens. It's completely lifeless — no fan, no lights, no nothing. What now?

The tricky thing about no-power problems is that a lot of times the problem isn't the obvious thing — the power supply. A variety of other components can cause a system to appear dead to the world. See how much you know about these dead-PC situations.

Test your knowledge of troubleshooting no-power problems:

1. What two physical cable connections are essential for a PC to have power to boot up?

    A. From the _____ to the _____.

    B. From the _____ to the _____.

2. Assuming that those connections from Question 1 are snug, you next want to check what component with a multimeter?

    _____

    _____

3. On an ATX system, what color wire from the power supply to the motherboard represents the Power_Good line?

    _____

    _____

4. What voltage should the Power_Good line show when the PC is powered on?

    _____

5. What voltage should the Power_Good line measure when the PC is powered off?

    _____

6. What setting should the multimeter be set at to test the Power_Good line: AC volts or DC volts?

    _____

7. Which of the following situations can prevent the power supply fan from spinning up? Mark as many as apply.

    A. _____ Monitor powered off

    B. _____ Dead motherboard

    C. _____ Dead display adapter

    D. _____ Incorrect jumper settings on motherboard for installed CPU

    E. _____ Monitor not connected

    F. _____ Keyboard not connected

G. _____ Dead CPU

H. _____ Attached printer powered off

I. _____ UPS powered off

J. _____ No drives installed

K. _____ Legacy COM ports disabled

Exercise 16-1: Dealing with Power Supplies

Even if you aren't having any problems currently with the PC powering on, you might still want to practice troubleshooting by doing the following:

1. Check that a power cord is plugged into the PC's power supply and to a wall outlet, surge suppressor, or UPS. Make sure the connections are snug.

2. Inside the PC case, check that the connector between the power supply and the motherboard is snug.

3. Check the surge suppressor or UPS to which your PC is attached. Does it have a power switch? If so, remember to check its on/off status if you're troubleshooting a no-power situation.

4. Remove the cover from the PC's case, with the PC running.

5. Set your multimeter to DC Volts, and if it isn't an autoranging model, set its upper limit to 20V.

6. Stick the red probe down the back of one of the red wires that runs from the power supply to the motherboard. (Don't unplug the connector from the motherboard).

7. Stick the black probe down the back of one of the black wires. Read the multimeter's display. It should read approximately 5V.

8. Test each of the other wires on the power supply connector.

   You can keep the black probe in the same black wire the whole time; black wires are for grounding only.

Troubleshooting Blank-Screen Errors

Okay, so the power supply fan spins up, and you seem to be getting some sort of electrical juice to the PC. But other than that, nothing.

Blank-screen errors are among the most frustrating to troubleshoot simply because no information is provided. It could be almost anything, from a motherboard problem to a display adapter malfunction to someone playing a prank on you by disconnecting your monitor. Where to start? What to do? See whether you know.

Test your ability to troubleshoot blank-screen situations:

8. Which of the following can cause a situation where the power supply fan spins up but nothing appears on-screen? Mark as many as apply.

A. _____ Monitor powered off

B. _____ Monitor not connected to PC

C. _____ Defective motherboard

D. _____ Incorrect jumper settings on motherboard

E. _____ Wrong voltage supplied on Power_Good pin

F. _____ No cooling fan installed

G. _____ Defective display adapter

H. _____ CRT brightness turned all the way down

I. _____ Keyboard not connected

J. _____ Dead CPU

K. _____ Attached scanner powered off

L. _____ UPS powered off

M. _____ No drives installed

N. _____ Legacy COM ports disabled

9. One of the tools you can use to troubleshoot a blank-screen situation is a POST card.

A. What does POST stand for?

_____

_____

B. What can you find out by using a POST card as the PC is attempting to boot?

_____

_____

C. How does a POST card provide that information to you?

_____

_____

D. How does a POST card connect to a PC?

_____

_____

Exercise 16-2: Working with POST cards

If you have a POST card available, try it out by doing the following:

1. Open up the PC case with the PC turned off.

2. Insert the POST card into an appropriate slot for the model. (Most are PCI.)

3. Boot the PC and watch the LED readout on the POST card.

   The numbers change as it cycles through the boot process.

4. Quickly write down several of the numbers you see during the process.

5. Look up those numbers in the reference manual that came with the POST card.

   These numbers tell you what the problem would have been if the PC had stalled during the boot process with those numbers displayed on the LED.

6. Power off the PC, remove the POST card, and then power it back up again.

Troubleshooting Common System Problems

In this section, you test your knowledge of troubleshooting techniques and tools through a variety of general problem scenarios. These scenarios represent a cross-section of issues that don't specifically have to do with no-power or blank-screen conditions but can still be challenging to diagnose.

See whether you can identify the correct procedures and tools to use in each of the following scenarios:

10. Suppose a user claims that his computer locks up or restarts every day about 15 minutes after he turns it on in the morning, and it continues to give him problems with lockups and restarts all day long. If he turns it off and lets it sit for awhile, it will work fine again for about 15 minutes, and then the problems resume.

A. What do you suspect is causing this?

_____

_____

_____

B. What hardware would you check first?

_____

_____

_____

C. What tools or spare parts would be useful in diagnosing this problem?

_____

_____

_____

11. Suppose an LCD monitor has thin white vertical stripes that affect about ¼ inch of the screen.

A. How can you determine whether this is a problem with the Windows display driver?

_____

_____

_____

B. If this is a desktop PC with an attached LCD monitor, what tools or spare parts would be useful in diagnosing the problem?

_____

_____

_____

C. If this is a notebook LCD screen, what tools or spare parts would be useful in diagnosing the problem?

_____

_____

_____

12. Suppose that a CRT screen's image appears distorted and wavy on one side.

     A. When you boot into Safe Mode, the problem remains. From this, what can you eliminate from suspicion as the cause of the problem?

     _____

     _____

     _____

     B. What external factors can cause distortion on one side of a CRT display?

     _____

     _____

     _____

     C. What monitor setting/feature can you use to eliminate any residual magnetic fields in the CRT that might cause distortion?

     _____

     _____

     _____

13. You just installed a floppy disk drive, and it doesn't work. The light on the front of the drive stays on all the time. What did you do wrong?

     _____

     _____

     _____

14. Suppose a floppy disk drive works fine except that when you remove one floppy disk and insert a different one, Windows and a command prompt file listing both still show the contents of the previous floppy disk. What part needs to be replaced?

     _____

     _____

15. You've just installed Windows 2000 on a home-built PC. Windows recognizes the USB ports as USB 1.1 compliant, but you know from the specs that came with the motherboard that they should be USB 2.0–compliant ports. Would a Windows update be likely to help with this problem? Why or why not?

_____

_____

_____

_____

16. Suppose a system has one hard drive and one DVD drive. The hard drive is the master on IDE0 (PATA), and the DVD drive is the slave on IDE0. You decide to move the DVD drive over to be the master on IDE1 (also PATA). You physically change over the cabling, and you set the jumper on the DVD drive to Master. The system boots up, and the DVD drive is recognized by the BIOS, but the hard drive is not.

A. What have you forgotten to do to the hard drive?

_____

_____

_____

B. Can you do what needs to be done without shutting down the PC?

_____

_____

17. Windows XP boots up to the login screen, but your wireless keyboard is unresponsive.

A. Check the PC's USB ports. What device must be plugged into one of them for a wireless keyboard to work?

_____

_____

B. Suppose that you've verified the physical connectivity in the preceding question. What should you check next?

_____

_____

18. On an older system, data CDs work just fine in the CD drive, but music CDs don't play. The owner of the PC says that music CDs have never played through the PC's speakers. However, he can attach headphones directly to the jack on the front of the drive to hear the music.

A. What is missing?

_____

B. After acquiring the missing part, how will you attach it?

_____

Exercise 16-3: Diagnosing Hardware Issues

This exercise requires the help of a techie friend or a lab partner.

Take turns "sabotaging" the hardware on each other's PCs in harmless, temporary ways while the other person isn't looking. Then trade back and see how quickly you can identify the problem.

Here are some suggestions for problems to create:

✔ Put a ribbon cable on a device or on the motherboard backwards, if the connector isn't keyed to disallow that.

✔ Disconnect or loosen a cable connection to a drive or peripheral.

✔ Disconnect the power to a drive.

✔ Partially unseat an expansion card.

✔ Change a jumper setting on an expansion card or the motherboard. (Be careful, though, not to change a jumper setting that involves voltage, or you could fry the CPU.)

✔ Partially unseat a stick of RAM.

Troubleshooting Problems with Peripheral Devices

This section rounds out the review of hardware troubleshooting by taking a look at some scenarios involving peripherals (that is, stuff that isn't inside the PC case). In many cases, a problem with a peripheral is actually a problem with the driver for the device, rather than the device itself, but you never know until you dive into it.

PRACTICE

19. Suppose your wireless keyboard works great in Windows, but you can't use it to enter the BIOS Setup program. What can you do?

_____

_____

_____

_____

20. A user complains that his CRT monitor, which has always worked fine before, suddenly looks like it has a strong purple tinge, and there is no green at all in the display. Upon questioning him, you find out that the problem started right after he moved his PC to a different office. What's the "easy fix" to check for first?

_____

_____

21. A user complains that after a lightning storm, his cable modem has stopped working, and the usual lights on the front aren't illuminated. Instead, a couple of the lights flash on and off intermittently. What's the first thing he should try before assuming it is damaged and returning the unit?

_____

_____

22. A user complains that when she connects her portable music player to the USB port on the front of her PC, nothing happens. Windows doesn't see the device.

A. What Windows utility tells you whether the USB root hub is functioning?

_____

_____

B. How can you determine whether the problem is with that one individual USB port or all the USB ports in the system?

_____

_____

C. Suppose you determine that all the USB ports are working correctly, but the device still isn't detected. Assuming that you don't have another portable music player to swap out, what other spare part would be useful to have to swap out?

_____

_____

23. A user complains that his optical mouse has suddenly become very hard to control, and the cursor jumps all over the screen wildly. Is this likely to be a problem with the mouse being dirty? Why or why not?

_____

_____

_____

_____

24. A user complains that her trackball no longer moves the cursor up and down — only side to side. Is this likely to be a problem with the trackball's driver? Why or why not?

_____

_____

_____

_____

Answers to Troubleshooting Hardware Problems

The following are the answers to the practice questions presented earlier in this chapter:

1. **What two physical cable connections are essential for a PC to have power to boot up?**

   A. From the <u>wall outlet</u> to the <u>power supply</u>.

   B. From the <u>power supply</u> to the <u>motherboard</u>.

2. **Assuming that those connections from Question 1 are snug, you next want to check what component with a multimeter?**

   Power supply

3. **On an ATX system, what color wire from the power supply to the motherboard represents the Power_Good line?**

   Gray

4. **What voltage should the Power_Good line show when the PC is powered on?**

   +5V (acceptable range is +3V to +6V)

5. **What voltage should the Power_Good line measure when the PC is powered off?**

   None

6. **What setting should the multimeter be set at to test the Power_Good line: AC volts or DC volts?**

   DC volts

7. **Which of the following situations can prevent the power supply fan from spinning up,? Mark as many as apply.**

   A. _____ Monitor powered off

   B. __X__ Dead motherboard

   C. __X__ Dead display adapter

   D. __X__ Incorrect jumper settings on motherboard for installed CPU

   E. _____ Monitor not connected

   F. _____ Keyboard not connected

   G. __X__ Dead CPU

   H. _____ Attached printer powered off

   I. _____ UPS powered off

   J. _____ No drives installed

   K. _____ Legacy COM ports disabled

8. **Which of the following could cause a situation where the power supply fan spins up but nothing appears on-screen? Mark as many as apply.**

   A. __X__ Monitor powered off

   B. __X__ Monitor not connected to PC

   C. __X__ Defective motherboard

   D. __X__ Incorrect jumper settings on motherboard

   E. _____ Wrong voltage supplied on Power_Good pin

   F. _____ No cooling fan installed

   G. __X__ Defective display adapter

   H. __X__ CRT brightness turned all the way down

   I. _____ Keyboard not connected

   J. _____ Dead CPU

   K. _____ Attached scanner powered off

   L. _____ UPS powered off

   M. _____ No drives installed

   N. _____ Legacy COM ports disabled

9. **One of the tools you can use to troubleshoot a blank-screen situation is a POST card.**

   A. **What does POST stand for?**

   Power-On Self Test

   B. **What can you find out by using a POST card as the PC is attempting to boot?**

   You can find out at what process during the POST the boot process is stalling.

   C. **How does a POST card provide that information to you?**

   It provides a two-digit numeric code, which you then look up in a command reference.

   D. **How does a POST card connect to a PC?**

   It fits into an expansion slot in the motherboard (usually PCI).

10. **Suppose a user claims that his computer locks up or restarts every day about 15 minutes after he turns it on in the morning, and it continues to give him problems with lockups and restarts all day long. If he turns it off and lets it sit for awhile, it will work fine again for about 15 minutes, and then the problems resume.**

    A. **What do you suspect is causing this?**

    Overheating, probably caused by a defective fan

    B. **What hardware would you check first?**

    Check the fans to make sure they're all operating.

    C. **What tools or spare parts would be useful in diagnosing this problem?**

    Extra fans to replace any defective ones would be useful. Canned compressed air might also be useful for cooling down a chip to verify that overheating was the problem.

11. Suppose an LCD monitor has thin white vertical stripes that affect about ¼ inch of the screen.

A. How can you determine whether this is a problem with the Windows display driver?

You can boot the PC in Safe Mode, which uses a generic VGA monitor driver. You can also observe whether the stripes remain on-screen during the text mode portion of the boot process.

B. If this is a desktop PC with an attached LCD monitor, what tools or spare parts would be useful in diagnosing the problem?

An extra monitor would be useful to swap out with the current monitor to check whether the monitor is the problem. If you determine that the monitor isn't at fault, a spare display adapter card would be useful for swapping out.

C. If this is a notebook LCD screen, what tools or spare parts would be useful in diagnosing the problem?

On a notebook PC, the display adapter and monitor are both built-in, so it's difficult to swap them out. You can connect an external monitor via the VGA or DVI port, however, to check whether the problem is with the built-in monitor. The built-in monitor uses the same display adapter as is fed by the external monitor ports on the notebook PC, so if the problem occurs on both monitors, you have narrowed down the problem to the display adapter.

12. Suppose that a CRT screen's image appears distorted and wavy on one side.

A. When you boot into Safe Mode, the problem remains. From this, what can you eliminate from suspicion as the cause of the problem?

The display adapter

B. What external factors can cause distortion on one side of a CRT display?

Typically it's a magnetic field of some sort, such as unshielded speakers being too close to the side of the monitor. It could also be magnetic disturbance built up in the monitor (in which case, degaussing would help), or it could be that you're running the monitor in a higher refresh rate than it can support at the current resolution.

C. What monitor setting/feature can you use to eliminate any residual magnetic fields in the CRT that might cause distortion?

Degaussing

13. You just installed a floppy disk drive, and it doesn't work. The light on the front of the drive stays on all the time. What did you do wrong?

The ribbon cable is connected backwards at one end or the other.

14. Suppose a floppy disk drive works fine except that when you remove one floppy disk and insert a different one, Windows and a command prompt file listing both still show the contents of the previous floppy disk. What part needs to be replaced?

Replace the floppy drive cable; one of the wires is broken in the current cable.

15. You've just installed Windows 2000 on a home-built PC. Windows recognizes the USB ports as USB 1.1 compliant, but you know from the specs that came with the motherboard that they should be USB 2.0–compliant ports. Would a Windows update be likely to help with this problem? Why or why not?

It might help; a service pack for Windows 2000 adds USB 2.0 support. If the problem is that Windows isn't up to date, that could solve the problem. You might also check whether there are drivers available for the motherboard's chipset that would add USB 2.0 support.

16. Suppose a system has one hard drive and one DVD drive. The hard drive is the master on IDE0 (PATA), and the DVD drive is the slave on IDE0. You decide to move the DVD drive over to be the master on IDE1 (also PATA). You physically change over the cabling, and you set the jumper on the DVD drive to Master. The system boots up, and the DVD drive is recognized by the BIOS, but the hard drive isn't.

A. What have you forgotten to do to the hard drive?

The hard drive might have a separate setting for Single versus Master. If so, you have forgotten to switch it over to Single.

B. Can you do what needs to be done without shutting down the PC?

No. Drive jumpers must be moved while the PC is off.

17. Windows XP boots up to the login screen, but your wireless keyboard is unresponsive.

A. Check the PC's USB ports. What device must be plugged into one of them for a wireless keyboard to work?

A USB transmitter (RF, Bluetooth, or Infrared) must be attached to the PC so that the PC has a way of communicating with the wireless device.

B. Suppose that you've verified the physical connectivity in the preceding question. What should you check next?

Next, do a synchronize operation between the device and the transmitter. This usually involves pressing a button on each.

18. On an older system, data CDs work just fine in the CD drive, but music CDs don't play. The owner of the PC says that music CDs have never played through the PC's speakers. However, he can attach headphones directly to the jack on the front of the drive to hear the music.

A. What is missing?

An audio cable

B. After acquiring the missing part, how will you attach it?

One end to the sound card and the other to the back of the CD drive

19. Suppose your wireless keyboard works great in Windows, but you can't use it to enter the BIOS Setup program. What can you do?

USB ports have limited functionality until the operating system is loaded. Some BIOS Setup programs have a Legacy USB setting that can be enabled to allow better USB support outside of Windows, but generally, you will want to keep a wired keyboard on hand to talk to a PC's BIOS Setup program when needed.

20. **A user complains that his CRT monitor, which has always worked fine before, suddenly looks like it has a strong purple tinge, and there is no green at all in the display. Upon questioning him, you find out that the problem started right after he moved his PC to a different office. What's the "easy fix" to check for first?**

    When one color disappears like that, it is usually because the monitor plug isn't firmly seated or because there is a bent or broken pin in the connector at one end. Check the cable and bend any pins back into place that have gotten bent.

21. **A user complains that after a lightning storm, his cable modem has stopped working, and the usual lights on the front aren't illuminated. Instead, a couple of the lights flash on and off intermittently. What's the first thing he should try before assuming it is damaged and returning the unit?**

    The first thing to try is to turn it off (unplug if needed), wait 15 seconds, and turn it back on again. You might also need to power the router off and on (if there is one) and the PC.

22. **A user complains that when she connects her portable music player to the USB port on the front of her PC, nothing happens. Windows doesn't see the device.**

    A. **What Windows utility tells you whether the USB root hub is functioning?**

       Device Manager

    B. **How can you determine whether the problem is with that one individual USB port or all the USB ports in the system?**

       Connect the device to each of the ports in turn to see whether it makes any difference.

    C. **Suppose you determine that all the USB ports are working correctly, but the device still isn't detected. Assuming that you don't have another portable music player to swap out, what other spare part would be useful to have to swap out?**

       The cable that connects the device to the PC might be faulty; try swapping it if possible.

23. **A user complains that his optical mouse has suddenly become very hard to control, and the cursor jumps all over the screen wildly. Is this likely to be a problem with the mouse being dirty? Why or why not?**

    No, this is probably not a "dirty" problem because it's an optical mouse (no ball) and because the cursor jumping around wildly is usually a symptom of a problem with the display adapter driver, not the mouse.

24. **A user complains that her trackball no longer moves the cursor up and down — only side to side. Is this likely to be a problem with the trackball's driver? Why or why not?**

    No, this isn't likely to be a driver problem. It's almost certainly a problem with the trackball unit itself. The up/down roller is broken or is so dirty that its contacts aren't registering. Clean it thoroughly and try again. If the problem persists, replace the unit.

Chapter 17

Troubleshooting Boot and Startup Problems

his chapter looks at troubleshooting as it relates to the myriad reasons why a Windows PC doesn't start up normally. The problems can involve hardware, Windows, applications, drivers, the Registry, or any number of other factors, so you need to be ready for almost anything.

Troubleshooting Missing or Corrupt Startup File Issues

Windows needs many different files to be available in order to start up correctly. If any one of them is missing or corrupted, the process fails.

If a file is completely missing (for example, if a user deleted it), Windows generally provides an error message letting you know which file it can't find. If the file is corrupted, though, it's a crapshoot — you might get an error message, or the system might simply lock up during the boot process. If you know the boot sequence for the Windows version you're using, as reviewed in Chapter 15, or if you can log or step through the boot process, you might be able to tell which file is causing the problem and replace it from the Windows Setup CD. You might also be able to use the System File Checker to scan the protected system files and replace any incorrect versions it finds.

PRACTICE

See how much you know about missing and corrupt startup file problems:

1. Suppose you can determine what Windows system file is missing or corrupted, and you have the Windows CD. You review the CD's contents using another computer, but you don't see the file you want. Why not?

_____

_____

_____

2. How can you browse the contents of a CAB file in Windows?

_____

_____

_____

3. What command-line utility extracts files from CABs at a command prompt or in the Recovery Console?

_____

4. Suppose you want to extract the file IIS_winxp.gif from d:\i386\iis6.cab to the root of the C: drive. What command syntax should you use?

_____

_____

5. What executable file runs the System File Checker from a command line?

_____

6. What command-line syntax would you use to run the System File Checker so that you could scan the integrity of all protected system files and (when possible) make repairs?

_____

_____

Exercise 17-1: Working with the System File Checker

Follow these steps to try out the System File Checker utility on your system:

1. Open a command prompt window.

2. Type **sfc /?** to see the command-line syntax help for the System File Checker.

   Depending on the Windows version you have, the syntax will be different. In particular, the switches are very different between Windows XP and Windows Vista.

3. If you have Windows Vista, type **sfc /verifyonly** to check system files without making any changes to them. Wait for the results of the test.

OR

If you have Windows XP, type **sfc /scannow** to check system files and repair them if needed. (Windows XP doesn't have the /verifyonly option.)

4. If you have your Windows Setup CD, insert it in the drive and browse it in Windows Explorer. Locate a cabinet file (.cab extension) and double-click it to see what's inside it. If you don't have the required CD, stop the exercise here.

5. Drag a file out of the cabinet listing and onto the desktop.

This is one way to extract a file from a compressed archive (cabinet).

6. Open a command prompt window and, using the EXPAND command, expand the same file you extracted in Step 5 to the root directory of your hard drive.

Creating an Emergency Repair Disk

An Emergency Repair Disk (ERD) is *not* a bootable disk (remember that for the test!), but rather a helper disk that works with the Windows NT, 2000, or XP Setup program to repair a damaged Windows installation. When you boot into the Windows Setup program, you have an option for repairing the current Windows installation, and at some point during that repair process, the program asks whether you have an Emergency Repair Disk. If you do, you pop it in, or you point the program to the location containing those files, and it reads them and does a better job repairing than it otherwise would.

ERDs were very useful for Windows NT and 2000, but for Windows XP, all the needed files won't fit on a floppy, so you can't create an ERD floppy. Instead, the Windows XP emergency repair process stores its backup copy of the registry files in the Windows folder. You can still use those backups to repair a system by pointing the path to that folder, provided the hard drive hasn't failed, but there's not really a *D* in ERD anymore.

See whether you know how to create ERDs:

7. What is the command for creating an ERD in Windows NT?

_____

8. The command in Question 7, when used alone, doesn't update SAM or SECURITY. What switch can you add to force it to do so?

_____

9. After the command in Question 7 runs under Windows NT, you must manually copy the files from the folder it creates to a floppy disk. Where is that folder located on the hard drive?

_____

_____

10. In Windows 2000, you can write the files for an ERD directly onto a floppy by using what Windows GUI-based utility program?

_____

Exercise 17-2: Creating an Emergency Repair Disk

Do the following to create an ERD in Windows 2000:

1. Start the Backup utility (Start⇨All Programs⇨Accessories⇨System⇨Tools⇨Backup).

2. On the Welcome tab, click the option to create an Emergency Repair Disk.

3. Follow the prompts to create the ERD.

Exercise 17-3: Using an Emergency Repair Disk

Here's an exercise for using the ERD during a Windows repair:

1. If needed, set up the BIOS to boot first from the CD. Then restart the PC from the Windows 2000 CD-ROM.

2. At the setup program's opening screen, press R to Repair.

3. Press R to start the emergency repair process.

4. Press F to select Fast Repair.

5. At the prompt, press Enter to indicate that you have an ERD available.

6. Insert the ERD floppy and press Enter.

7. Follow the prompts to allow the setup program to repair Windows.

Using the Recovery Console

Windows 9x enables you to make a startup floppy that will let you work from a command-line interface to perform repairs on a Windows system that won't boot normally. Windows NT, 2000, XP, and Vista don't have that capability because their startup files are so radically different. (See Chapter 15 for more on the Windows 9x/Everything After Windows 9x divide.) But that doesn't mean you're out in the cold. You can boot into a command-line interface called the Recovery Console to do much of the same things that you can do with a Win9x floppy.

You have two ways of getting into the Recovery Console. You can boot from the Windows Setup CD and choose the Recovery Console as an option in the Setup utility, or you can install the Recovery Console on your hard drive so that it's an option every time you boot. (If you do the latter, a boot menu appears every time you start the PC, so you can choose between booting Windows or booting into the Recovery Console.)

In the Recovery Console, you can use most of the familiar commands for file management, such as ATTRIB, CD, MD, COPY, DEL, CHKDSK, DIR, EXIT, EXPAND, FORMAT, MD, RD, and RN. You can also use extra commands that are specific to the Recovery Console, such as BATCH, DISABLE, DISKPART, ENABLE, FIXBOOT, FIXMBR, and LISTSYS.

TIP

Extensive Recovery Console familiarity isn't required for the A+ exam; you should simply know what it is, how to get into and out of it, and how to issue basic commands through its interface.

PRACTICE

Test your knowledge of starting and using the Recovery Console:

11. Assuming that your CD-ROM drive is `E:`, what command installs the Recovery Console on your hard drive from the Windows 2000 or XP Setup CD?

_____

_____

12. What can you type at the Recovery Console's command prompt to get a list of valid commands?

_____

Match up the following commands available in the Recovery Console with their purposes.

    A. BATCH

    B. DISABLE

    C. DISKPART

    D. ENABLE

    E. FIXBOOT

    F. FIXMBR

    G. LISTSVC

    H. CHKDSK

    I. EXPAND

    J. EXIT

    K. MD

13. _____ Manages hard drive partitions; roughly equivalent to FDISK

14. _____ Lists all the available drivers, services, and startup types

15. _____ Creates a new folder

16. _____ Quits the Recovery Console

17. _____ Enables a particular Windows service or driver

18. _____ Writes a new boot sector on the boot partition

19. _____ Extracts a file from a CAB

20. _____ Checks a disk for file system errors

21. _____ Executes batch commands in a specified text file

22. _____ Repairs the master boot record on the disk

23. _____ Disables a particular Windows service or driver

Exercise 17-4: Installing the Recovery Console

Do the following to install the Recovery Console on your hard drive:

1. While Windows is running normally, insert the Windows CD in the drive. If a window opens automatically for the CD, close it.

2. Use the Run command to run `x:\i386\win32 /cmdcons`, where *x* is the drive letter of your CD drive, and click OK.

3. At the confirmation that appears, click Yes.

4. After the installation, another confirmation appears; click OK.

Exercise 17-5: Booting Into (And Trying Out) the Recovery Console

You need to do the following to boot into the Recovery Console from your hard drive:

1. Restart the PC. When the menu appears asking what you want to start, press the number on the menu that corresponds to the Recovery Console.

2. Press 1 and press Enter to select the first Windows installation on the system.

3. If prompted for the administrator password, type it and press Enter.

   You are now at a `C:\WINNT` or `C:\Windows` command prompt.

Then try out the Recovery Console by doing the following:

1. Type **DIR** and press Enter to see a file listing.

2. Type **LISTSVC** and press Enter to see a list of services.

3. Type **CHKDSK** and press Enter to check the disk for errors.

4. Type **EXIT** to leave the Recovery Console and then reboot normally.

Starting Windows in Safe Mode

Safe Mode is one of the alternative boot modes you can choose from the Windows Startup menu. This menu appears automatically the next time you try to boot after Windows fails to start normally. In Safe Mode, a minimal set of drivers loads, including a generic VGA video driver instead of the driver for your particular display adapter. This eliminates most problems with bad drivers preventing Windows from starting. Safe Mode also skips the loading of most programs set to load at startup, which eliminates most problems with bad applications preventing Windows from starting. After you get into Safe Mode, you can then roll back any problematic drivers and uninstall or disable any problematic programs.

The available commands on the Windows Startup menu depend on the Windows version:

Startup Mode	Description	Windows Versions
Safe Mode	Starts with a minimal set of drivers	95, 98, Me, 2000, XP
Safe Mode with Network Support	Same as Safe Mode but includes networking	95, 2000, XP
Safe Mode Command Prompt Only	Boots to a command prompt and bypasses all startup files	95, 98
Safe Mode with Command Prompt	Same as Safe Mode except a command prompt window opens within Safe Mode	2000, XP
VGA Mode / Enable VGA Mode	Starts normally but uses the plain VGA video driver	NT, 2000, XP

See how much you know about working in Safe Mode:

24. If the Windows Startup menu (from which you can choose Safe Mode) doesn't appear automatically, what key can you press as the PC is starting up to force the menu to appear?

_____

25. How can you tell that Windows is in Safe Mode? List at least two visual cues.

_____

_____

26. What type of keyboard can't you use to press F8 to open the Windows Startup menu? Why?

_____

_____

_____

_____

27. In a situation where you can't press F8 to get to the Windows Startup menu, you might still be able to get into Safe Mode. If you can start Windows at all (even if it isn't running properly), what utility can you use to force a Safe Mode boot the next time the PC starts up?

_____

28. After booting into Safe Mode, what utility can you use to roll back a device driver that was causing a problem?

_____

29. After booting into Safe Mode, what utility can you use to prevent a certain program from loading at startup?

_____

30. After booting into Safe Mode, what utility can you use to set a certain service to not start automatically at startup?

_____

Exercise 17-6: Working in Safe Mode

Do the following to experiment with Safe Mode:

1. Boot into Safe Mode.

If you have a wired keyboard, you can boot into Safe Mode by pressing F8 as the PC starts up.

The timing can be tricky for pressing F8. If you just hold it down, you get a Keyboard Stuck error. Try pressing it at one-second intervals as soon as you hear the power supply fan start spinning up. The ideal time to press F8 for the menu is when you hear the single beep as the PC starts up, but unless you're really quick, you'll miss the window of opportunity, so pressing and releasing F8 repeatedly is usually your best bet.

If your keyboard is wireless, do the following:

 a. In Windows, choose Start⇨Run, type **MSCONFIG** into the Run dialog box, and then click OK.

 b. In the System Configuration Utility, on the BOOT.INI tab, select the /SAFEBOOT check box.

 c. Click OK and reboot.

2. Open the My Computer window. Check to see whether your CD drive appears there.

In Safe Mode, the drive appears in some Windows versions but not others.

3. In the Control Panel, open the Sounds and Audio Devices Properties dialog box.

Notice that all the controls for the sounds are unavailable; that's because the sound card driver isn't loaded. Other devices might appear with reduced functionality too.

4. In the Control Panel, open System and click the Device Manager button (located on the Hardware tab). Examine the devices.

Is anything out of the ordinary? Probably not; even though not all device drivers load, the devices still appear here so that you can work with their drivers.

5. Display the properties for a device and display its Driver tab.

Note the Roll Back Driver button there. That's what you'd use if you needed to remove a newly installed driver that was causing problems.

6. In the Control Panel, open Administrative Tools and then Services. Sort the list of services by the Status column.

   Notice that there are very few services running. (If you come back here later, when Windows has booted normally, many more services will be running.)

7. Look in the Startup Type column.

   Services that have a type of Manual won't start automatically; if you were having a problem with a certain service, you could set it to Manual here.

8. Restart the PC normally.

Disabling Programs That Load at Startup

Lots of Windows startup errors are caused by a particular program trying to load but having a problem because of missing hardware files, file corruption, or the program itself being malware. If you can at least boot into Safe Mode, you can troubleshoot by systematically disabling the optional startup items one by one until you find out which one has been causing the problem.

Check your knowledge of disabling startup programs:

31. As Windows boots, it automatically runs programs with shortcuts found in which folder on the Start menu?

    _____

32. When you delete a shortcut from the folder from Question 31, how is the original executable file affected?

    _____

33. From the Run command, what utility can you run to disable certain startup programs?

    _____

34. Within that utility from Question 33, on which tab do you clear the check boxes for unwanted programs?

    _____

35. Suppose you're manually editing the Registry to remove a program that stubbornly persists in loading at startup, even after you disabled it. If you delete the reference to that program from HKEY_LOCAL_MACHINE\SOFTWARE\Microsoft\Windows\CurrentVersion\Run, will it affect all users of this PC or only the current user?

    _____

Exercise 17-7: Enabling and Disabling Programs at Startup

Do the following to examine the programs loading at startup and experiment with enabling and disabling them:

1. Choose Start⇨Run, type **%userprofile%\Start Menu\Programs\Startup** into the Run dialog box and then click OK.

   This step opens the folder for the current user's StartUp folder on the Start menu. You can delete shortcuts from here if needed.

2. Choose Start⇨Run, type **%allusersprofile%\Start Menu\Programs\Startup** into the Run dialog box and then click OK.

   This opens the folder for the global (all users) StartUp folder. You can also delete shortcuts from here if needed.

3. From the Run command, run MSCONFIG.

4. On the General tab, notice the options. (Don't select either of these now.)

   • **Selecting Normal Startup** selects all the cleared check boxes on the Startup tab.

   • **Selecting Diagnostic Startup** deselects all check boxes on the Startup tab.

If you accidentally select either of the preceding options and then change your mind about wanting to globally enable or disable everything, click Cancel to close MSCONFIG without saving your changes. Then reopen MSCONFIG.

5. On the Startup tab, select the check box for something that you don't want to load.

   Don't pick anything important (such as antivirus software); pick a program like QuickTime, Adobe Acrobat Launcher, or something related to a reminder.

   If you aren't sure what something is, enlarge the Command column so that you can see what folder it's running from; the folder can often give you a clue.

6. Click OK and, when prompted, click Restart. When the PC restarts, you might see a warning about selective startup; click OK to move past it.

   The warning is normal. If you want, you can select the check box in that dialog box to prevent it from redisplaying every time you restart.

7. Confirm that the program whose check box you cleared didn't load automatically.

   You might notice a difference in the icons in the notification area, for example.

8. Display the Task Manager (right-click the taskbar and click Task Manager) and look on the Processes tab. Confirm that the program isn't running there.

9. From the Run command, run MSCONFIG one more time and turn the program from Step 5 back on again on the Startup tab.

10. Restart the PC normally.

Setting and Using a Restore Point

System Restore is a utility that makes regular backups of the Registry and other system settings so that if something goes awry, you can go back to that earlier system configuration. Windows Me, XP, and Vista all come with System Restore; earlier versions of Windows do not.

A System Restore point is a wonderful thing to have when you install some harmless-looking program that turns out to be virulent malware, or when installing a new application makes some other application begin to misbehave. Just go through the System Restore utility and tell it what point to restore. After a reboot, it's like the unfortunate incident never happened.

If a virus has infected the system, you should turn off System Restore before removing the virus. Turning off System Restore deletes all saved restore points. Otherwise, the virus could infect the PC from a restore point that was created after the initial infection occurred.

Check your knowledge of the System Restore feature:

36. What is the Start menu path for starting System Restore?

_____

37. To set System Restore options, you need to use the System Restore tab. In which Control Panel applet is this tab located?

_____

38. When restoring the system to an earlier time, a calendar appears from which you can select a date, and then within that date, you can select a System Restore point that was created on that date. What does it mean if a particular date is bold on that calendar?

_____

39. Suppose you create a System Restore point, install Microsoft Word, and then create a document called `Notes.doc` and save it in the My Documents folder. Then you use System Restore to revert to a restore that was created before Microsoft Word was installed.

A. Will the file `Notes.doc` be available in the My Documents folder?

_____

B. Will the program files for Word still be on the hard drive?

_____

C. Will you be able to run Word from the Start menu?

_____

40. Now suppose you use System Restore to go forward again, to the time after you installed Word, and then reboot the PC.

A. Will the file Notes.doc be available in the My Documents folder?

_____

B. Will you be able to run Word from the Start menu?

_____

Exercise 17-8: Working with System Restore

Try out System Restore:

1. Start System Restore and set a restore point. Name it Before Desktop Changes.

2. Change the desktop background color.

3. Rearrange some items on the Start menu by dragging them up or down there.

4. Use System Restore to restore the point you created. When prompted to reboot, do so.

   When Windows reboots, none of the changes you made in Steps 2 and 3 are in effect.

5. Use System Restore to reverse the restore you just did.

   When you did the restore, System Restore took another snapshot of your system, so you can restore that snapshot.

   When Windows reboots, your earlier changes once again appear.

Answers to Questions in This Chapter

The following are the answers to the practice questions presented earlier in this chapter:

1. **Suppose you can determine what Windows system file is missing or corrupted, and you have the Windows CD. You review the CD's contents using another computer, but you don't see the file you want. Why not?**

   It's in a compressed archive, a cabinet (.cab) file.

2. **How can you browse the contents of a CAB file in Windows?**

   Double-click the CAB file to open it as a folder.

3. **What command-line utility extracts files from CABs at a command prompt or in the Recovery Console?**

   expand.exe

4. **Suppose you want to extract the file IIS_winxp.gif from d:\i386\iis6.cab to the root of the C: drive. What command syntax should you use?**

   expand.exe D:\i386\iis6.cab -F iis_winxp.gif C:\

5. **What executable file runs the System File Checker from a command line?**

   sfc.exe

6. **What command-line syntax would you use to run the System File Checker so that you could scan the integrity of all protected system files and (when possible) make repairs?**

   sfc /scannow

7. **What is the command for creating an ERD in Windows NT?**

   rdisk.exe

8. **The command in Question 7, when used alone, doesn't update SAM or SECURITY. What switch can you add to force it to do so?**

   /s

9. **After the command in Question 7 runs under Windows NT, you must manually copy the files from the folder it creates to a floppy disk. Where is that folder located on the hard drive?**

   C:\Windows\repair, or whatever the path to your Windows folder is, if it's different than that. This is typically written as %systemroot% or %windir% in most technical documentation, like this: %winroot%\repair.

10. **In Windows 2000, you can write the files for an ERD directly onto a floppy by using what Windows GUI-based utility program?**

    Microsoft Backup

11. **Assuming that your CD-ROM drive is `E:`, what command installs the Recovery Console on your hard drive from the Windows 2000 or XP Setup CD?**

    `E:\i386\winnt32 /cmdcons`

12. **What can you type at the Recovery Console's command prompt to get a list of valid commands?**

    HELP

13. C

14. G

15. K

16. J

17. D

18. E

19. I

20. H

21. A

22. F

23. B

24. **If the Windows Startup menu (from which you can choose Safe Mode) doesn't appear automatically, what key can you press as the PC is starting up to force the menu to appear?**

    F8

25. **How can you tell that Windows is in Safe Mode? List at least two visual cues.**

    The display is 640 x 480 16 colors (VGA), the words Safe Mode appear in the corners, and the Windows version number appears at the top of the screen. A Help window might also appear, depending on the Windows version.

26. **What type of keyboard can't you use to press F8 to open the Windows Startup menu? Why?**

    You can't use a wireless USB keyboard because the wireless adapter doesn't work until Windows loads, and you must press F8 before Windows loads.

27. **In a situation where you can't press F8 to get to the Windows Startup menu, you might still be able to get into Safe Mode. If you can start Windows at all (even if it isn't running properly), what utility can you use to force a Safe Mode boot the next time the PC starts up?**

    MSCONFIG, on the BOOT.INI tab

28. **After booting into Safe Mode, what utility can you use to roll back a device driver that was causing a problem?**

   Device Manager

29. **After booting into Safe Mode, what utility can you use to prevent a certain program from loading at startup?**

   MSCONFIG (the System Configuration Utility)

30. **After booting into Safe Mode, what utility can you use to set a certain service to not start automatically at startup?**

   `Services.exe`, from the Administrative Tools applet in the Control Panel

31. **As Windows boots, it automatically runs programs with shortcuts found in which folder on the Start menu?**

   The StartUp folder

32. **When you delete a shortcut from the folder from Question 31, how is the original executable file affected?**

   It is not affected at all.

33. **From the Run command, what utility can you run to disable certain startup programs?**

   MSCONFIG (the System Configuration Utility)

34. **Within that utility from Question 33, on which tab do you clear the check boxes for unwanted programs?**

   Startup

35. **Suppose you're manually editing the Registry to remove a program that stubbornly persists in loading at startup, even after you disabled it. If you delete the reference to that program from `HKEY_LOCAL_MACHINE\SOFTWARE\Microsoft\Windows\CurrentVersion\Run`, will it affect all users of this PC, or only the current user?**

   All users. If you wanted to affect only the current user, you would make the change from `HKEY_CURRENT_USER\SOFTWARE\Microsoft\Windows\CurrentVersion\Run`.

36. **What is the Start menu path for starting System Restore?**

   Start⇨All Programs⇨Accessories⇨System Tools⇨System Restore

37. **To set System Restore options, you need to use the System Restore tab. In which Control Panel applet is this tab located?**

   System

38. **When restoring the system to an earlier time, a calendar appears from which you can select a date, and then within that date, you can select a system restore point that was created on that date. What does it mean if a particular date is bold on that calendar?**

   A bold date means a restore point is available for that date.

39. Suppose you create a system restore point, install Microsoft Word, and then create a document called Notes.doc and save it in the My Documents folder. Then you use System Restore to revert to a restore that was created before Microsoft Word was installed.

    A. Will the file Notes.doc be available in the My Documents folder?

    Yes, System Restore doesn't delete data files.

    B. Will the program files for Word still be on the hard drive?

    Yes, System Restore doesn't delete program files.

    C. Will you be able to run Word from the Start menu?

    No, because all references to Word have been removed from the Registry.

40. Now suppose you use System Restore to go forward again, to the time after you installed Word, and then reboot the PC.

    A. Will the file Notes.doc be available in the My Documents folder?

    Yes, it never left.

    B. Will you be able to run Word from the Start menu?

    Yes, because the Registry has been restored to a version that knows Word is installed.

Part V
Networking

In this part . . .

These chapters look at networking theory and practice. You make sure you're up to date on networking terminology, and you practice setting up and troubleshooting Windows networking and Internet access. This part also looks at some basic security and privacy settings in Windows that might affect a user's ability to safely surf the Net.

Chapter 18

Understanding and Selecting Network Types

Most business PCs — and some home PCs, too — are part of one or more networks, and a good technician should be able to identify network types, configure network hardware and software, and connect and disconnect PCs from the network. The A+ exam expects you to understand the types of networks available and to select the appropriate network type and its associated hardware.

Understanding Client/Server and Peer-to-Peer Networks

Network is a very generic term that refers to a group of PCs and other devices that are connected for sharing data or devices. Under that broad umbrella are two main types of networks:

✔ **Client/server:** A network that consists of one or more *servers,* which are PCs dedicated to the running of the network, and one or more *clients,* which are ordinary desktop or notebook PCs.

✔ **Peer-to-peer:** A network that consists only of clients. Each client shares in the burden of maintaining the network connectivity. No PCs are dedicated to network administration.

Check your knowledge of the features and appropriate uses of peer-to-peer and client/server networks:

1. Which type of network is most appropriate in the following situations? Write *C* next to the descriptions for which client/server is most appropriate, and write *P* next to the descriptions where peer-to-peer is most appropriate.

   A. _____ A business has 25 PCs that all need to access a central database.

   B. _____ A home has 3 PCs that need to share a single DSL Internet connection.

   C. _____ A company has over 2,000 PCs that need to share printers, files, and Internet connectivity.

   D. _____ A business has 8 individual-user PCs that need to share a single printer.

   E. _____ A business has 8 PCs that are shared by 24 users, 8 on each shift. A user might use a different PC each time he or she logs in.

2. Which type of network is cheapest to create?

   _____

3. Which type of network requires a network operating system (NOS)?

   _____

4. Which type of network maintains user logins separately on each individual PC?

   _____

5. Which type of network is more secure?

   _____

Exercise 18-1: Verifying Network Types

1. If your computer is on a network, determine which type of network it is: client/server or peer-to-peer. Here are some things to look for:

   • Open the System Properties dialog box from the Control Panel and look for a workgroup or domain name. A workgroup name indicates a peer-to-peer network; a domain name indicates client/server.

   • Estimate the number of PCs in the network. A network with more than ten PCs is usually client/server.

   • Is there a system administrator or an IT department? If so, the network is probably client/server.

2. If possible, visit a business or organization that has the other type of network and examine it using the same criteria.

Understanding Network Topologies

A *topology* is a layout. It can be either a physical layout, as in what plugs into what, or a logical layout, as in how data is passed from point to point.

A lot of people get tripped up on topologies because a network's physical topology — that is, its physical layout — can be different from the way data is passed in that network. For example, an Ethernet network is logically a bus, but physically it can be either a bus or a star. In this section, I'm talking only about the physical topology.

For each of the following pictures, fill out the information requested:

6. Topology #1

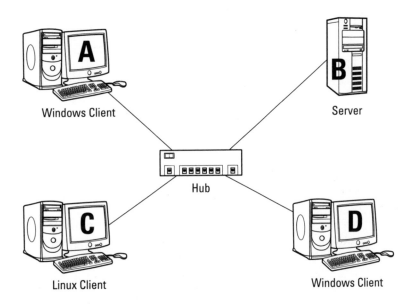

A. What type of topology is this?

_____

B. If PC A goes down, will PC C go down too?

_____

C. If PC A has data to send to PC C, will it go only to C, or will all the other PCs get it too?

_____

D. This topology can also be implemented with devices other than hubs at the center. Name two other devices that could be used instead of a hub.

_____

7. Topology #2

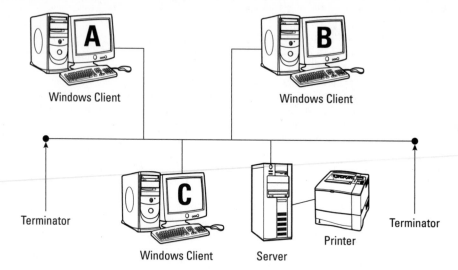

A. What type of topology is this?

_____

B. If PC A goes down, will PC C go down too?

_____

C. If PC A has data to send to PC C, will it go only to C, or will all the other PCs get it too?

_____

D. Will the network still work if the terminators were removed from the ends of the chain?

_____

8. Topology #3

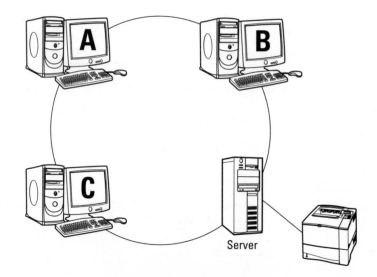

A. What type of topology is this?

_____

B. If the connection is broken between PCs A and C, will PC A be able to access PC B?

_____

9. Topology #4

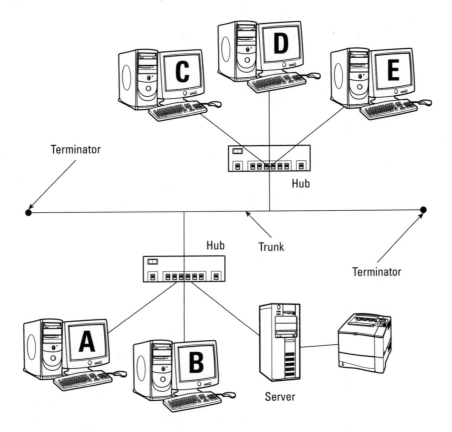

A. What type of topology is this?

_____

B. Which two other topologies does this combine?

_____

C. If PC A wants to send a message to PC E, will the fact that PC B is disconnected be a problem?

_____

Exercise 18-2: Defining Network Topologies

1. Identify the physical topology of your network.

2. Trace the physical connections of your wired network and draw a diagram illustrating the connections. Include not only the PCs but also any connection boxes such as routers, switches, and hubs. If it's a very large network, draw only your local segment. Use this space:

Identifying Network Cables

As part of building a network, you need to be able to select the appropriate cables. You need to be able not only to identify the cable types by sight but also to distinguish between cables that look physically identical but conform to different standards.

10. In the following picture:

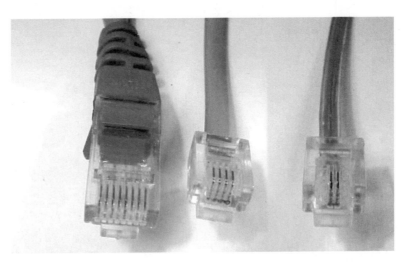

A. What type of cables are these: coaxial, twisted pair, or fiber optic?

_____

B. Circle the cable that will work in an Ethernet network.

11. In the following picture, what type of cables are these: coaxial, twisted pair, or fiber optic?

12. In the following picture:

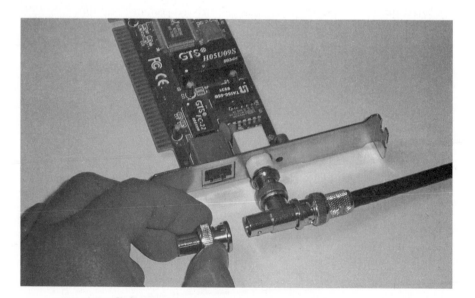

A. What type of network is this card and cable for: 10BaseT, 10Base5 (thicknet), or 10Base2 (thinnet)?

B. What is the purpose of the metal barrel being attached to the left end of the T connector in the picture?

13. In the following picture:

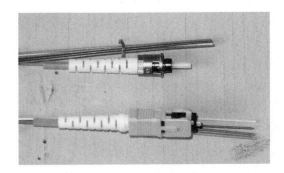

A. What type of cables are these: coaxial, twisted pair, or fiber optic?

B. Circle the Strait Tip (ST) connector in the picture.

14. Fill in the following chart with the maximum data transfer speeds for unshielded twisted pair (UTP) cabling:

Category	Speed
CAT3	
CAT5	
CAT5e	
CAT6	

15. What is the maximum cable length, in meters, for twisted pair cable?

16. What type of cable is also known as RG-58, and what is its maximum cable length and data transfer speed?

_____

17. What type of cable is also known as RG-8, and what is its maximum cable length and data transfer speed?

_____

18. In shielded twisted pair cabling, what is the shielding protecting the conduit from?

_____

Exercise 18-3: Working with Network Cabling

1. Visit a computer store that sells network cables. Physically inspect as many different kinds of cables as you can so that you can better identify them on sight.

2. Visually compare a CAT5e cable with a CAT6 cable. What differences do you note? Check for writing on the cable's casing.

3. If possible, find some 10Base2 T connectors and cable and practice connecting and disconnecting the coaxial cable from the BNC connectors.

4. If possible, get the following types of cables and cut them open with a knife to examine the conduits inside them:

- Fiber optic (Don't sweat it if you can't get one of these easily; they can be expensive. You can find pictures on the Internet showing the innards of these.)

- Unshielded twisted pair

- Shielded twisted pair

- RG-58 coaxial

Comparing Network Architectures

The *network architecture* is the technology that the network uses. Some people use the term to mean physical topology, but that's not really accurate. The topology is the layout, whereas the architecture is the topology, the cable type, and the access method combined.

Ethernet is the most popular network architecture. Other architectures in use today include Token Ring and FDDI.

The thing about Ethernet is that there are many subtypes of it because it has been around so long and is so popular. You can connect various types of Ethernet architectures. For instance, you can combine a wired Ethernet network with a wireless one, or a fiber-optic Ethernet network with a 100BaseT one. However, the overall transfer speed will be limited to the speed of the slowest part.

PRACTICE

19. What IEEE project number defines the requirements for:

A. Ethernet: _____

B. Token Ring: _____

20. What does CSMA/CD stand for?

_____

_____

21. What is the purpose of CSMA/CD in a network?

_____

_____

_____

22. With which network architecture is CSMA/CD most closely associated: Ethernet, Token Ring, or FDDI?

_____

23. Logically, the Token Ring network operates as a ring. What is the most common physical topology for it?

_____

24. What does MAU stand for?

_____

25. What is the purpose of a MAU in a Token Ring network?

_____

26. What does FDDI stand for?

_____

27. What collision avoidance method does FDDI use?

_____

28. Name two differences between Token Ring and FDDI.

_____

_____

_____

_____

29. What is the IEEE standard governing wireless networking, also called Wi-Fi?

_____

30. Of 802.11a, 802.11b, and 802.11g, which two are compatible with one another?

_____

31. What is the (theoretical maximum) data transfer rate for each of the following:

A. 802.11a: _____

B. 802.11b: _____

C. 802.11g: _____

D. 802.11n: _____

32. What is the typical range, in meters, for each of the following:

A. 802.11a: _____

B. 802.11b: _____

C. 802.11g: _____

D. 802.11n: _____

33. Which of the four wireless standards listed in Question 32 use the 2.4 GHz spectrum and therefore can potentially conflict with 2.4 GHz cordless phones?

_____

_____

Match up the following types of Ethernet with their descriptions:

A. 10BaseT

B. 10Base2

C. 10Base5

D. 10BaseFL

E. 100BaseT

        F. 100BaseFX

        G. 1000BaseT

        H. 1000BaseSX

        I. 1000BaseLX

34. _____ Operates at 1 gigabit per second and uses CAT5e UTP cabling

35. _____ Operates at 10 Mbps and uses a bus or hybrid star-bus topology with thinnet coaxial cabling

36. _____ Operates at 10 Mbps and uses fiber-optic cabling

37. _____ Operates at 10 Mbps and uses star or hybrid star-bus topology with CAT3 UTP cabling

38. _____ Operates at 1 gigabit per second and uses multimode fiber-optic cabling; suitable for short distances

39. _____ Operates at 10 Mbps and uses a bus topology with thicknet coaxial cabling

40. _____ Operates at 100 Mbps and uses a star or hybrid star-bus topology with CAT5 UTP cabling

41. _____ Operates at 100 Mbps and uses fiber-optic cable

42. _____ Operates at 1 gigabit per second and uses single-mode fiber-optic cabling; suitable for long distances

Understanding and Selecting Network Devices

Part of your job description as a PC technician might include buying and installing network hardware. Each PC needs a *network interface card* (NIC) or an equivalent built-in or USB device, and you need various connector boxes for linking the PCs together physically, either via cables or via wireless interface.

PRACTICE

Check your knowledge of network hardware:

43. What is a MAC address?

_____

_____

_____

44. What does the acronym MAC stand for?

_____

_____

45. In the MAC address 00-20-3F-6B-25-13, what portion of that address identifies the card manufacturer?

_____

Match the following hardware types to their descriptions:

    A. Repeater

    B. Bridge

    C. Router

    D. Gateway

    E. Switch

    F. Hub

    G. Wireless access point

    H. Network interface card

46. _____ Physically joins PCs together in a star topology and sends data only to the port of the destination system.

47. _____ Regenerates the signal to increase the maximum distance a signal can travel.

48. _____ Intelligently routes packets of data between networks based on the packet addresses; the Internet is based upon an interconnected system of these.

49. _____ Accepts data from wireless clients and passes it on to other wireless clients and/or to a wired network.

50. _____ Converts information from one format to another so that different types of networks can share data.

51. _____ Connects network segments and also regenerates the signal and filters the data so that it is sent only to the proper segment.

52. _____ Provides network connectivity to individual PCs, via a PCI card, PCMCIA, or USB interface.

53. _____ Physically joins PCs together in a star topology but doesn't do any analysis of the packets passing through; it forwards all data to all ports.

Exercise 18-4: Designing Network Topologies

Suppose you have a customer who has an existing five-machine Token Ring network that she wants to preserve, but she also has four new PCs with built-in 1000BaseT Ethernet cards that she wants to use to create a new network segment as well as two older PCs that don't have NICs and two notebook PCs that have wireless Ethernet.

1. Make a list of the hardware you will need to create a single network for this office that will enable all users to access the Internet through a single DSL connection and will allow them to share files and printers.

_____

_____

_____

_____

_____

_____

2. Using the Internet, develop a rough estimate of how much the hardware for this project is going to cost, including cable. Assume that each PC will be 50 feet away from the switch, hub, router, or whatever you decide to use to join them, and that the two network segments will be 75 feet away from one another.

3. Draw a diagram showing how you will connect everything.

Answers to Questions in This Chapter

The following are the answers to the practice questions presented earlier in this chapter:

1. **Which type of network is most appropriate in the following situations? Write *C* next to the descriptions for which client/server is most appropriate, and write *P* next to the descriptions where peer-to-peer is most appropriate.**

   A. _C_ A business has 25 PCs that all need to access a central database.

   B. _P_ A home has 3 PCs that need to share a single DSL Internet connection.

   C. _C_ A company has over 2,000 PCs that need to share printers, files, and Internet connectivity.

   D. _P_ A business has 8 individual-user PCs that need to share a single printer.

   E. _C_ A business has 8 PCs that are shared by 24 users, 8 on each shift. A user might use a different PC each time he or she logs in.

2. **Which type of network is cheapest to create?**

   Peer-to-peer

3. **Which type of network requires a network operating system (NOS)?**

   Client/server

4. **Which type of network maintains user logins separately on each individual PC?**

   Peer-to-peer

5. **Which type of network is more secure?**

   Client/server

6. **Topology #1**

   A. What type of topology is this?

   Star

   B. If PC A goes down, will PC C go down too?

   No

   C. If PC A has data to send to PC C, will it go only to C, or will all the other PCs get it too?

   All will get it.

   D. This topology can also be implemented with devices other than hubs at the center. Name two other devices that could be used instead of a hub.

   Switches and routers

7. **Topology #2**

   A. What type of topology is this?

   Bus

B. **If PC A goes down, will PC C go down too?**

Yes

C. **If PC A has data to send to PC C, will it go only to C, or will all the other PCs get it too?**

It will go to all.

D. **Will the network still work if the terminators were removed from the ends of the chain?**

No

8. **Topology #3**

A. **What type of topology is this?**

Ring

B. **If the connection is broken between PCs A and C, will PC A be able to access PC B?**

No

9. **Topology #4**

A. **What type of topology is this?**

Hybrid

B. **Which two other topologies does this combine?**

Bus and star

C. **If PC A wants to send a message to PC E, will the fact that PC B is disconnected be a problem?**

No, it will still work.

10. **In the picture associated with this question:**

A. **What type of cables are these: coaxial, twisted pair, or fiber optic?**

Twisted pair

B. **Circle the cable that will work in an Ethernet network.**

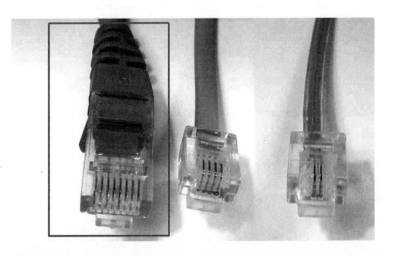

11. **In the picture associated with this question, what type of cables are these: coaxial, twisted pair, or fiber optic?**

    Coaxial

12. **In the picture associated with this question:**

    A. **What type of network is this card and cable for: 10BaseT, 10Base5 (thicknet), or 10Base2 (thinnet)?**

    10Base2

    B. **What is the purpose of the metal barrel being attached to the left end of the T connector in the picture?**

    It is a terminator.

13. **In the picture associated with this question:**

    A. **What type of cables are these: coaxial, twisted pair, or fiber optic?**

    Fiber optic

    B. **Circle the Strait Tip (ST) connector in the picture.**

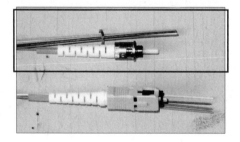

14. **Fill in the following chart with the maximum data transfer speeds for unshielded twisted pair (UTP) cabling:**

Category	Speed
CAT3	10 Mbps
CAT5	100 Mbps
CAT5e	1,000 Mbps
CAT6	10 Gbps

15. **What is the maximum cable length, in meters, for twisted pair cable?**

    100 meters

16. **What type of cable is also known as RG-58, and what is its maximum cable length and data transfer speed?**

    Thinnet, 185 meters at 10 Mbps

17. **What type of cable is also known as RG-8, and what is its maximum cable length and data transfer speed?**

    Thicknet, 500 meters at 10 Mbps

18. **In shielded twisted pair cabling, what is the shield protecting the conduit from?**

    Electromagnetic interference (EMI)

19. **What IEEE project number defines the requirements for:**

    A. Ethernet: <u>802.3</u>

    B. Token Ring: <u>802.5</u>

20. **What does CSMA/CD stand for?**

    Carrier Sense Multiple Access/Collision Detection

21. **What is the purpose of CSMA/CD in a network?**

    It detects packet collisions and resends packets after a random interval to avoid repeated collisions.

22. **With which network architecture is CSMA/CD most closely associated: Ethernet, Token Ring, or FDDI?**

    Ethernet

23. **Logically, the Token Ring network operates as a ring. What is the most common physical topology for it?**

    Star

24. **What does MAU stand for?**

    Multistation Access Unit

25. **What is the purpose of a MAU in a Token Ring network?**

    It functions as a physical hub.

26. **What does FDDI stand for?**

    Fiber Distributed Data Network

27. **What collision avoidance method does FDDI use?**

    Token passing

28. **Name two differences between Token Ring and FDDI.**

    Token ring uses a single ring with coaxial or twisted pair cabling. FDDI uses a double ring with fiber-optic cable.

29. **What is the IEEE standard governing wireless networking, also called Wi-Fi?**

    802.11

30. **Of 802.11a, 802.11b, and 802.11g, which two are compatible with one another?**

   802.11b and 802.11g

31. **What is the (theoretical maximum) data transfer rate for each of the following:**

   A. 802.11a: <u>54 Mbps</u>

   B. 802.11b: <u>11 Mbps</u>

   C. 802.11g: <u>54 Mbps</u>

   D. 802.11n: <u>248 Mbps</u>

32. **What is the typical range, in meters, for each of the following:**

   A. 802.11a: <u>30 meters</u>

   B. 802.11b: <u>30 meters</u>

   C. 802.11g: <u>30 meters</u>

   D. 802.11n: <u>50 meters</u>

33. **Which of the four wireless standards listed in Question 32 use the 2.4 GHz spectrum and therefore can potentially conflict with 2.4 GHz cordless phones?**

   802.11b, g, and n

34. G

35. B

36. D

37. A

38. H

39. C

40. E

41. F

42. I

43. **What is a MAC address?**

   It is the unique hardware ID, like a serial number, for a network interface card.

44. **What does the acronym MAC stand for?**

   Media Access Control

45. **In the MAC address 00-20-3F-6B-25-13, what portion of that address identifies the card manufacturer?**

   The first three base-16 numbers are the card manufacturer's ID. In this case, that would be 00-20-3F.

46. E

47. A

48. C

49. G

50. D

51. B

52. H

53. F

Chapter 19

Managing Windows Networking

· ·

In This Chapter

▶ Connecting to a wired network

▶ Connecting to a wireless network

▶ Sharing folders and printers

▶ Troubleshooting common network connectivity problems

· ·

*N*etwork hardware is only half the equation — and some would say less than half, because it seems like most of the work that technicians do and most of the problems they troubleshoot have to do more with the Windows configuration of the network than with the network itself. In this chapter, you check your knowledge of Windows-based network setup, configuration, and troubleshooting.

Connecting to a Wired Network

As discussed in Chapter 18, a peer-to-peer network consists of all clients — no servers. This type of network works well when just a few PCs need to be connected to one another but you don't have a dedicated PC to function as a server. A client/server network, on the other hand, is based on a domain created with a dedicated server.

Connecting to either type of network is basically the same from a client standpoint. You make the physical connections to hook into the network (wired or wireless) and then you run the Network Setup Wizard on the PC (in Windows XP).

If the PC has been part of a network before and/or if you specified a computer name and a workgroup or a domain when you installed Windows, the PC might have enough information already to make the network connection work without running the Network Setup Wizard. If so, the network simply starts working when you connect the cable.

Test your knowledge of setting up a wired networking connection:

1. In a peer-to-peer network, which PC controls the network administration?

_____

2. Microsoft recommends that fewer than _____ computers be part of a peer-to-peer network.

3. How do you start the Network Setup Wizard in Windows XP?

_____

_____

4. If each PC is set up for obtaining an IP address automatically but no DHCP server is available, how does each PC get an IP address?

_____

_____

5. Assuming that IP addresses have been assigned using the method you specified in Question 4, in what IP address range do those assignments fall?

_____

6. In a peer-to-peer network, if one of the PCs shares its Internet connection with the others via Internet Connection Sharing (ICS), that PC functions as a DHCP server for the network.

   A. What IP address does it assign to itself?

_____

   B. In what range are the IP addresses it assigns to the other PCs in the workgroup?

_____

7. From which Control Panel applet in Windows XP can you change the workgroup or domain to which a PC has been assigned?

_____

8. From which Control Panel applet in Windows XP can you change the computer's name as it appears to others on the network?

_____

9. What are the steps for manually assigning an IP address to a network connection in Windows XP?

_____

_____

_____

_____

_____

Exercise 19-1: Setting Up a Peer-to-Peer Network in Windows XP

To set up a two-computer peer-to-peer network in Windows XP, start by ensuring that both PCs have network adapters installed and that those adapters are recognized in Device Manager. Connect both PCs to a hub, switch, or router and then do the following on each PC:

1. Choose Start⇨Connect To⇨Show All Connections.

   The Network Connections window opens.

2. Look for a Local Area Connection icon.

   If it already shows Connected, Windows might have automatically configured the network for you. You can then skip to Step 6. If the status is not Connected, continue on to the following step.

3. Click Set Up a Home or Small Office Network in the lists of tasks at the left in the Network Connections window.

4. Follow the steps in the Network Setup Wizard to configure the network connection and install the needed software. During this process, the wizard asks you about several things:

   • **Whether this computer shares its Internet connection with other computers on the network:** If it does, it will be set up with Internet Connection Sharing (ICS).

   • **What workgroup name and computer name you want to use:** Each computer must have a unique name; all computers must use the same workgroup name. The default name is WORKGROUP or MSHOME depending on the Windows version.

   • **Whether to turn on file and printer sharing:** This isn't necessary if you just want to use a shared Internet connection, but you need to do it if you plan on sharing that PC's files or printers with others.

   • **Whether to make a network setup disk:** You don't have to do this if the other PC in the network has Windows XP, but if it has some earlier version of Windows, it's a good idea to do so; then take the disk to the other PC and run this same setup wizard from that disk.

5. To test the network connectivity, check the Network Connections window again and confirm that the network connection's status is Connected.

6. If you enabled file and printer sharing on the PCs, try browsing the shared resources on the other PC by choosing Start⇨My Network Places.

Connecting to a Wireless Network

You need to take some special considerations and configuration steps when connecting to wireless networks rather than wired ones, chiefly because of the increased security measures. With a wired network, unless someone has access to the switch, hub, or router, they can't get on the network. With a wireless network, however, it's an open-air free-for-all unless you have some security in place. That's why you see so much emphasis on security and encryption, both in real life and on the A+ exams.

Test your knowledge of setting up a wireless networking connection:

10. Windows XP Service Pack 2 and higher contains a Wireless Network Setup Wizard that you can use to set up the preferred network and enter any security codes needed to connect to it. What are two ways of starting this wizard?

_____

_____

_____

11. What does WEP stand for, and what does it do?

_____

_____

_____

12. What does WPA stand for, and what does it do?

_____

_____

_____

13. What is an SSID, and what does the acronym stand for?

_____

14. There are pros and cons of broadcasting the SSID.

A. What is one reason you might want to broadcast the SSID?

_____

_____

B. What is one reason you might *not* want to broadcast the SSID?

_____

_____

15. What device would you configure in order to choose whether to broadcast the SSID?

_____

16. Suppose you know the IP address for the device you named in Question 15. What application would you use to access its configuration page?

_____

_____

Exercise 19-2: Working with Wireless

Practice setting up a wireless network from scratch:

1. Acquire a wireless access point or wireless router. Turn it on. Do not do any configuration to it yet. If it already had a configuration stored in it, you might want to wipe out its CMOS (by doing a hard reset; see the documentation) for the extra challenge of reconfiguring it.

2. Turn on a PC that has a wireless network adapter. It should be able to find the access point. If it can't, you might need to connect a PC to the access point with a cable to get it configured.

3. Consult the documentation for the access point to find out its default IP address. Use Internet Explorer or another Web browser to connect to it. The username and password to enter should also be in the documentation.

4. Using the access point's Web-based configuration utility, set it up for open (unsecure) access.

5. Connect to the access point by using the wireless network adapter, to confirm that the connectivity is there.

6. On the access point, in the configuration utility, set up WEP security. Turn off SSID broadcasting and change the SSID to something other than the default.

7. On the PC containing the wireless adapter, set up WEP security and change the SSID, and verify that it can connect to the access point using those settings.

8. (Optional) If you have another wireless device, connect it to the access point, too. Keep in mind that SSID broadcasting is turned off, so you need to manually enter the network name.

Sharing Folders and Printers

As your momma probably told you, *sharing is good.* Each client PC can't only be a taker (that is, use network resources); each must also be a giver, making folders and printers available to others. For example, a user might want to share a particular folder on his or her hard drive that contains some documents that others need, or allow other network users to print to his or her personal printer.

Okay, it's not quite as simple as all that. Sharing isn't *always* good. Be careful about sharing entire drives, because there might be something on the drive that you wouldn't want others to see. It's best to share individual folders only, so that you can keep tabs on what's being shared. You might also want to share read access only, so that others can't change your files.

Test your knowledge of folder and printer sharing:

17. File and Printer Sharing for Microsoft Networks must be enabled before you can share specific folders or printers.

A. Suppose you want to check whether sharing is enabled for a particular connection. How would you do this from the Network Connections window?

_____

_____

_____

B. An easy way to turn File and Printer Sharing for Microsoft Networks on/off is to use what wizard?

_____

18. When you turn on File and Printer Sharing using the wizard named in Question 17B, which folder is automatically set up to be shared?

_____

_____

19. To share a folder, right-click it and choose what command from the menu that appears?

_____

20. Instead of doing what was described in Question 19, you could open up the folder's Properties box (right-click the folder and click Properties) and then click which tab?

_____

21. To share a printer, open the Printers folder, right-click the printer icon, and then choose what?

_____

22. If you need the shared printer to be accessible from MS-DOS workstations, how many characters, at maximum, can the share name be?

_____

23. If the printer is being shared from a Windows XP computer and you need the shared printer to be network-accessible from PCs running Windows 9x or other operating systems, what additional steps need to be taken after sharing the printer to make the additional drivers available?

_____

_____

_____

_____

Exercise 19-3: Initiating Folder and Printer Sharing

Try out folder and printer sharing by doing the following. You need two PCs for this. I call them A and B.

1. On computer A, check the network connection's Properties box from the Network Connections window and make sure the File and Printer Sharing for Microsoft Networks option is enabled. If it isn't, enable it from there or run the Network Setup Wizard to turn on file and printer sharing.

2. On computer B, browse the network and see what's available on computer A.

   You should be able to find a shared document folder that's available by default.

3. On computer A, create a new folder on the C: drive called **TestShare** and share it. Allow others to change its content.

4. Copy several document files into TestShare from some other location, such as My Documents.

5. On computer B, refresh the list of shared resources and open TestShare. Open one of the documents, make a change to it, and save and close it.

6. On computer A, open the document you changed from computer B and confirm that the changes appear.

7. On computer A, change the network sharing properties for TestShare so that others can read the content but can't change it.

8. On computer B, try to make another change to the same document you changed earlier, and note what happens.

9. On computer A, delete the TestShare folder.

10. On computer B, on the list of shared resources, try to open TestShare again. Note the error message you see.

Understanding Network Protocols and Services

When you view the Properties dialog box for a network connection, the box's General tab lists the network clients, services, and protocols. Here's an example:

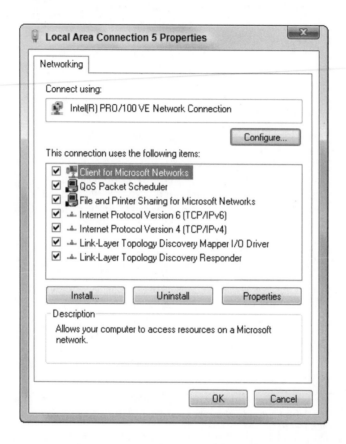

✔ **A client is the software that manages the connection.** For Microsoft networks, including peer-to-peer connectivity via Windows, the essential client is Client for Microsoft Networks.

✔ **A service is a component that creates some type of network functionality.** File and Printer Sharing for Microsoft Networks is a service, for example.

✔ **A protocol is a language to be spoken.** The most common protocol for a network is Internet Protocol (TCP/IP). Windows Vista has two versions of it: version 4 (the standard one in use on the Internet and nearly everywhere else) and version 6 (the up-and-coming new standard).

All those pieces are installed automatically when you set up networking on a Windows XP or Vista machine, but you might also want to add some other clients, services, and protocols.

Test your knowledge of networking protocols and services:

24. In Windows XP, suppose you need to connect to a Netware network. What network client would you need to install?

_____

25. What type of network might use the IPX/SPX-compatible protocol?

_____

_____

26. What type of network might use the NetBEUI protocol?

_____

_____

27. From the Network Connections window, how can you install a new protocol for a particular network connection?

_____

_____

_____

_____

28. Why would you ever want to clear the check box for a protocol to disable it rather than removing it completely with Uninstall?

_____

_____

_____

Exercise 19-4: Working with Network Protocols

Follow these steps to experiment with adding and removing network protocols under Windows XP:

1. Open the Properties dialog box for your network connection.

2. On the General tab, click Install. Choose Protocol and click Add.

3. Choose Microsoft TCP/IP Version 6 and click OK.

4. Wait for the protocol to be installed.

   When the window closes and you see the Properties dialog box again, installation is complete.

5. Confirm that Microsoft TCP/IP Version 6 appears on the list on the General tab. Clear its check box.

   It is now installed but not enabled for this connection.

6. Click Close.

7. Reopen the Properties dialog box for the network connection.

8. Click Microsoft TCP/IP Version 6 and click Uninstall.

9. A warning appears about the uninstall being for all connections. Click Yes.

10. When prompted, click Yes to restart your computer.

Troubleshooting Common Network Connectivity Problems

When troubleshooting network problems, the key is to start at the local machine and gradually expand your search until you get to the part that doesn't work. For example, first you check that the local PC has a network adapter installed and the appropriate client (Client for Microsoft Networks) and protocol (TCP/IP), and you check to make sure it can see its own IP address. Then you take things a step further and test whether it can see the switch/hub/router and some other device that's also connected to that same box. Then outward you go until you find the disconnect.

See how much you know about the tools and procedures for network troubleshooting:

29. Wireless types IEEE 802.11b, g, and n all use what frequency spectrum, which puts them at risk of conflicting with cordless telephones?

   _____

30. If a conflict with a cordless telephone occurs, what can you change on the wireless access point and the client configurations to possibly overcome the conflict?

   _____

31. Suppose a network connection is set to be assigned an IP address automatically.

   A. From Windows XP's GUI interface, how can you determine what that IP address is?

   _____

   B. From a command prompt, how can you determine what that IP address is?

   _____

32. From a command prompt, how can you renew the current IP address?

   _____

33. What is the loopback IP address — that is, the address that you can ping to test whether a network connection can see itself?

_____

34. What is the command syntax for pinging the loopback address at a command prompt?

_____

35. Suppose you ping the loopback address and you see the following:

```
Pinging 127.0.0.1 with 32 bytes of data:

Reply from 127.0.0.1: bytes=32 time<1ms TTL=128
Reply from 127.0.0.1: bytes=32 time<1ms TTL=128
Reply from 127.0.0.1: bytes=32 time<1ms TTL=128
Reply from 127.0.0.1: bytes=32 time<1ms TTL=128

Ping statistics for 127.0.0.1:
    Packets: Sent = 4, Received = 4, Lost = 0 (0% loss),
Approximate round trip times in milli-seconds:
    Minimum = 0ms, Maximum = 0ms, Average = 0ms
```

Was the ping successful?

_____

36. Suppose the PC is connected to a router, and the router is connected to a cable modem, which is in turn connected to the Internet. The PC can ping itself, but it cannot ping any Web sites.

A. What would be the most logical choice to ping next?

_____

B. How do you find out the IP address of the item from Question A?

_____

37. To trace the path from point A to point B on a network, one method is to manually ping the default gateways of the routers at each stop along the way.

A. What command can you use at a command prompt that traces the route between points, without having to know the exact IP addresses at each stop?

_____

B. What would be the syntax if you wanted to use the command to trace the route between the local PC and `http://www.wiley.com`?

_____

_____

Answers to Questions in This Chapter

The following are the answers to the practice questions presented earlier in this chapter:

1. **In a peer-to-peer network, which PC controls the network administration?**

All computers control it collectively.

2. **Microsoft recommends that fewer than 10 computers be part of a peer-to-peer network.**

3. **How do you start the Network Setup Wizard in Windows XP?**

There are two ways. You can do it from the Control Panel or from the Start menu (Start⇨ All Programs⇨Accessories⇨Communication).

4. **If each PC is set up for obtaining an IP address automatically but no DHCP server is available, how does each PC get an IP address?**

Automatic Private IP Addressing (APIPA)

5. **Assuming that IP addresses have been assigned using the method you specified in Question 4, in what IP address range do those assignments fall?**

169.254.0.1 to 169.254.255.254

6. **In a peer-to-peer network, if one of the PCs shares its Internet connection with the others via Internet Connection Sharing (ICS), that PC functions as a DHCP server for the network.**

A. What IP address does it assign to itself?

192.168.0.1

B. In what range are the IP addresses it assigns to the other PCs in the workgroup?

192.168.0.2 to 192.168.0.254

7. **From which Control Panel applet in Windows XP can you change the workgroup or domain to which a PC has been assigned?**

System, on the Computer Name tab

8. **From which Control Panel applet in Windows XP can you change the computer's name as it appears to others on the network?**

System, on the Computer Name tab

9. **What are the steps for manually assigning an IP address to a network connection in Windows XP?**

Right-click the network connection icon in the Network Connections window and choose Properties. On the General tab, double-click Internet Protocol (TCP/IP) and select Use the Following Address. Then type the IP address you want to assign.

10. **Windows XP Service Pack 2 and higher contains a Wireless Network Setup Wizard that you can use to set up the preferred network and enter any security codes needed to connect to it. What are two ways of starting this wizard?**

    Via the Control Panel or the Start menu (Start➪All Programs➪Accessories➪ Communication➪Wireless Network Setup Wizard)

11. **What does WEP stand for, and what does it do?**

    Wired Equivalent Privacy. It's a type of security for wireless networks. It uses a 64-bit or 128-bit encryption key. It's easy to configure on both the access point and the client and provides security against the casual unauthorized wireless user, although it won't keep out a determined hardcore hacker.

12. **What does WPA stand for, and what does it do?**

    Wi-Fi Protected Access. It's a more robust form of security than WEP for wireless networks. Rather than using a single WEP key, WPA uses per-session keys that are agreed upon by the wireless client and the access point after an initial handshaking process.

13. **What is an SSID, and what does the acronym stand for?**

    Service Set ID. It's another name for the network name, assigned by the wireless access point or wireless router.

14. **There are pros and cons of broadcasting the SSID.**

    A. **What is one reason you might want to broadcast the SSID?**

    To allow other users to connect to your network without having to tell them the SSID, to save support costs. For example, a hotel that provides wireless access to guests would want to broadcast the SSID because many people will be coming and going on the network and a support person is not always available.

    B. **What is one reason you might *not* want to broadcast the SSID?**

    For greater security. If the SSID isn't broadcast and it isn't a default or easily guessable name, you have one more level of security in preventing unauthorized people from accessing a network.

15. **What device would you configure in order to choose whether to broadcast the SSID?**

    The wireless access point or wireless router

16. **Suppose you know the IP address for the device you named in Question 15. What application would you use to access its configuration page?**

    A Web browser, such as Internet Explorer

17. **File and Printer Sharing for Microsoft Networks must be enabled before you can share specific folders or printers.**

    A. **Suppose you want to check whether sharing is enabled for a particular connection. How would you do this from the Network Connections window?**

    Right-click the network connection and choose Properties. The File and Printer Sharing for Microsoft Networks option will be listed on the General tab of the Properties dialog box if it is installed.

B. **An easy way to turn File and Printer Sharing for Microsoft Networks on/off is to use what wizard?**

The Network Setup Wizard

18. **When you turn on File and Printer Sharing using the wizard named in Question 17B, which folder is automatically set up to be shared?**

The `C:\Documents and Settings\All Users\Documents` folder. On the network, its default share name is Shared or Shared Documents.

19. **To share a folder, right-click it and choose what command from the menu that appears?**

Sharing, or Sharing and Security

20. **Instead of doing what was described in Question 19, you could open up the folder's Properties box (right-click the folder and click Properties) and then click which tab?**

Sharing

21. **To share a printer, open the Printers folder, right-click the printer icon, and then choose what?**

Sharing

22. **If you need the shared printer to be accessible from MS-DOS workstations, how many characters, at maximum, can the share name be?**

8

23. **If the printer is being shared from a Windows XP computer and you need the shared printer to be network-accessible from PCs running Windows 9x or other operating systems, what additional steps need to be taken after sharing the printer to make the additional drivers available?**

In the printer's Properties dialog box, on the Sharing tab, click Additional Drivers.

24. **In Windows XP, suppose you need to connect to a Netware network. What network client would you need to install?**

Client Service for Netware

25. **What type of network might use the IPX/SPX-compatible protocol?**

A Netware network

26. **What type of network might use the NetBEUI protocol?**

A small workgroup-based network with fewer than ten PCs. NetBEUI isn't routable (it doesn't work across routers), so it can't be used for large networks.

27. **From the Network Connections window, how can you install a new protocol for a particular network connection?**

Right-click the connection and choose Properties. On the General tab, click Install. Select what you want to install (Client, Service, or Protocol) and click OK. Select the item to install (use Have Disk if you have a disk for it) and follow the prompts.

28. Why would you ever want to clear the check box for a protocol to disable it rather than removing it completely with Uninstall?

Disabling an item is for that connection only; removing it with Uninstall affects every network connection. You might have some services or protocols that you want to use only with certain networks.

29. Wireless types IEEE 802.11b, g, and n all use what frequency spectrum, which puts them at risk of conflicting with cordless telephones?

2.4 GHz

30. If a conflict with a cordless telephone occurs, what can you change on the wireless access point and the client configurations to possibly overcome the conflict?

Set a different channel on the wireless access point and on the clients.

31. Suppose a network connection is set to be assigned an IP address automatically.

A. From Windows XP's GUI interface, how can you determine what that IP address is?

Open the Status window for a connection by double-clicking the connection's icon in the Network Connections window.

B. From a command prompt, how can you determine what that IP address is?

Use IPCONFIG.

32. From a command prompt, how can you renew the current IP address?

`IPCONFIG /RENEW`

33. What is the loopback IP address — that is, the address that you can ping to test whether a network connection can see itself?

127.0.0.1

34. What is the command syntax for pinging the loopback address at a command prompt?

`PING 127.0.0.1`

35. Suppose you ping the loopback address and you see the following:

```
Pinging 127.0.0.1 with 32 bytes of data:

Reply from 127.0.0.1: bytes=32 time<1ms TTL=128
Reply from 127.0.0.1: bytes=32 time<1ms TTL=128
Reply from 127.0.0.1: bytes=32 time<1ms TTL=128
Reply from 127.0.0.1: bytes=32 time<1ms TTL=128

Ping statistics for 127.0.0.1:
    Packets: Sent = 4, Received = 4, Lost = 0 (0% loss),
Approximate round trip times in milli-seconds:
    Minimum = 0ms, Maximum = 0ms, Average = 0ms
```

Was the ping successful?

Yes

36. Suppose the PC is connected to a router, and the router is connected to a cable modem, which is in turn connected to the Internet. The PC can ping itself, but it cannot ping any Web sites.

    A. What would be the most logical choice to ping next?

    Ping the default gateway of the router.

    B. How do you find out the IP address of the item from Question A?

    Use the configuration page for the router via Web interface, or in the connection's status, click Details and look for the Default Gateway information.

37. To trace the path from point A to point B on a network, one method is to manually ping the default gateways of the routers at each stop along the way.

    A. What command can you use at a command prompt that traces the route between points, without having to know the exact IP addresses at each stop?

    TRACERT

    B. What would be the syntax if you wanted to use the command to trace the route between the local PC and www.wiley.com?

    TRACERT www.wiley.com

Chapter 20

Configuring Internet Access and Security

*T*hese days it's becoming rare to find a computer that *isn't* connected to the Internet in some way, whether the connection is dial-up or broadband. As more and more places get always-on, network-based Internet access, the job of setting up Internet service becomes easier for technicians. That's good, but along with that comes the increased need for security measures, because always-on access means always vulnerable, and because the explosion of Internet popularity has brought with it an explosion of cyber ne'er-do-wells.

Security isn't *just* about the Internet, though. In a corporate environment, local security is an issue too. Will someone unauthorized sit down at the CFO's PC and snoop the financial data? In this chapter, you look at Internet access and various types of security, both on and off the Net.

Working with Modems

The dial-up connection is separate from — but related to — the modem functionality, so this chapter deals with them separately. First up: modems.

Modem usage and troubleshooting used to be a *huge* topic for A+ techies a decade or so ago, when you had to use cryptic commands in a terminal program to talk to the modem in a language it understood, and when nearly everyone was using a modem to go online.

Nowadays, you might be tempted to say that dial-up Internet access is passé, but sad to say, for many people it's still today's reality. You need to be able to create dial-up connections in Windows 2000 and XP and troubleshoot problems with them, including problems involving the modem hardware.

See how much you know about modem configuration:

1. From the Control Panel, how can you run a diagnostic check on an installed modem?

_____

_____

_____

2. Where in Windows XP's Control Panel do you specify your home area code and whether to dial a number for an outside line?

_____

3. How do a hardware modem and a software-assisted modem differ in terms of the operating systems in which they can operate?

_____

_____

_____

4. Regarding AT commands issued to modems:

A. What is AT an abbreviation for?

_____

B. What program in Windows 2000 and XP can you use to send AT commands to a modem?

_____

5. Which tab of the modem's Properties dialog box would you use to enter an initialization string, including AT commands to send to the modem prior to each call?

_____

Match the following AT commands to their purposes:

    A. ATDT

    B. ATDP

    C. ATA

    D. ATH

    E. ATL

    F. ATM

    G. ATZ

6. _____ Sets the speaker volume

7. _____ Instructs the modem to answer

8. _____ Dials using tone dialing

9. _____ Mutes the speaker

10. _____ Resets the modem to the default settings

11. _____ Dials using pulse dialing

12. _____ Instructs the modem to hang up

Exercise 20-1: Working with Modem Settings

In Windows XP, do the following to experiment with modem settings:

1. In the Control Panel, open Phone and Modem Options.

2. On the Modems tab, double-click the modem.

   Its Properties dialog box opens.

3. Note the device status on the General tab.

4. On the Modem tab, adjust the speaker volume if desired.

5. On the Diagnostics tab, click Query Modem and wait for the results.

   If at least some commands report "Success" in the Response column, the modem is probably installed and working correctly.

   Notice those commands in the Command column and how they all start with AT. Those are the same type of AT commands that I quizzed you about in this section. If you have some extra time on your hands, find an AT command reference online and decipher what each of those commands is asking of the modem.

6. Click the Advanced tab.

   Here's where you can enter any extra AT commands you wanted to send to the modem each time it dialed a connection. For example, if you want to reset it every time, you might enter **ATZ** here. Leave this blank for now.

7. Click OK.

Using Dial-Up Internet Connections

When the modem is up and running and passes all its tests, you're ready to create the dial-up connection. (Yes, I know — *yuck* — but sometimes it's necessary.) Windows takes care of sending the dial command to the modem (that whole ATDT thing), so all you have to do is work through the New Connection Wizard to get things going. After you create the connection, you can modify its properties by right-clicking it and choosing Properties.

Exercise 20-2: Setting Up a Dial-Up Connection

Follow these steps in Windows XP to create a dial-up connection to an ISP. For this exercise, you need an account with an ISP and a local phone number to dial for it, or you can fake your way through with a phony name and number (but don't call it when you're done!).

1. From the Control Panel, open Network Connections.

2. In the Network Connections window, click Create a New Connection.

3. In the New Connection Wizard, click Next.

4. Click Connect to the Internet and click Next.

5. Click Set Up My Connection Manually and click Next.

6. Click Connect Using a Dial-Up Modem and click Next.

7. Type the name of the ISP and click Next.

8. Type the phone number to dial (including a 1 if needed) and click Next.

9. Fill in the username and password and click Next.

10. Click Finish.

    The Connect dialog box appears for the new connection.

11. Click Cancel to skip trying out the connection.

12. Right-click the connection and choose Properties. Browse the tabs in the Properties dialog box to get an idea of what you can change for a connection. (You can change the phone number, for example.) Click Cancel when you're finished looking.

13. If you don't need it, delete the icon for the connection you just created. (Select the icon, press Delete, and click Yes.)

Understanding Protocols

A *protocol* is a language spoken between devices or applications. TCP/IP is the most common protocol used on the Internet (and in networking in general), but it's actually a suite of protocols rather than one single protocol, and many individual protocols can be in use simultaneously.

That happens because different protocols execute at different levels of the Open System Architecture (OSI) model. It's a seven-layer model that explains how data is passed on a network, starting with the bottommost level (the physical level) and going all the way up to the highest level (the application level). Along the way, the packets of data are modified and passed along in various ways, and each level has different protocols associated with it. As you can see in the following graphic, the high-level protocols that interact with the applications include FTP, SMTP, POP3, Telnet, and SNMP. At the lower levels are TCP and IP (which, as you can see, are actually two separate things that operate at different levels). Those top-level protocols can all be acting at once, each talking to a different application. That's what makes it possible for an e-mail program to send mail at the same time as a Web page is being retrieved by the browser, to take one example.

A Breakdown of the TCP/IP Protocol Suite

FTP	SMTP	POP3	Telnet	SNMP		MS Network Client	Other NetBIOS Application

Sockets	NetBIOS

UDP	TCP

ARP	IGMP	IP
ICMP		

Physical

For the A+ exams, you don't have to know the specifics of the OSI model, but you do need a passing familiarity with the various protocol acronyms, their meanings, and what types of applications they interface with.

See how much you know about Internet protocols. For each protocol, give both the acronym and the spelled-out version:

13. Which protocols are typically used in an e-mail program such as Outlook . . .

A. To send outgoing mail?

_____

B. To receive incoming mail?

_____

14. What mail protocol is used with Outlook and other mail programs on mail systems that leave the mail on the server, rather than transferring it to the local PC?

_____

15. What protocol is used to access Web sites?

_____

16. What protocol is used to transfer files?

_____

17. What protocol is used to connect one computer to another with a terminal program?

_____

Understanding IP Addressing

IP stands for Internet Protocol, and it's part of the TCP/IP suite. IP addresses are the basis of all Internet addressing, as well as the basis of most companies' networking systems.

For the A+ exams, you need to understand three things about IP addressing, including how to determine them and how to change them:

- ✔ **IP address:** The unique address assigned to the computer or other device. You need to know valid ranges of IP addresses.

- ✔ **Subnet mask:** The mask that determines how the IP address breaks down between a _network ID_ (which is like the area code of a phone number) and a _host ID_ (which is like a phone number sans area code). You need to be able to look at the subnet mask and determine whether an address is Class A, B, or C.

- ✔ **Default gateway:** The IP address on the outgoing port on the router that leads out of your local subnet.

IP addressing is a fairly complex topic to learn (and to teach). College courses spend many days on it; it's not something you can easily pick up on your own. Check out _CompTIA A+ Certification All-in-One Desk Reference For Dummies,_ by Glen E. Clarke and Ed Tetz (Wiley Publishing), for a good explanation of the basic principles.

Check your knowledge of IP addressing:

18. An IP address consists of four sets of eight-digit binary numbers (octets) separated by periods. Each octet is converted to a decimal number for easier reading. Each of those octets must be between 0 (zero) and what number in decimal?

_____

19. What is the IP address 131.107.2.200 if converted to binary? (Use a calculator if needed.)

_____

20. What would the default subnet mask be for a . . .

A. Class A address?

_____

B. Class B address?

_____

C. Class C address?

_____

21. You can determine an IP address's class by looking at the first octet. What is the range of values for the first octet for a . . .

A. Class A address?

_____

B. Class B address?

_____

C. Class C address?

_____

22. Referring to the address 255.0.255.255:

A. Could that be a valid subnet mask?

_____

B. Why or why not?

_____

_____

_____

_____

23. Referring to the address 255.255.255.0:

A. Could that be a valid subnet mask?

_____

B. Why or why not?

_____

_____

_____

_____

24. What type of server assigns IP addresses to computers on a network? (Give the acronym and also spell out what it stands for.)

_____

_____

_____

25. On the Internet, what type of server translates IP addresses to fully qualified domain names (FQDN) and vice versa? (Give the acronym and also spell out what it stands for.)

_____

_____

_____

Configuring the Windows Firewall

The Windows Firewall (called the Internet Firewall in Windows XP prior to Service Pack 2) is a software means of stopping data packets from reaching your system without your permission.

Incoming data packets come in on certain ports; different protocols and applications use different port numbers. There are many unused ports, and one way a hacker gets into a system is via an open port. A firewall closes off the unused ports and allows packets in only if they have a recognized destination within your system.

Exercise 20-3: Examining Windows Firewall

Follow these steps to experiment with the Windows Firewall in Windows XP:

1. From the Control Panel, open Windows Firewall.

2. Looking at the General tab, make sure that the firewall is set to On.

3. Click the Exceptions tab. Scroll through the list of programs. The ones that have check marks next to them are allowed to receive incoming network connections. If you see any that you don't recognize or don't want to receive network traffic from, clear the corresponding check box.

4. Sometimes you might need to add access to a particular port number, rather than a specific application. Click Add Port. Notice that you can set up a port name and a port number here. Click Cancel here without creating a new port.

5. Click the Advanced tab. On the Network Connection Settings list are the network connections for your PC. You can set exceptions differently for each connection here. To try it, click one of the connections and then click the Settings button. Click Cancel to close that dialog box without making any changes.

6. Click OK to close the Windows Firewall.

Configuring Internet Security and Privacy Settings

In Internet Explorer, you can set up security and privacy settings that control how much outside "influence" the browser lets in. This can range from running or not running ActiveX controls on pages to storing or not storing cookies on the hard drive. The settings are somewhat different depending on the version of IE you have (6.0 comes with Windows XP, but 7.0 is available for free via Windows Update and also with all versions of Windows Vista). The A+ exam covers these settings only in a general way, though, focusing on their concepts rather than their execution.

Test your knowledge of Internet privacy and security settings in Windows:

26. Name two ways of opening the Internet Options (Internet Properties) dialog box — one from within IE and one from outside it.

_____

_____

Match the following security and privacy features to their descriptions:

    A. Cookies

    B. Offline content

    C. Temporary Internet files

    D. History

    E. ActiveX controls

    F. Pop-up blocker

    G. Content Advisor

    H. Certificates

    I. AutoComplete

27. _____ A feature that verifies the publisher of Web content and verifies that the content hasn't been tampered with since it was published.

28. _____ A record of the Web sites visited, in reverse chronological order (newest to oldest).

29. _____ Small text files stored on the hard drive to remember settings for re-visits to Web sites.

30. _____ Web pages cached on the hard drive so that the page can be redisplayed even when the Internet isn't available.

31. _____ Downloaded applets that provide enhanced functionality and interactivity on some Web sites.

32. _____ Web pages cached on the hard drive so that the page can be more quickly redisplayed when revisited.

33. _____ A feature that prevents Web pages from opening additional windows automatically.

34. _____ A feature that remembers your typing in text boxes and helps with retyping by suggesting content.

35. _____ A screening utility that blocks pages that might contain objectionable content.

Exercise 20-4: Ensuring Internet Privacy

Follow these steps to clean a system so that it retains no traces of the previous user's Internet habits and so that it can't store any new data about the user's habits:

1. Open the Internet Options dialog box, either from the Control Panel or from the Tools menu in Internet Explorer.

2. On the General tab, do the following:

   - Click Delete Cookies and click OK.
   - Click Delete Files, mark the Delete All Offline Content check box, and click OK.
   - Click Settings. Set the Amount of Disk Space to Use to 1MB. Click OK.
   - Click Clear History and click Yes to confirm.
   - Set the Days to keep pages in history to 0.

3. On the Privacy tab, drag the Settings slider all the way to the top so that the setting changes to Block All Cookies.

4. On the Content tab, do the following:

   - Click Clear SSL State and click OK.
   - Click AutoComplete. In the AutoComplete Settings dialog box, clear all check boxes. Click the Clear Forms button and click OK. Click the Clear Passwords button and click OK. Then click OK to close the AutoComplete Settings dialog box.

5. On the Programs tab, click Reset Web Settings, click OK, and then OK again.

6. Click OK to close the Internet Options dialog box.

Answers to Questions in This Chapter

The following are the answers to the practice questions presented earlier in this chapter:

1. **From the Control Panel, how can you run a diagnostic check on an installed modem?**

Open Phone and Modem Options and then double-click the modem icon to test. On the Diagnostics tab, click Query Modem.

2. **Where in Windows XP's Control Panel do you specify your home area code and whether to dial a number for an outside line?**

Open Phone and Modem Options and then set up locations on the Dialing Rules tab.

3. **How do a hardware modem and a software-assisted modem differ in terms of the operating systems in which they can operate?**

A hardware modem can run on any operating system; a software-assisted modem requires software that runs in a specific OS (Windows, for example) to function.

4. **Regarding AT commands issued to modems:**

A. What is AT an abbreviation for?

Attention

B. What program in Windows 2000 and XP can you use to send AT commands to a modem?

Hyperterminal can be used; however, it isn't included in Windows Vista.

5. **Which tab of the modem's Properties dialog box would you use to enter an initialization string, including AT commands to send to the modem prior to each call?**

Advanced

6. E

7. C

8. A

9. F

10. G

11. B

12. D

13. **Which protocols are typically used in an e-mail program such as Outlook . . .**

A. To send outgoing mail?

SMTP — Simple Mail Transport Protocol

B. To receive incoming mail?

POP3 — Post Office Protocol version 3

14. **What mail protocol is used with Outlook and other mail programs on mail systems that leave the mail on the server, rather than transferring it to the local PC?**

    IMAP — Internet Message Access Protocol

15. **What protocol is used to access Web sites?**

    HTTP — Hypertext Transport Protocol

16. **What protocol is used to transfer files?**

    FTP — File Transfer Protocol

17. **What protocol is used to connect one computer to another with a terminal program?**

    Telnet (not an acronym)

18. **An IP address consists of four sets of eight-digit binary numbers (octets) separated by periods. Each octet is converted to a decimal number for easier reading. Each of those octets must be between 0 (zero) and what number in decimal?**

    255, because that's 11111111 in binary and because there are only eight digits, and each digit can be either a 0 (zero) or a 1 only. You can't go higher than 255.

19. **What is the IP address 131.107.2.200 if converted to binary? (Use a calculator if needed.)**

    10000011.01101011.00000010.11001000

20. **What would the default subnet mask be for a . . .**

    A. **Class A address?**

       255.0.0.0

    B. **Class B address?**

       255.255.0.0

    C. **Class C address?**

       255.255.255.0

21. **You can determine an IP address class by looking at the first octet. What is the range of values for the first octet for a . . .**

    A. **Class A address?**

       1 to 126

    B. **Class B address?**

       128 to 191

    C. **Class C address?**

       192 to 223

22. **Referring to the address 255.0.255.255:**

    A. **Could that be a valid subnet mask?**

       No

B. Why or why not?

When converted to binary, subnet masks must have all the 1s at the left and all the 0s at the right, like this: 11111111000000000000000000000000. The example, when converted to binary, would be 11111111000000001111111111111111. The 0s are in the middle; this is an improper subnet mask.

23. **Referring to the address 255.255.255.0:**

    A. Could that be a valid subnet mask?

    Yes

    B. Why or why not?

    This is the standard subnet mask for a Class C address.

24. **What type of server assigns IP addresses to computers on a network? (Give the acronym and also spell out what it stands for.)**

    A Dynamic Host Configuration Protocol (DHCP) server

25. **On the Internet, what type of server translates IP addresses to fully qualified domain names (FQDN) and vice versa? (Give the acronym and also spell out what it stands for.)**

    A Domain Name Service (DNS) server

26. **Name two ways of opening the Internet Options (Internet Properties) dialog box — one from within IE and one from outside it.**

    From inside IE, choose Tools⇨Internet Options. Or, from the Control Panel, double-click the Internet Options icon.

27. H

28. D

29. A

30. B

31. E

32. C

33. F

34. I

35. G

Part VI
The Part of Tens

"They can predict earthquakes and seizures, why <u>not</u> server failures?"

In this part . . .

This part contains some handy Top Ten lists that can help you not only study for the A+ exams, but also prepare for real-life situations you'll encounter as a PC technician. You find out about some problems that end-users create for themselves and how to fix them, review the important system files, and practice with handy command-line utilities for troubleshooting and repair.

Chapter 21

Ten Things End-Users Do to Mess Up Their PCs (And How to Fix Them)

*L*ike it or not, a large part of most IT tech support jobs involves saving users from themselves. They get into the darnedest messes because they aren't educated about things that the techno-elite take for granted, such as virus definitions and spyware. Here's a quick look at some of the most common mistakes they make and how to fix them.

Falling for Fake Error Messages

Beginning computer users have little ability to differentiate between the various warnings, offers, and other stuff that pops up on their screens. And therein lies a problem. They end up falling prey to unscrupulous pop-ups, fake error messages, and promises of free gift certificates and prizes. When they click a seemingly innocuous OK button, they get spyware or adware gunk installed on their PCs, or they get redirected to a phishing site that steals their personal information.

The best defense against this ignorance is to educate your users by showing them some examples of fake messages and too-good-to-be-true offers and showing them how to close a pop-up dialog box with the X in the upper-right corner rather than by using the OK and Cancel buttons (which can sometimes be rigged).

You can also use tools that help them cut down on pop-ups and that recognize and report phishing sites. (Internet Explorer 7, for instance, has both a pop-up blocker and a phishing filter.)

Installing Junk

You can find all manner of free (and not-free) utilities out there, including memory optimizers, browser toolbars, search enhancers, and so on. Most of them are pretty worthless, but users get suckered into them all the time and end up with spyware, adware, or just annoyance-ware on their systems.

If you can't train your users not to install this stuff, you can at least train them to run antimalware programs regularly, such as Spybot-S&D, Windows Live OneCare, Spy Sweeper, or other similar apps. You can also show them how to use Add/Remove Programs to remove anything that looks suspicious.

Accidentally Shrinking the Taskbar

Okay, picture this. You're on the phone with a user who says that his taskbar is gone. The first thing you think is that he has it set to Autohide, and moving the cursor down into that area will make it pop up. However, that trick doesn't work.

What has happened here? Well, you can be 99 percent certain that he has accidentally resized the task bar right out of existence. Ask him whether there's a thin line where the taskbar should be. If there is, tell him to rest the cursor over it till he sees an up/down arrow on the cursor, and then tell him to drag upward. *Voilà.*

By the way, this isn't an issue in Windows Vista. Apparently Microsoft figured out that people were having a problem with this, so the taskbar in Vista can't be shrunk down that far.

Installing Unsigned Drivers

Windows XP and Windows Vista are both fairly insistent upon using signed drivers — and for good reason. Generally speaking, signed drivers don't cause the crashes, incompatibilities, and other headaches that unsigned ones can. All kinds of warning messages appear if the user tries to install an unsigned driver, but users are doggedly persistent when it comes to messing up their systems, and occasionally an unsigned driver slips in there and starts causing problems.

If the problem is with a driver for anything other than the display adapter, you can simply roll back the driver by using the Roll Back Driver button in the device's Properties dialog box (from Device Manager). If it's with the display adapter, however, you might not be able to get into Windows at all in normal mode; you might need to boot into Safe Mode to take care of the problem.

Surfing without Virus Protection

Windows doesn't come with any virus protection, and that fact lulls unsuspecting users into believing that none is needed. And that's how many home users' systems get infected with all kinds of nasty stuff.

Some users complain that they can't afford the subscription fees on the major antivirus applications such as Norton Antivirus or McAfee VirusScan. True, these programs aren't free, but there are free antivirus applications for people who can't pay, such as AVG AntiVirus (`http://free.grisoft.com/freeweb.php/doc/2/`).

Many companies find it more economical to buy a corporate version of a virus protection application, such as Norton Antivirus Corporate Edition, and then manage the virus definition updates from their own server.

Opening Unknown E-Mail Attachments

The most common kind of infection these days isn't actually a traditional virus, but rather a worm that arrives as an e-mail attachment. Users open an attachment that runs a script or program that installs the infection. These nasty mass mailers send themselves to everyone in the address book of an infected user. This trick is particularly insidious because then the infection arrives in other people's inboxes disguised in e-mail from someone they know, so they unwittingly install the worm on their own PCs by trusting and opening the attachment.

Most antivirus programs have e-mail–scanning capabilities, and turning those on prevents most infections, but you should also counsel your users not to open attachments that they aren't expecting, even from known sources. You should also explain to them about double-extensions, like `file.doc.vbs`, which can indicate a Visual Basic script that someone is trying to disguise as a Word document.

Not Updating Virus Definitions

Most antivirus programs are only as good as their most recent set of virus definitions because they work by comparing their definitions to what they find in the computer's file system and in its memory.

If a user claims to have an antivirus program installed but still managed to get a virus infection, the first thing to check is that he or she has automatic updates turned on for the program. (Even automatic updates can be foiled, however, if the user doesn't have a full-time Internet connection.) If needed, teach the user how to initiate an update and either set it up to run automatically or have him or her put reminders on the calendar to download them every week.

Allowing the Desktop to Fill Up with Junk

Applications are often pushy. When users install them, they put shortcuts for themselves not only on the Start menu, but also on the desktop and sometimes in the Quick Launch toolbar. Over time, a user's desktop can become a virtual landmine of shortcuts, often to programs that the user has no interest in and might not even understand. One particularly bad offender is Quicken. Not only do you get a Quicken shortcut, but you get umpteen links to various promotional Web sites for other Intuit products and services.

One easy way for users to take control of the desktop is with the Desktop Cleanup Wizard. This places all infrequently used shortcuts into a single folder on the desktop, from which any shortcuts that the user actually needs can easily be retrieved.

To run the Desktop Cleanup Wizard from Windows XP, follow these steps:

1. Right-click the desktop and choose Properties to display the Properties dialog box.
2. On the Desktop tab, click Customize Desktop.
3. On the General tab, click Clean Desktop Now.

Users can also manually organize their desktop shortcuts, of course. You can show them how to create a folder on the desktop and then drag shortcuts into it or delete them entirely by dragging them to the Recycle Bin.

The Desktop Cleanup Wizard is not available in Windows Vista.

Not Organizing the Favorites Menu into Categories

The Start menu can become a real quagmire of folders and shortcuts, with endless mazes of nested folders. One way around this problem is to show your users how to reorganize their Start menu structure into categories. For example, you could have them create a folder called Graphics and then put all the folders for the individual graphics applications in there. They can then do the same with Utilities, Business Applications, Games, and so on.

To change the folder structure of the Start menu, follow these steps:

1. Right-click the Start button and choose Explore All Users.

   A Windows Explorer window opens with the Start Menu folder displayed.

2. If you see any shortcuts at the top level that you want to remove from the top of the Start menu, delete their icons here.

3. Double-click the Programs folder.

4. Create new folders here, one for each category.

5. Drag the existing folders into the new folders to organize them. Do the same for any standalone program shortcuts.

6. Click the Start button and point to All Programs to test the new menu structure.

In Windows Vista, you don't have to wade through folders to find a particular program on the Start menu; just start typing its name and the Start menu narrows down to show just the matching shortcuts.

Not Installing Windows Updates

It seems like nearly every week, the press is talking about some new hole or exploit that some evil computer hacker has found in Windows. Microsoft releases patches and updates for Windows to block these, but unless a user has automatic updates turned on, he or she might not receive the updates that will prevent the problem.

If possible, users should configure Windows Update to run automatically so that it downloads and installs all updates for them. If that's not viable for some reason, train your users to use the Tools⇨Windows Update command in Internet Explorer to manually check for updates at regular intervals (such as once a week).

Chapter 22

Ten (More or Less) Windows System Files You Need to Know About

- -

In This Chapter

▶ Startup files

▶ Files for loading drivers/startup items

▶ Files for choosing your OS

▶ Files for opening a prompt window

▶ Registry files

▶ Files to manage memory

- -

*T*he A+ exams expect you to know dozens of various system-related files on sight and to identify how they fit into the scheme of things in a particular operating system version. Here's a quick rundown of some of the most critical ones to memorize.

IO.SYS and MSDOS.SYS

IO.SYS and MSDOS.SYS, along with COMMAND.COM, are the three files necessary for a bootable floppy disk, such as the emergency startup disk you can make in any of the 9x/Me versions of Windows.

IO.SYS and MSDOS.SYS were the core system files, along with COMMAND.COM, of the venerable MS-DOS operating system. Back in the days, IO.SYS loaded the very basic input/output drivers, and MSDOS.SYS loaded the operating system core. These files continued to exist in Windows 95, 98, and Me, but in a different capacity. All the functions previously performed by IO.SYS and MSDOS.SYS were combined into a new MSDOS.SYS, and IO.SYS became a text file containing configuration settings.

CONFIG.SYS

CONFIG.SYS is another old file. It originated in the days of MS-DOS and was used to load device drivers into memory at startup. You can still use it to load real-mode device drivers if you need any, but with modern versions of Windows, you probably don't. (In fact, real-mode device drivers can slow down Windows.)

CONFIG.SYS is a plain text file even though it has a .sys extension. You can open it in Notepad or any other text editor. Inside, you can find lines that set up the operating environment and load device drivers, like this:

```
FILES=20
DEVICE=C:\Windows\HIMEM.SYS
DOS=HIGH,UMB
DEVICE=C:\Drivers\Mouse.sys
```

If CONFIG.SYS exists on a Windows system, it will be processed for backward compatibility, but it isn't necessary.

AUTOEXEC.BAT

AUTOEXEC.BAT is the other half of the team with CONFIG.SYS for loading startup items in the MS-DOS environment. Like CONFIG.SYS, it isn't necessary on a Windows system, but if it's present, it gets processed at startup.

The main difference between AUTOEXEC.BAT and CONFIG.SYS is that AUTOEXEC.BAT contains commands to run and programs to load — things that ostensibly can be done at any time, not just at startup. On the other hand, CONFIG.SYS calls drivers and system settings that can be processed only at startup.

Here are some example lines from an AUTOEXEC.BAT file:

```
@ECHO OFF
LOAD=C:\utility\manager.com
PROMPT $p$g
```

BOOT.INI

When you have more than one operating system installed, and one of them is Windows NT/2000/XP/Vista, the BOOT.INI file controls the menu from which you choose the OS you want at startup. If you have only one OS installed, BOOT.INI still exists; it just has only one OS represented in it.

Here's an example of a BOOT.INI where there is only one OS:

```
[boot loader]
timeout=30
default=multi(0)disk(0)rdisk(0)partition(2)\WINDOWS
[operating systems]
multi(0)disk(0)rdisk(0)partition(2)\WINDOWS="Microsoft Windows XP
        Professional" /fastdetect /noexecute=optin
```

WIN.COM

WIN.COM is the primary executable file for running Windows 9x. In early versions of Windows, such as Windows 3.1, you could start up MS-DOS and then start up Windows separately by typing **Win.com** at a command prompt. Modern versions of Windows run WIN.COM automatically at startup.

CMD.EXE and COMMAND.COM

In NT versions of Windows (Windows NT 4, Windows 2000, Windows XP, and Windows Vista), CMD.EXE is the command that opens a prompt window. It's the command interpreter, the utility that accepts keyboard command input. To open a command prompt window, choose Start⇨Run, type **CMD** in the Run box, and click OK.

In 9x versions of Windows (Windows 95, 98, and Me), COMMAND.COM is used instead. You might remember COMMAND.COM from MS-DOS as the third of the three files essential for a boot disk. (The other two are IO.SYS and MSDOS.SYS.)

The Registry Hives

Although the Registry appears to be a single database file when you work with it in the Registry Editor, it actually consists of several files.

In NT versions of Windows (NT 4, 2000, XP, and Vista), the Registry is stored in a set of files called the *hives*. Collectively, they hold all the data in the Registry. These files are

- ✔ Sam
- ✔ Security
- ✔ System
- ✔ Software
- ✔ Default

They're all stored in the Windows\System32 folder.

USER.DAT and SYSTEM.DAT

USER.DAT and SYSTEM.DAT are the Windows 9x versions of the hive files. Together they comprise the Registry. As the names imply, SYSTEM.DAT contains settings related to the hardware and other system portions of Windows, and USER.DAT contains user preferences.

WIN.INI and SYSTEM.INI

Windows 3.x didn't have a Registry. Instead, it had two text files, WIN.INI and SYSTEM.INI, that served much the same purpose. Some 16-bit Windows programs write their settings to these files when you install them. These are plain-text files that you can edit with Notepad or any other text editor.

These files don't exist in 32-bit versions of Windows (Windows NT 4, Windows 95, and higher), but if a system has them, Windows reads the data in them and processes it at startup, for backward compatibility.

HIMEM.SYS

HIMEM.SYS is the extended memory manager. It has been around since the days of MS-DOS and is still a critical part of Windows today. It enables the PC to recognize and use more than the first 1MB of RAM.

Back in the DOS days, you had to load HIMEM.SYS with a line in CONFIG.SYS, but Windows 95 and higher load HIMEM.SYS automatically at startup if it has not already been loaded during the CONFIG.SYS process.

Chapter 23

Ten Command-Prompt Commands That Can Save the Day

*T*he command prompt is one of the tools that separates the true techies from the wannabes. Especially with the older versions of Windows and DOS, command-line utilities abound, and they can help you handle many system configuration and trouble-shooting tasks that the regular Windows GUI can't. This chapter lists some of the most useful command-line commands to know. (To open the command prompt, choose Start➪Run and type CMD.)

HELP or /?

Are you unsure about the syntax of a command? Or are you unsure what commands are available? The HELP command or the /? switch can answer these questions and provide other information, too.

To get a list of all available commands, type **HELP** and press Enter at a command prompt.

To get help with a particular command, type that command followed by **/?**, as shown at the top of the figure here:

Here's how to interpret the syntax example in the preceding figure:

- Anything in square brackets is optional. For example, for the PING command, only one item is *not* in square brackets, and that's the target_name. So the only thing required following this command is a target. (In the case of PING, that target is a URL or an IP address.)

- Anything preceded by a – sign should be entered literally. For example, if the syntax calls for -t, you would type **–t** just like that.

- Anything following a – sign and a letter is a variable. For example, if the syntax calls for –n count, you would enter **–n**, a space, and then a number for the count.

CHKDSK

CHKDSK is a very old command, from way back in the early days of MS-DOS. It checks for file system errors and optionally fixes them. It was replaced by Scandisk in later versions of MS-DOS and Windows 9x and by a GUI utility called Check Disk in NT versions of Windows.

You can still use the old CHKDSK command at a prompt anytime you like. For example, if you can't boot into the GUI of a Windows 9x system but you can boot from a startup floppy, you can run CHKDSK on the hard drive to make sure that the problem isn't arising from any file system errors.

The only gotcha to watch out for is that it finds the errors but doesn't actually fix them unless you use the /F switch.

SYS

The SYS command is available only in MS-DOS and in 9x versions of Windows (because those are the ones that use IO.SYS and MSDOS.SYS as the first-level system files). It copies those two files, plus COMMAND.COM, to whatever drive you point it to, making that drive bootable.

For example, suppose you have a bootable floppy disk that contains those three files, and you have a hard drive that for some reason isn't wanting to boot up correctly. From the A:> prompt, you can type **SYS C:** to copy the files to the hard drive, replacing any corrupted versions that might be there.

Why not just copy the files with the COPY command? Well, for system startup files, that won't work. They have to be placed in a specific physical location on the disk, and the COPY command won't put them there. Only the SYS command will do it right.

TYPE

The TYPE command prints the contents of a file on-screen. It's most useful with plain text files because anything else would have unreadable characters in it.

For example, suppose you had a LOG.TXT file on your hard drive, and you wanted to know what was in it. You could open it in a text editor, but for a quick look, it might be easier to use TYPE:

```
TYPE LOG.TXT
```

If the file scrolls by too quickly for you to read, add | MORE on the end to make it scroll one page at a time:

```
TYPE LOG.TXT | MORE
```

Then press Enter to advance the file one screenful at a time. To end the typing early, without seeing the whole file, press Ctrl+C.

FORMAT

The FORMAT command formats (and reformats) disk drives. You might use this from a Windows 9x startup floppy, for example, in preparation for reinstalling Windows from scratch. Include the drive letter in the command:

```
FORMAT C:
```

To speed up the formatting process on a disk that has been previously formatted, you can use the /Q switch after the drive letter:

```
FORMAT C: /Q
```

You can assign a volume label to the disk as you're formatting it by including a /V switch and a label. For example:

```
FORMAT C: /V:mylabel
```

ATTRIB

The ATTRIB command shows the attributes for the files: Archive, Read-Only, System, and/or Hidden. These are useful to know in general, but there are a couple of really important things you can do with it, too: You can remove the Hidden attribute from a group of files so that you can find out what's in a folder; and you can remove the Read-Only attribute from files so that they can be deleted. (You have to know files are there before you can delete them, and you have to delete them before you can delete the folder/directory they are in.)

To see all the files and their attributes, use ATTRIB all by itself:

```
ATTRIB
```

To just see certain files, add a file spec. For example, to see all files with a .SYS extension, use this command:

```
ATTRIB *.SYS
```

To add or remove an attribute, use a minus or plus sign with the first letter of the attribute type (A for Archive, R for Read-Only, and so on). For example, to remove the Hidden attribute from .SYS files, use this command:

```
ATTRIB -H *.SYS
```

EDIT

Edit starts the MS-DOS–based text editor that comes with DOS and that is included on emergency startup disks made via Windows 95, 98, and Me. It's like Notepad except that it doesn't require Windows; you can use it to modify plain-text configuration files like AUTOEXEC.BAT and CONFIG.SYS.

EXTRACT

The EXTRACT command, provided on a Windows 9x startup floppy, enables you to decompress a file from a .CAB archive, such as what you'll find on the Windows setup CD. This command is useful if Windows won't start up because a certain critical system file is corrupted or missing; it helps you avoid having to completely reinstall Windows in order to get that one file back. (This command is available only in Windows 95, 98, Me, and NT.)

The syntax for the EXTRACT command is somewhat cumbersome and not at all obvious from looking at the EXTRACT /? syntax help, so here are a few examples.

If you know what cabinet file contains the file you want to extract, use this syntax:

```
extract <cabinet> <filename> /l <destination>
```

For example, here's how you can extract the file Unidrv.dll from the cabinet file A:\Windows\System\Win95_10.cab to the C:\Windows\System folder:

```
extract a:\win95_10.cab unidrv.dll /l c:\Windows\System
```

If you want to extract multiple files, use a wildcard spec. For example, you can extract all the .dll files from the preceding example:

```
extract a:\win95_10.cab *.dll /l c:\Windows\System
```

A more common situation, though, is that you don't know which cabinet file contains the file you're looking for. In that case, use the /a switch and tell it which cabinet file to start with. The command then looks in all the cabinet files, starting with the specified one, until it finds the file you chose.

For example, suppose you aren't sure where unidrv.dll is. Use this command to look in all the .CAB files starting with win95_02.cab:

```
extract /a a:\win95_02.cab unidrv.dll /l c:\windows\system
```

PING

The PING command checks connectivity between the local PC and some other network location. You can use it with an IP address, a Web URL, or a network path.

For example, suppose you are trying to figure out why a computer can't get out of its local subnet. You know that the default gateway on the router is 192.168.0.1, so you ping that address like this:

```
PING 192.168.0.1
```

If a reply comes back, as shown in the preceding figure, you know there's connectivity. If the request times out, you have a problem.

You can use PING with Web sites, too. For example:

```
PING www.sycamoreknoll.com
```

Be aware, however, that some Web servers block PING access, so just because a particular site times out doesn't necessarily mean that it's down. Microsoft blocks PING access to Microsoft.com, for example.

TRACERT

Short for *trace route,* the TRACERT command goes beyond PING to actually tell you the path taken between points A and B on a network. For example, suppose you can't ping a particular Web site; the connection keeps timing out. But where's the problem? You can use TRACERT to tell you where the communication is breaking down.

For example, you can trace the route to www.sycamoreknoll.com:

```
TRACERT www.sycamoreknoll.com
```

The results come back as server addresses and IP addresses, as shown here:

Appendix A

About the A+ Certification Exams

Until 2006, the A+ certification exams consisted of two tests: one on hardware and the other on software. That made sense on the surface, but in some cases, the distinction was rather tenuous. For example, if you're fixing a problem with a device and the fix happens to include doing something in Windows, is that hardware or software? Issues like that sprang up all the time.

The 2006 version of the A+ exams takes a job-centered approach instead, which is much more true to real life. To become A+ certified, you must past two exams. All candidates must take the A+ Essentials exam (220-601), and then candidates must take at least one other exam, depending on the specialty for which they are preparing:

220-602: IT Technician

220-603: Remote Support Technician

220-604: Depot Technician

For complete information about these exams, visit the CompTIA Web site, www. comptia.org.

About the A+ Essentials Exam

The first exam, CompTIA A+ Essentials, is required for all candidates. It measures the necessary competencies for an entry-level IT professional with the equivalent knowledge of at least 500 hours of hands-on experience in the lab or field. Hands-on experience or equivalent knowledge includes installing, building, upgrading, repairing, configuring, troubleshooting, optimizing, diagnosing, and performing preventive maintenance of basic PC hardware and operating systems.

Domain	Percentage
1.0 Personal Computer Components	21%
2.0 Laptops and Portable Devices	11%
3.0 Operating Systems	21%
4.0 Printers and Scanners	9%
5.0 Networks	12%
6.0 Security	11%
7.0 Safety and Environmental Issues	10%
8.0 Communication and Professionalism	5%
Total	**100%**

Here's an outline of the main sections you can expect to see:

1.0 Personal Computer Components

- ✔ 1.1 Identify the fundamental principles of using personal computers
- ✔ 1.2 Install, configure, optimize, and upgrade personal computer components
- ✔ 1.3 Identify tools, diagnostic procedures, and troubleshooting techniques for personal computer components
- ✔ 1.4 Perform preventive maintenance on personal computer components

2.0 Laptops and Portable Devices

- ✔ 2.1 Identify the fundamental principles of using laptops and portable devices
- ✔ 2.2 Install, configure, optimize, and upgrade laptops and portable devices
- ✔ 2.3 Identify tools, basic diagnostic procedures, and troubleshooting techniques for laptops and portable devices
- ✔ 2.4 Perform preventive maintenance on laptops and portable devices

3.0 Operating Systems (Unless otherwise noted, the operating systems referred to include Microsoft Windows 2000, XP Professional, XP Home, and Media Center.)

- ✔ 3.1 Identify the fundamentals of using operating systems
- ✔ 3.2 Install, configure, optimize, and upgrade operating systems (references to upgrading from Windows 95 and NT may be made)
- ✔ 3.3 Identify tools, diagnostic procedures, and troubleshooting techniques for operating systems
- ✔ 3.4 Perform preventive maintenance on operating systems

4.0 Printers and Scanners

- ✔ 4.1 Identify the fundamental principles of using printers and scanners
- ✔ 4.2 Identify basic components of installing, configuring, optimizing, and upgrading printers and scanners
- ✔ 4.3 Identify tools, basic diagnostic procedures, and troubleshooting techniques for printers and scanners

5.0 Networks

- ✔ 5.1 Identify the fundamental principles of networks
- ✔ 5.2 Install, configure, optimize, and upgrade networks
- ✔ 5.3 Identify tools, diagnostic procedures, and troubleshooting techniques for networks

6.0 Security

✔ 6.1 Identify the fundamental principles of security

✔ 6.2 Install, configure, upgrade, and optimize security

✔ 6.3 Identify tools, diagnostic procedures, and troubleshooting techniques for security

✔ 6.4 Perform preventive maintenance for computer security

7.0 Safety and Environmental Issues

✔ 7.1 Describe the aspects and importance of safety and environmental issues

✔ 7.2 Identify potential hazards and implement proper safety procedures, such as taking ESD precautions, establishing a safe work environment, and properly handling equipment

✔ 7.3 Identify proper disposal procedures for batteries, display devices, and chemical solvents and cans

8.0 Communication and Professionalism

✔ 8.1 Use good communication skills, including listening and tact/discretion, when communicating with customers and colleagues

✔ 8.2 Use job-related professional behavior, including notation of privacy, confidentiality, and respect for the customer and customer's property

About the IT Technician Exam

This exam is targeted to individuals who work or intend to work in a mobile or corporate technical environment with a high level of face-to-face client interaction. Job titles in some organizations that describe this role might be enterprise technician, IT administrator, field service technician, PC technician, and so on. Some people in nontechnical roles might also find this exam useful, such as students, salespersons, and small business office managers.

Domain	Percentage
1.0 Personal Computer Components	18%
2.0 Laptops and Portable Devices	9%
3.0 Operating Systems	20%
4.0 Printers and Scanners	14%
5.0 Networks	11%
6.0 Security	8%
7.0 Safety and Environmental Issues	5%
8.0 Communication and Professionalism	15%
Total	**100%**

Here are the main objectives for this exam:

1.0 Personal Computer Components

- ✓ 1.1 Install, configure, optimize, and upgrade personal computer components
- ✓ 1.2 Identify tools, diagnostic procedures, and troubleshooting techniques for personal computer components
- ✓ 1.3 Perform preventive maintenance of personal computer components

2.0 Laptops and Portable Devices

- ✓ 2.1 Identify fundamental principles of using laptops and portable devices
- ✓ 2.2 Install, configure, optimize, and upgrade laptops and portable devices
- ✓ 2.3 Use tools, diagnostic procedures, and troubleshooting techniques for laptops and portable devices.

3.0 Operating Systems (Unless otherwise noted, the operating systems referred to include Microsoft Windows 2000, XP Professional, XP Home, and Media Center.)

- ✓ 3.1 Identify the fundamental principles of operating systems
- ✓ 3.2 Install, configure, optimize, and upgrade operating systems (References to upgrading from Windows 95 and NT might be made.)
- ✓ 3.3 Identify tools, diagnostic procedures, and troubleshooting techniques for operating systems
- ✓ 3.4 Perform preventive maintenance for operating systems

4.0 Printers and Scanners

- ✓ 4.1 Identify the fundamental principles of using printers and scanners
- ✓ 4.2 Install, configure, optimize, and upgrade printers and scanners
- ✓ 4.3 Identify tools and diagnostic procedures to troubleshoot printers and scanners
- ✓ 4.4 Perform preventive maintenance of printers and scanners

5.0 Networks

- ✓ 5.1 Identify the fundamental principles of networks
- ✓ 5.2 Install, configure, optimize, and upgrade networks
- ✓ 5.3 Use tools and diagnostic procedures to troubleshoot network problems
- ✓ 5.4 Perform preventive maintenance of networks including securing and protecting network cabling

6.0 Security

   ✔ 6.1 Identify the fundamentals and principles of security

   ✔ 6.2 Install, configure, upgrade, and optimize security

   ✔ 6.3 Identify tools, diagnostic procedures, and troubleshooting techniques for security

   ✔ 6.4 Perform preventive maintenance for security

7.0 Safety and Environmental Issues

   ✔ 7.1 Identify potential hazards and proper safety procedures including power supply, display devices, and environment (for example, trip, liquid, situational, atmospheric hazards, and high-voltage and moving equipment)

8.0 Communication and Professionalism

   ✔ 8.1 Use good communication skills, including listening and tact/discretion, when communicating with customers and colleagues

   ✔ 8.2 Use job-related professional behavior including notation of privacy, confidentiality, and respect for the customer and customer's property

About the Remote Support Technician Exam

This exam is targeted to people who work in a remote-based environment where client interaction, client training, operating system, and connectivity issues are emphasized. People with the following positions might find this exam's skills useful: remote support technician, help desk technician, call center technician, and technical support representative.

Domain	Percentage
1.0 Personal Computer Components	15%
2.0 Operating Systems	29%
3.0 Printers and Scanners	10%
4.0 Networks	11%
5.0 Security	15%
6.0 Communication and Professionalism	20%
Total	**100%**

Here are the exam objectives:

1.0 Personal Computer Components

   ✔ 1.1 Install, configure, optimize, and upgrade personal computer components

   ✔ 1.2 Identify tools, diagnostic procedures, and troubleshooting techniques for personal computer components

   ✔ 1.3 Perform preventive maintenance on personal computer components

2.0 Operating Systems (Unless otherwise noted, the operating systems referred to include Microsoft Windows 2000, X Professional, XP Home, and Media Center.)

- ✔ 2.1 Identify the fundamental principles of using operating systems
- ✔ 2.2 Install, configure, optimize, and upgrade operating systems
- ✔ 2.3 Identify tools, diagnostic procedures, and troubleshooting techniques for operating systems
- ✔ 2.4 Perform preventive maintenance for operating systems

3.0 Printers and Scanners

- ✔ 3.1 Identify the fundamental principles of using printers and scanners
- ✔ 3.2 Install, configure, optimize, and upgrade printers and scanners
- ✔ 3.3 Identify tools, diagnostic procedures, and troubleshooting techniques for printers and scanners

4.0 Networks

- ✔ 4.1 Identify the fundamental principles of networks
- ✔ 4.2 Install, configure, optimize, and upgrade networks
- ✔ 4.3 Identify tools, diagnostic procedures, and troubleshooting techniques for networks

5.0 Security

- ✔ 5.1 Identify the fundamental principles of security
- ✔ 5.2 Install, configure, optimize, and upgrade security
- ✔ 5.3 Identify tools, diagnostic procedures, and troubleshooting techniques for security issues
- ✔ 5.4 Perform preventive maintenance for security

6.0 Communication and Professionalism

- ✔ 6.1 Use good communication skills, including listening and tact/discretion, when communicating with customers and colleagues
- ✔ 6.2 Use job-related professional behavior, including notation of privacy, confidentiality, and respect for the customer and customer's property

About the Depot Technician Exam

The Depot Technician exam is for people who work in settings where there is limited customer interaction, and where hardware-related activities are emphasized, such as repair shops. Job titles might include depot technician, bench technician, and so on.

Domain	Percentage
1.0 Personal Computer Components	45%
2.0 Laptops and Portable Devices	20%
3.0 Printers and Scanners	20%
4.0 Security	5%
5.0 Safety and Environmental Issues	10%
Total	**100%**

Here are the exam objectives:

1.0 Personal Computer Components

- ✔ 1.1 Install, configure, optimize, and upgrade personal computer components
- ✔ 1.2 Identify tools, diagnostic procedures, and troubleshooting techniques for personal computer components
- ✔ 1.3 Perform preventive maintenance on personal computer components

2.0 Laptops and Portable Devices

- ✔ 2.1 Identify the fundamental principles of using laptops and portable devices
- ✔ 2.2 Install, configure, optimize, and upgrade laptops and portable devices
- ✔ 2.3 Identify tools, diagnostic procedures, and troubleshooting techniques for laptops and portable devices

3.0 Printers and Scanners

- ✔ 3.1 Identify the fundamental principles of using printers and scanners
- ✔ 3.2 Install, configure, optimize, and upgrade printers and scanners
- ✔ 3.3 Identify tools, diagnostic procedures, and troubleshooting techniques for printers and scanners
- ✔ 3.4 Perform preventive maintenance of printer and scanner problems

4.0 Security

- ✔ 4.1 Identify the names, purposes, and characteristics of physical security devices and processes
- ✔ 4.2 Install hardware security

5.0 Safety and Environmental Issues

- ✔ 5.1 Identify potential hazards and proper safety procedures including power supply, display devices, and environment (for example, trip, liquid, situational, atmospheric hazards, and high-voltage and moving equipment)

Appendix B

About the CD-ROM

Check out this appendix for info on how to use the CD-ROM accompanying this book.

System Requirements

Make sure that your computer meets the minimum system requirements shown in the following list. If your computer doesn't meet most of these requirements, you might have problems using the software and files on the CD. For the latest and greatest information, please refer to the ReadMe file located at the root of the CD-ROM.

- A PC with a Pentium or faster processor; or a Mac OSX computer with a G3 or faster processor
- Microsoft Windows 2000 or later; or Mac OSX system software 10.1 or later
- A CD-ROM drive

Using the CD

To install the items from the CD to your hard drive, follow these steps:

1. **Insert the CD into your computer's CD-ROM drive.**

The license agreement appears.

Note to Windows users: The interface won't launch if you have autorun disabled. In that case, run the file start.exe on the CD. (Choose Start⇨Run. In the dialog box that appears, type **D:\start.exe** and click OK. Replace D with the proper letter if your CD-ROM drive uses a different letter. If you don't know the letter, see how your CD-ROM drive is listed under My Computer.

Note for Mac Users: The CD icon appears on your desktop. Double-click the icon to open the CD and double-click the Start icon.

2. **Read through the license agreement and then click the Accept button if you want to use the CD.**

3. **The CD interface appears.**

   The interface allows you to install the software by following the prompts.

What You'll Find on the CD

The CD that accompanies this book contains a Prep Test designed to simulate the actual A+ situation — questions with multiple choice answers. The Prep Test on the CD-ROM isn't adaptive and it isn't timed, but you may time yourself to gauge your speed. After you answer each question, you will find out whether you answered the question correctly. If you answered correctly, you're on your way to A+ success. If you answered incorrectly, you are told the correct answer with a brief explanation of why it is the correct answer.

If you perform well on the Prep Test, you're probably ready to tackle the real thing.

Troubleshooting

The software on this book's CD should work on most computers with the minimum system requirements.

If you have trouble using it, the two likeliest problems are that you don't have enough memory (RAM) or that you have other programs running that are affecting installation or running of a program. If you get an error message such as `Not enough memory` or `Setup cannot continue`, try one or more of the following suggestions and then try using the software again:

- ✔ **Turn off any antivirus software running on your computer.** Installation programs sometimes mimic virus activity and might make your computer incorrectly believe that it's being infected by a virus.

- ✔ **Close all running programs.** The more programs you have running, the less memory is available to other programs. Installation programs typically update files and programs, so if you keep other programs running, installation might not work properly.

- ✔ **Add more RAM to your computer.** Adding more memory can really help the speed of your computer and allow more programs to run at the same time.

If you have trouble with the CD-ROM, please call the Wiley Product Technical Support phone number at (800) 762-2974. Outside the United States, call 1(317) 572-3994. You can also contact Wiley Product Technical Support at `http://support.wiley.com`. John Wiley & Sons will provide technical support only for installation and other general quality control items. For technical support on the applications themselves, consult the program's vendor or author.

To place additional orders or to request information about other Wiley products, please call (877) 762-2974.

Index

• T •

• U •

• V •

Wiley Publishing, Inc.
End-User License Agreement

READ THIS. You should carefully read these terms and conditions before opening the software packet(s) included with this book "Book". This is a license agreement "Agreement" between you and Wiley Publishing, Inc. "WPI". By opening the accompanying software packet(s), you acknowledge that you have read and accept the following terms and conditions. If you do not agree and do not want to be bound by such terms and conditions, promptly return the Book and the unopened software packet(s) to the place you obtained them for a full refund.

1. **License Grant.** WPI grants to you (either an individual or entity) a nonexclusive license to use one copy of the enclosed software program(s) (collectively, the "Software") solely for your own personal or business purposes on a single computer (whether a standard computer or a workstation component of a multi-user network). The Software is in use on a computer when it is loaded into temporary memory (RAM) or installed into permanent memory (hard disk, CD-ROM, or other storage device). WPI reserves all rights not expressly granted herein.

2. **Ownership.** WPI is the owner of all right, title, and interest, including copyright, in and to the compilation of the Software recorded on the physical packet included with this Book "Software Media". Copyright to the individual programs recorded on the Software Media is owned by the author or other authorized copyright owner of each program. Ownership of the Software and all proprietary rights relating thereto remain with WPI and its licensers.

3. **Restrictions on Use and Transfer.**

    (a) You may only (i) make one copy of the Software for backup or archival purposes, or (ii) transfer the Software to a single hard disk, provided that you keep the original for backup or archival purposes. You may not (i) rent or lease the Software, (ii) copy or reproduce the Software through a LAN or other network system or through any computer subscriber system or bulletin-board system, or (iii) modify, adapt, or create derivative works based on the Software.

    (b) You may not reverse engineer, decompile, or disassemble the Software. You may transfer the Software and user documentation on a permanent basis, provided that the transferee agrees to accept the terms and conditions of this Agreement and you retain no copies. If the Software is an update or has been updated, any transfer must include the most recent update and all prior versions.

4. **Restrictions on Use of Individual Programs.** You must follow the individual requirements and restrictions detailed for each individual program in the "About the CD" appendix of this Book or on the Software Media. These limitations are also contained in the individual license agreements recorded on the Software Media. These limitations may include a requirement that after using the program for a specified period of time, the user must pay a registration fee or discontinue use. By opening the Software packet(s), you agree to abide by the licenses and restrictions for these individual programs that are detailed in the "About the CD" appendix and/or on the Software Media. None of the material on this Software Media or listed in this Book may ever be redistributed, in original or modified form, for commercial purposes.